Library of
Davidson College

ANCIENT PHILOSOPHY

Editions
Commentaries
Critical Works

Edited by
LEONARDO TARÁN
Columbia University

A Garland Series

J. COOK WILSON

ON THE
INTERPRETATION OF
PLATO'S *TIMAEUS*

ON THE
PLATONIST DOCTRINE OF
THE ἀσύμβλητοι ἀριθμοί

GARLAND PUBLISHING, INC.
NEW YORK & LONDON
1980

For a complete list of the titles in this series,
see the final pages of this volume.

The volumes in this series are printed on acid-free,
250-year-life-paper.

Bibliographical note:
The facsimile of *On the Interpretation of Plato's 'Timaeus'*
has been made from a copy in the University of
Southern California Library; that of *On the Platonist Doctrine*
has been made from a copy in the Yale University Library.

Library of Congress Cataloging in Publication Data

Wilson, John Cook, 1849–1915.
On the interpretation of Plato's Timaeus.

(Ancient philosophy)
Reprint of two works, the first published in 1889
by D. Nutt, London; and the second published
in 1904 in the journal Classical review, v. 18.
Includes bibliographical references.
1. Plato. Timaeus. 2. Cosmology—Early works
to 1800. 3. God. 4. Idea (Philosophy)
I. Wilson, John Cook, 1849–1915. On the Platonist
doctrine of asymblētoi arithmoi. II. Title.
III. Series.
B387.W54   1980   113   78-66577
ISBN 0-8240-9571-5

Printed in the United States of America

ON THE INTERPRETATION

OF

PLATO'S TIMAEUS

Critical Studies

WITH SPECIAL REFERENCE TO
A RECENT EDITION

BY

J. COOK WILSON, M.A.

LONDON

DAVID NUTT, 270 STRAND, W.C.

1889

CONTENTS.

		PAGE
PREFACE	. . . .	5

PART I. Relation of the Edition to Preceding Commentaries.

§ 1.—Obligations to Stallbaum . . .	Paragraphs 1–7 ...	9–19
§ 2.—Criticisms of Stallbaum	„ 8–22 ...	20–47
§ 3.—Obligations to Martin and some others .	„ 23–33 ...	47–61
§ 4.—Acquaintance with Ancient Authors quoted	„ 34–40 ...	61–68
§ 5.—Obligations to Daremberg . . .	„ 41–47 ...	68–79

PART II. Text and Apparatus Criticus . . . . „ 48–50 ... 80–85

PART III. Interpretation of the Language . . . „ 51–64 ... 86–128

PART IV. The Editor's Note on the Motion of the Planets Venus and Mars, and some Points in his Reply . . . . „ 65–70 ... 129–145

PREFACE.

THIS pamphlet originates in a criticism of a recent edition[1] of the Timaeus of Plato in the 'Classical Review' for March this year. The editor replied to my review in the April number. My full answer was reserved for a pamphlet because the subject could not be adequately treated in a review: and yet the editor's statements were such that I could not let them remain long unchallenged. Rather therefore than wait for the pamphlet, I wrote a preliminary answer for the same number of the 'Classical Review.' In it was given, among other things, a test instance of the trustworthiness of the editor's allegations. Eventually the editor accepted the test without reserve, in a tone of contempt and with an appearance of great confidence. How completely unfortunate the result was for him, may be seen from an article of mine which followed in the 'Academy' of June 8, 1889, and if mere success in controversy had been my object there would have been no need for me to say anything more.

But there seemed to be a reason for redeeming my promise about the pamphlet. In the editing of the Timaeus there are a number of different departments: all are undertaken in the edition in question, in all the work seemed of the same character, and thus the number and nature of things to be noticed was so great that a full description could not be conveniently given in a review. Hence I was obliged to give a general account of them, working out a

[1] The Timaeus of Plato. Edited with Introduction and Notes by R. D. Archer-Hind, M.A.

few typical examples, and giving sufficient indications of the nature of others to enable any reader acquainted with the subject to verify what was said of them. Now as the editor apparently presumed in his answer on the number of readers who could not or would not do this, it seemed advisable to publish a pamphlet to supply omitted details. It is not my fault that in some cases the editor's notes and those of others or portions of his reply have had to be given with such fulness. The method which he chose in his reply made this absolutely necessary. This is partly why repetition of examples given in the review has not been avoided, for I am now justified in showing more fully than before the nature of the mistakes involved in some of them. Others have been challenged, and on that account alone may be restated. The editor's answer, which was disfigured by personalities, was an evasion that amounted to confession. He said he would not have felt called upon to notice the review, if I had not 'freely scattered accusations of dishonesty,' or as he also expresses it, of 'piracy' and 'mala fides.' It is, by the way, a part of the misrepresentation of his reply to give the reader the impression that I was as intemperate in my language as himself. I did not use the above terms, and I take the opportunity of saying that the severest form of comment I allowed myself, consisted in pointing out how entirely applicable to himself were the phrases which he used of other people.

If the charges to which the editor thus referred were his only reason for replying, he was committed to answering them. But the main counts against him resting on the use made of the notes of Stallbaum and Martin are not denied, much less controverted. In the case of the former, he produces the appearance of an answer by professing to prove with an air of triumph that he had not pirated from Stallbaum in one particular place. It is a place where he was not even suspected of piracy. He professed also to defend himself with regard to Daremberg, to whom his obligations would in any case be small as compared with that to the two editors. But here the evasion is so palpable that it would not escape any careful reader, even if he had not my own review before him to test it by. What he did beside was to try to discredit my whole review, by trying to shew me wrong upon several points which were not relevant to the only issue which, according to his own statement, had moved him to answer. The total effect therefore of his reply was a tacit confession on this issue. The reply itself is considered in detail in paragraphs 15, 31, 32, 41–47, 65–70 in this pamphlet; and of the examination of the several arguments in it, it need only be said here, that one who wished to clear himself of an imputation of 'mala fides,' should for his own sake have avoided such forms of controversy as are there brought to light. With the fatality of unconscious self-criticism which attends him so constantly, he has quoted in the Introduction of his reply—ἀξιῶ ἀμφισβητεῖν μέν, ἐρίζειν δὲ μή.

It is not always thought necessary to tell the whole truth about a book in a review, but it was necessary in this case to tell a good deal of it not only in justice to the editor's predecessors, for reasons which will appear, but also in justice to his contemporaries, because it will not do to allow foreign critics to think our standard of an edition of a classical author so far below theirs, or our notion of the interpretation of ancient philosophy so anachronistic. There was another reason—something very different to the truth had been told about this book. In such circumstances though the reviewer's duty is clear, it has its dangers, for partisans are not always scrupulous, as I was speedily to learn.

The vindication of the rights of Stallbaum and Martin and of others besides will find sympathy with those who are trying to do genuine work, and who hope that posterity will both find it useful and not forget their share in it.

As to Stallbaum, it is not uncommon to find him merely depreciated at first by students, partly because his treatment of the philosophical questions does not satisfy them. But this onesidedness is but a sign of immaturity and of imperfect acquaintance with modern books on Greek philology. Stallbaum, in his editions of the Platonic dialogues, made an important contribution to the subject, as may be seen on even a casual inspection of the most important German literature on Greek Grammar. The attitude to Stallbaum (as well as to others) in this edition would be inexcusable even if the obligation to him was less than it is: for in respect of accuracy, Greek scholarship, learning (especially such as subserves the criticism of the Greek text), and in the general conception of what an edition of a Greek author should aim at, there is no comparison to be drawn.

Academical and literary engagements have delayed the publication of this pamphlet, and even now I am not ready with the parts which treat of the philosophy and what may conveniently be called the scientific subjects in the Timaeus.

J. COOK WILSON.

October, 1889.

CORRIGENDA.

Page 61, note, 1st line, *for* πήγην *read* πηγήν

,, 74, l. 9, *for* νενοημένον *read* νενοημένου

,, 83, *transpose the two sentences*
          Of the emendations . . . Part III.
          But, as we have also seen . . . had before him.

25 1.15 for ταυτοῦ read τούτου

J. Cook Wilson's Timaeus.

PART I.

RELATION OF THE EDITION TO PRECEDING COMMENTARIES.

§ 1.—Obligations to Stallbaum.

1. Some of the notes seem mere translation of Stallbaum; but generally there are modifications. Thus when Stallbaum quotes a passage from an ancient author, the editor occasionally gives the sense, but oftener he writes out the words of the original where Stallbaum has only given the reference, or he quotes a little more than Stallbaum has done, or a little less; or the form of the reference is modified, more especially by giving the more modern or more convenient method. The changes often shew that the editor has looked out the passages for himself; this is, of course, so far to his credit, but it can hardly give proprietary rights. Sometimes the notes of Stallbaum seem to be abridged, sometimes they are added to with not altogether fortunate results.

It may be easily verified, by comparing the two books, that there is a good deal of such reproduction without any sort of acknowledgment; but some specimens of different kinds will be given.

2. The first two are notes (on 17 B and 35 B) which require the original from which they appear derived to make them intelligible or complete.

17 B.

ὅσα ὑμῖν] ᵃThis is doubtless the right reading. Sokrates had bargained with his friends, as we may learn from 20 B, that they should supply the sequel to his discourseᵃ: and this they had consented to do.

ᵇThus in recapitulating his own contribution Sokrates recalls to their minds what is expected of themᵇ.

Stallbaum.

ᵇ 'Num meministis, &c.' Quod est modeste suspicantis, ut alteri recordentur, quid ipse postulaveritᵇ. * * *

ᵃMale Bekkerus e duobus libris ἡμῖν dedit quod servavit etiam Astius. Nam etsi Socrates ipse partem disputationis profligaverat, tamen ceteros voluerat de iisdem rebus suam ferre sententiamᵃ.

[10]

The reader will vainly look in the editor's commentary or apparatus criticus for the alternative reading which is rejected, but will find it (ἡμῖν) in Stallbaum's. Otherwise the notes are identical, though the order of the subjects is reversed.

35 B.

	Stallbaum.
(N.B.—The editor's note is given without omissions exactly as it stands.) ἤρχετο δὲ διαιρεῖν ὧδε] Here Plato is really pythagorising. The numbers which follow are those which compose the geometrical τετρακτὺς of the Pythagoreans. This τετρακτὺς is double, proceeding in one branch from 1 to 2^3, in the other from 1 to 3^3, thus: 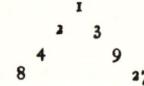 It will be observed that the sum of the first six numbers, 1, 2, 3, 4, 8, 9 equals the last, 27. This τετρακτὺς was significant of many things to the Pythagoreans: of these it will suffice to mention one which Plato may have had in view in selecting these numbers: 1 denotes the point; then in the διπλάσια διαστήματα 2 stands for the straight line, 4 for the rectilinear plane, 8 for the rectilinear solid. In the τριπλάσια διαστήματα 3 is the curved line, 9 the curvilinear superficies, 27 the curvilinear solid. These numbers also, as we presently see, form the basis of a musical scale. The simple Pythagorean τετρακτύς, 1 + 2 + 3 + 4 = 10 is not employed by Plato.	(Stallbaum after stating that there were said to be several forms of the Pythagorean tetractys, two of which were numerical, the first of them being a series in arithmetical progression, continues, p. 140, col. 2): Verum hujus quidem tetractyos nunc a Platone non habita est ratio, qui potius ob oculos habuit alteram, quae efficitur multiplicatione atque proportione nititur geometrica. Est autem ea duplex, prouti ex numeris vel paribus vel imparibus composita est, ita quidem ut in illis binario, in his ternario exponendi tribuatur vis et potentia. Speciem ejus atque formam haecce figura repraesentabit, quam apud Macrobium l. c. vidimus appictam; (here comes the editor's figure) * * (141, col. 2) . . . cujus sex priora membra aequant summam ultimi, h. e. viginti septem efficiunt. (Stallbaum after giving various meanings assigned in Theon Smyrnaeus to some of the numbers in the 'arithmetical' tetractys continues) Quae vides quam vaga sint et ambigua, ut vix quidquam inde ad Platonis interpretationem proficiamus. Plus momenti ad rem nostram facit geometrica illorum numerorum explicatio. Nam monas puncti dyas lineae, trias planitiei, tetras cubi signum esse putabatur. Id quod prorsus etiam in geometricam convenit tetractyn, in qua et ipsa terni numeri ex unitate prognati lineae, planitiei, atque cubi vel solidi corporis imaginem exhibent, hoc tamen discrimine, ut tetractys ex paribus numeris conflata figuras rectis lineis constantes denotet; altera autem, quae impares habet numeros, curvarum linearum indicium faciat. * * Duotetractys illa . . . a Pythagoreis etiam pro fundamento habita est systematis harmonici, s. tonici. * * (140. 2) tetractys, quae ex primis quattuor numeris, 1, 2, 3, 4, composita est atque habet arithmeticam proportionem,

> quippe additione effecta, qui quidem numeri quum gignant numerum denarium, factum est, ut hic ipse numerus pro perfectissimo sanctissimoque haberetur. Verum hujus quidem tetractyos Platone non est habita ratio.

There are several points worthy of attention in the relation of the English note and the Latin.

(1) The former begins at once with something about 'the geometrical tetractys,' which implies (cf. 'this tetractys') that there are other forms of tetractys. Yet nothing has been said about any others. Quite at the end of the English note another tetractys is mentioned, but we are not told whether these two are all, or what the general meaning of 'tetractys' is. The corresponding passage in Stallbaum is preceded, as it should of course be, by the information that there were several forms of tetractys. The English transcript should have begun at an earlier point.

(2) Why is 'this tetractys' called 'geometrical'? The English does not say, and might from what is said of the geometrical relations symbolised by the tetractys suggest a wrong answer. From the part of the Latin not reproduced we learn that the geometrical tetractys is so called because its terms are in geometrical proportion (or progression), and it is opposed to the arithmetical tetractys whose terms are in arithmetical proportion (or progression).

(3) The reader would not know from the English whether the lambda-shaped figure had any special meaning, or whether it is the editor's way of representing the two series, which start from the same term. It appears from the corresponding part by Stallbaum that the figure is an ancient tradition. (Compare also Martin i. 384.)

(4) It is said 'this tetractys was significant of many things, &c.' as if it were only a question of choosing, to suit the passage, one of several known meanings of the geometrical tetractys. This looks like an inaccurate reading of the corresponding Latin. Stallbaum quotes various meanings assigned in ancient authorities, not to the geometrical but the *arithmetical* tetractys, and puts forward an interpretation of the geometrical tetractys, based on the analogy of one of the meanings of the arithmetical tetractys, as may be seen from what is quoted above. It is significant in this connexion that the editor does not say why the other meanings of the geometrical tetractys, which his language would imply known to him, will not suit. He does not even say why the meaning of it, which he assigns, will suit. Such things are characteristic of notes of this dependent kind.

The mathematical phraseology in the same part of the note is very odd—'rectilinear plane'—'rectilinear solid'—'curvilinear superficies'—'curvilinear solid.' Their origin seems to be an attempt to render the Latin of Stallbaum 'figuras rectis lineis constantes,' &c., &c. One must wonder what the editor thought it all meant.

(5) The last sentence of the note is careless. The 'simple tetractys' should have of course been represented as a series, and not as a sum, and if it had been called 'arithmetical,' the right meaning of 'geometrical tetractys' would have been at least suggested. The bare fact that the sum of the four terms of the arithmetical tetractys is ten is repeated without its context, and so without a hint as to whether it had any significance for the Pythagoreans. So it is with the statement earlier in the note, that the sum of the first six numbers in the double tetractys is equal to the last. Information on both points is given in Stallbaum: some of it is quoted above.

(6) The opening sentence—'Here Plato is really pythagorising,' illustrates what the editor thinks will do for a note in this kind of subject.

In any case such a statement is valueless unless the authority for it is given, and more especially here, since there has been so much doubt as to what is 'really' Pythagorean and what is not.

(7) Stallbaum, besides referring to the ancient authorities, acknowledges his obligation to Boeckh. The English note contains no acknowledgment whatever.

3. The next set of instances concern the learning by which the Timaeus is illustrated.

21 C.

διὰ τὰς στάσεις κ.τ.λ. ἠναγκάσθη καταμελῆσαι.

	Stallbaum.
διὰ τὰς στάσεις] Plutarch, *Solon*, c. 31 says it was old age, not civil troubles, which prevented Solon from carrying out his designs.	Senectute eum impeditum esse scribit Plutarchus vit. Solon. c. 31.

21 E.

Νηίθ] This goddess is identified by Plutarch with Isis, *de Iside et Osiride*, § 9 τὸ δ' ἐν Σάει τῆς Ἀθηνᾶς, ἣν καὶ Ἶσιν νομίζουσιν, ἕδος ἐπιγραφὴν εἶχε τοιαύτην, Ἐγώ εἰμι πᾶν τὸ γεγονὸς καὶ ὂν καὶ ἐσόμενον· καὶ τὸν ἐμὸν πέπλον οὐδείς πω θνητὸς ἀπεκάλυψεν.	De dea Aegyptia, cui Neith nomen fuit quamque etiam Herodotus . . . Plutarch. de Isid. et Osir. p. 354 pro Minerva habent.

[13]

29 E.

The vulgar notion of τὸ θεῖον φθονερόν was extremely distasteful to Plato, cf. *Phaedrus* 247 A φθόνος γὰρ ἔξω θείου χοροῦ ἵσταται.

ἀγαθῷ ... δ' οὐδεὶς φθόνος] Ita Phaedr. 247 A φθόνος γὰρ ἔξω θείου χόρου (sic) ἵσταται, de quo vid. &c.

So Aristotle *Metaph.* A. ii. 983ᵃ 2 ἀλλ' οὔτε τὸ θεῖον φθονερὸν ἐνδέχεται εἶναι, ἀλλὰ καὶ κατὰ τὴν παροιμίαν πολλὰ ψεύδονται ἀοιδοί.

Aristot. Metaphys. p. 8 ed. Brandis εἰ δὴ λέγουσίν τι κ.τ.λ. ... ἀλλ' οὔτε τὸ θεῖον φθονερὸν ἐνδέχεται εἶναι ἀλλὰ καὶ κατὰ τὴν παροιμίαν πολλὰ ψεύδονται ἀοιδοί, οὔτε κ.τ.λ.

In his preface the editor excuses himself for excluding much 'linguistic exegesis' on the ground that 'the commentary would have been swelled to an unwieldy bulk.' (A better ground will probably suggest itself later on.) When self-denial is professed in the matter of useful notes, suspicion is provoked by the borrowing of such entirely superfluous learning as in some of the following instances, which seems only to serve for a 'gelehrten Anstrich.'

19 B.

οἷον εἴ τις] This passage is referred to by Athenaeus XI. 507 D in support of the truly remarkable charge of φιλοδοξία which he brings against Plato.

Stallbaum.

ceterum hoc initio orationis Socraticae usus est Athenaeus XI. 507 D, E, ut Platonem more suo calumniaretur.

So also at the beginning of the dialogue, is repeated, without acknowledgment to Boeckh or Stallbaum the useless gossip from Athenaeus (IX. 382) given in Boeckh's note, and the remark of Quintilian (IX. iv. 78), to which Boeckh also refers: where Stallbaum rightly says, 'Ceterum non attinet hic narrare quid Athenaeus IX. p. 382 ... et Quintilian. IX. iv. 78 de hoc Timaei initio judicaverint.'

24 A.

παραδείγματα is of course not put for εἰκόνας, as Proklos would have it, but signifies samples, specimens.

Stallbaum.

... de quo vocabulo Proclus: παραδείγματα νῦν τὰς εἰκόνας καλεῖ ... Imo παραδείγματα dicuntur quasi specimina quaedam, &c. (Stallbaum also renders 'Proben' = samples.)

At the end of the note on the reflection from mirrors (46 A) is added a quotation from Seneca, which might well have been spared as will be seen.

46 A.

Seneca *natur. quaest.* I. v. 1 clearly expresses the distinctive character of Plato's theory of reflections:

Stallbaum.

Brevius rem tractavit Alcinous ... ad cujus verba Jacobus Carpentarius: 'Quamquam non omnes, inquit, hanc rationem eorum, quae in speculis apparent, admittent, sed, ut ait Seneca Natur. Quaest.

'de speculis duae opiniones sunt ; alii enim in illis simulacra cerni putant id est corporum nostrorum figuras a nostris corporibus emissas ac separatas,
alii non imagines in speculo, sed ipsa adspici corpora retorta oculorum acie et in se rursus reflexa.

ᵃThe italicised words express Plato'ᵣ opinion.ᵃ

I. 5, omnino de illis duae opiniones sunt. Alii enim in iis simulacra cerni putant, i. e. corporum nostrorum figuras a nostris corporibus per aërem sparsas et in illis acceptas. ᵃAlii cum Platone aiuntᵃ nullas re vera imagines in speculo esse, quemadmodum neque in iride colores, sed ipsa adspici corpora, oculorum acie retorta et in se rursus reflexa.'

Seneca does not mention Plato here. If Plato is really meant Charpentier should have (as he has in Stallbaum's note) the credit of pointing it out. The editor, who makes no acknowledgments, reproduces in his last sentence ('The italicised words, &c.') Charpentier's remark 'alii cum Platone aiunt,' without observing that the words of Seneca referred to do *not* 'clearly express the distinctive character of Plato's theory of reflections,' for in that the 'oculorum acies' is no more supposed to be 'turned back on itself' than it is in the theory of direct vision[1]. The single case which it might suit is that where a man sees his own eye in a mirror, but though Plato speaks of a man seeing his own face (which certainly involves no 'retorta oculorum acies') it happens that he does not consider what would take place in the peculiar case of the eye seeing itself.

4. A couple of instances follow of philological notes, which are a kind of variant on Stallbaum's.

45 A.
σκέλη μὲν οὖν χεῖρές τε ταύτῃ καὶ διὰ ταῦτα προσέφυ πᾶσι.

προσέφυ] With this remarkable use of the singular compare the still stronger case in *Symposium* 188 B καὶ γὰρ πάχναι καὶ χάλαζαι καὶ ἐρυσίβαι ἐκ πλεονεξίας καὶ ἀκοσμίας περὶ ἄλληλα τῶν τοιούτων γίγνεται ἐρωτικῶν.
The construction is of course distinct from the so-called 'schema Pindaricum,' in which the verb precedes its subject, and which is not so very uncommon in Attic writers.

Stallbaum.
De numero verbi singulari v. ad Symposium 188 B, Coll. Matthiae Gr. § 203.

The addition *de suo* is an instance of the inaccuracy of the philological notes which will be more fully illustrated hereafter. On the one hand there is no danger of confusion with the particular construction to which the editor is referring because the verb is always εἶναι or something cognate: an important feature which the editor does not notice. On the other hand, in the 'schema Pindaricum' in the wider sense the verb does not necessarily come first, and the construction of

---

[1] See below, par. 63.

the present passage may be well compared with it, and, as it happens, is compared with it by Kühner.

23 B.
τὸ κάλλιστον καὶ ἄριστον γένος ἐπ' ἀνθρώπους.

Stallbaum.

ἐπί signifies extension over : a use exceedingly rare in Attic prose but occurring again in *Critias* 112 E ἐπὶ πᾶσαν Εὐρώπην καὶ Ἀσίαν κατά τε σωμάτων κάλλη καὶ κατὰ τὴν τῶν ψυχῶν παντοίαν ἀρετὴν ἐλλόγιμοί τε ἦσαν καὶ ὀνομαστότατοι πάντων τῶν τότε : and a similar, though not identical, use is to be found in Protagoras 322 D. It is not uncommon in Homer, e.g. *Iliad* X. 213 μέγα κέν οἱ ὑπουράνιον κλέος εἴη | πάντας ἐπ' ἀνθρώπους.

ἐπ' ἀνθρώπους . . . quod similiter dictum est atque Critia p. 112 E ἐπὶ πᾶσαν Εὐρώπην—ἐλλόγιμοι ἦσαν, et fere idem valet quod ἐν ἀνθρώποις.
Homer, Iliad XXIV. v. 202 ὤμοι, πῇ δή τοι φρένες οἴχονθ' ἧς τὸ πάρος περ, ἔκλε' ἐπ' ἀνθρώπους. Ibid. v. 535 πάντας γὰρ ἐπ' ἀνθρώπους, κ.τ.λ.

The matter is not put quite accurately in the English note. ἐπί, signifying 'extension over,' is common enough in Attic prose in expressions of time (cf. e.g. in this same context ἐπὶ πολλὰς γενεάς), though not apparently common in those of space. The present use of ἐπί should have been represented rather as a derivative from that of 'extension over,' for, as Stallbaum says, it comes to be equivalent to ἐν with the dative. The passage from the Protagoras is the one quoted in Ast's lexicon along with the other two (Critias and Timaeus), but it should have been stated that it is an instance of ἐπί with νέμειν—a use sufficiently established both with νέμειν and διανέμειν.

5. The following are examples in matters of general interpretation.

19 D.

Stallbaum.

τὸ μιμητικὸν ἔθνος] [b]See *Republic* 392 D, 398 A, 597 E foll. Poetry, says Plato, is an imitative art;[b] and [a]poets cannot imitate what is outside of their experience.[a] [f]For the use of ἔθνος compare *Sophist* 242 D, *Gorgias* 455 B, *Politicus* 290 B.[e]
ἔτι δὲ χαλεπώτερον λόγοις] [f]Proklos raises needless difficulties about this.[f] [d]Plato simply means[d] that to describe such things worthily requires [c]a rare literary gift: it is far easier to find an Agamemnon than a Homer.[c]

[a]Dicuntur poetae ea tantum scite imitari posse quibus quasi innutriti sint; quae ab ipsius vitae usu et consuetudine sint remota, ea vero imitari non posse.[a] Hujus enim generis res, quum actione exprimi vix queant, tum [c]oratione omnium difficillime exprimi solere.[c]
[b]Enimvero Platonem constat poesin omnem in imitatione positam judicavisse, de qua re philosophus explicavit Reip. III. p. 392 C sqq. p. 398 A al.[b]
Jam vero quoniam qui id, quod non didicerunt et cui disciplina non sunt assuefacti, ora*' ne imitari instituunt, praeter rerum peritiam [c]etiam eloquentiam habeant necesse est,[c] [d]facile est ad intelligendum, quibus causis et rationibus notatur hoc philosophi judicium,[d] [f]de quo Proclus rursus multa frustra nugatur.[f]
(From a preceding note.)
[e]ἔθνος . . . Gorg. 455 B ἢ περὶ ναυπηγῶν ἢ περὶ ἄλλων τινὸς δημιουργικοῦ ἔθνους. De Rep. 351 C, 420 B, 421 C, Sophist. 242 D τὸ Ἐλεατικὸν ἔθνος, Politic. 290 B τὸ κηρυκικὸν γένος [l. ἔθνος]. Legg. 776 D τὸ Θετταλῶν πενεστικὸν ἔθνος.[e]

[16]

24 B.

τῶν περὶ τὴν 'Ασίαν] Egypt was commonly regarded in Plato's time as belonging to Asia rather than Africa. All Africa was indeed often regarded as part of Asia; but that Plato distinguished them is made clear below in 24 E.

Stallbaum.

Magis etiam lapsi sunt quidam in interpretandis verbis proximis: οἷς ἡμεῖς πρῶτοι τῶν περὶ 'Ασίαν ὡπλίσμεθα. Nempe ignorarunt isti Egyptum a veteribus pro Asiae parte habitam esse, siquidem multi totius orbis terrarum duas fecerunt partes, Asiam et Europam, Libyam nunc Asiae nunc Europae accensentes. Hanc rationem Plato nunc ex parte sequitur quandoquidem mox πορευομένην ἅμα ἐπὶ πᾶσαν Εὐρώπην καὶ 'Ασίαν; quanquam ibidem Libyam at Asiae discernit verbis ἡ δὲ νῆσος ... &c. [24 E.]

19 A.

Τὰ μὲν τῶν ἀγαθῶν θρεπτέον ἔφαμεν εἶναι, τὰ δὲ τῶν κακῶν εἰς τὴν ἄλλην λάθρᾳ διαδοτέον πόλιν.

Plato has here somewhat mitigated the rigour of his ordinance in the *Republic*: see 459 D τοὺς ἀρίστους ταῖς ἀρίσταις συγγίγνεσθαι ὡς πλειστάκις, τοὺς δὲ φαυλοτάτους ταῖς φαυλοτάταις τοὐναντίον, καὶ τῶν μὲν τὰ ἔκγονα τρέφειν τῶν δὲ μή. Compare too 460 C τὰ δὲ τῶν χειρόνων, καὶ ἐάν τι τῶν ἄλλων ἀνάπηρον γίγνηται, ἐν ἀπορρήτῳ τε καὶ ἀδήλῳ κατακρύψουσιν ὡς πρέπει: and again, 461 C μάλιστα μὲν μηδ' εἰς φῶς ἐκφέρειν κύημα μηδέ γ' ἕν, ἐὰν γένηται, ἐὰν δέ τι βιάσηται, οὕτω τιθέναι ὡς οὐκ οὔσης τροφῆς τῷ τοιούτῳ. But in 415 B the milder course is enjoined: ἐάν τε σφέτερος ἔκγονος ὑπόχαλκος ἢ ὑποσίδηρος γένηται, μηδενὶ τρόπῳ κατελεήσουσιν, ἀλλὰ τὴν τῇ φύσει προσήκουσαν τιμὴν ἀποδόντες ὤσουσιν εἰς δημιουργοὺς ἢ εἰς γεωργούς. Probably then, when Plato speaks of not rearing the inferior children, he merely means that they are not to be reared by the state as infant φύλακες.

Stallbaum.

Legendus de hac re locus est de Rep. III. p. 415 A, B ; V. p. 461 A sqq. unde apparet εἰς τὴν ἄλλην πόλιν esse *in reliquam civitatis partem*, h. e. in ceteros civium ordinem, operarios et agricolas.

Itaque θρεπτέον εἶναι est *tanquam futuros civitatis custodes educari opportere*, neque cogitandum de infantum expositione.

The enlargement of Stallbaum's note has resulted in a characteristic confusion. First we are told that Plato in the Timaeus has somewhat mitigated the rigour of his ordinance in the Republic: as though the Republic was all one way. Secondly, it turns out in the course of the note that 'the milder course is enjoined' in the Republic itself, but it does not occur to the editor to qualify his first statement. Thirdly, the confusion is completed by the last sentence—'Probably then when Plato,' &c. For since Plato does not speak in the Timaeus of 'not rearing the inferior children,' but in some of the passages from the Republic, quoted in the English note, this last sentence can only mean that there is no 'rigorous ordinance' at all in the Republic. It looks as though this had been occasioned by the last sentence in Stallbaum's note which relates to the Timaeus and not to the Republic.

ἀπείρους ... ἀπείρου] For the play on the word compare *Philebus* 17 E τὸ δὲ ἄπειρόν σε ἑκάστων καὶ ἐν τούτοις πλῆθος ἄπειρον ἑκάστοτε ποιεῖ τοῦ φρονεῖν καὶ οὐκ ἐλλόγιμον οὐδ' ἐνάριθμον, ἅτ' οὐκ εἰς ἀριθμὸν οὐδένα ἐν οὐδένι πώποτε ἀπιδόντα.

Plato is at issue with Demokritos, who consistently with his whole physical theory maintained that the number of κόσμοι was infinite : Plato is equally consistent in affirming that there is only one.

The oddest fancy in this way is one ascribed by Plutarch *de defectu oraculorum*, § 22, to Petron of Himera[1], who declared there were 183 κόσμοι, disposed in the form of an equilateral triangle. The eternal fitness of the arrangement is not explained by Plutarch.

Apaturia was the name of a festival in honour of Dionysos, held in the month Pyanepsion, which corresponded, roughly speaking, to our October.

It lasted three days, of which the first was called δόρπεια, the second ἀνάρρυσις, the third κουρεῶτις. On the third day the names of children three or four[2] years of age were enrolled on the register of their φρατρία.

Proklos seems mistaken in making ἀνάρρυσις the first day ; all other authorities place δόρπεια first.

55 D.
Stallbaum.

Ceterum observabis elegantem dilogiam verborum ἀπείρους—ἀπείρου (imperiti) τινὸς εἶναι quae reperitur etiam Phileb. 17 E τὸ δ' ἄπειρόν σε ἑκάστων καὶ ἐν ἑκάστοις πλῆθος ἄπειρον ἑκάστοτε ποιεῖ.

Praeterea notabis rideri haud dubie Democritum de quo Diog. Laert. IX. 44 ἀπείρους (ἡγήσατο) εἶναι κόσμους &c. &c.

* *

Plutarchus De εἶ apud Delphos, p. 389, &c. (here follows a quotation reproduced with additions by the Editor in his next note).

... r ulta idem De Oraculor. Defectu 426 sqq. = 682 sqq. ed. Reisk.... quae omnia describere non vacat.

21 B
Stallbaum.

Apaturia quotannis colebant mense Pyanepsione, h. e. Octobri, per triduum, &c. .... de quo v. Meurs. Graecia feriat. &c. &c.

Primus dies vocabatur δόρπεια, quia ut Suidas ait, φράτορες ὀψίας συνελθόντες εὐωχοῦντο. Alter dicebatur ἀνάρρυσις, ... Tertius erat κουρεῶτις, qui nomen habebat ἀπὸ τοῦ τοὺς κούρους καὶ τὰς κόρας ἐγγράφειν εἰς τὰς φρατρίας.

Disputarunt de Apaturiis Meursius, &c. &c.

Ceterum Proclus ad h. l. quem sequitur Scholiastes, primum Apaturiorum diem ἀνάρρυσιν, secundum δορπίαν (δόρπειαν) . . vocatum esse narrat, quod non tantum Suidae testimonio adversatur, sed etiam cum iis pugnat quae Hesychius, Harpocratio, &c. &c. memoriae prodiderunt.

Martin.

Plutarque (Du silence des Oracles, c. 22) cite une opinion d'après laquelle il aurait tout juste cent quatre-vingt-trois mondes rangés en forme de triangle.

---

[1] This is not quite accurate. The opinion is cited in § 22, but it is not till afterwards (§ 23) that reasons are given for attributing it to Petron of Himera.

[2] Cf. in Martin's note, ' les garçons et les filles de trois à quatre ans.'

B

6. The following is an instance where the debt to Stallbaum is not so obvious to the eye.

31 A.

σωματοειδὲς δὲ δὴ καὶ ὁρατὸν ἁπτόν τε δεῖ τὸ γενόμενον εἶναι.

ὁρατὸν ἁπτόν τε] Visibility and tangibility are the two most conspicuous characteristics of matter, therefore the fundamental constituents of the universe are fire and earth. This agrees with the view of Parmenides: cf. Aristotle, *Physica* I. v. 188ᵃ 20 καὶ γὰρ Παρμενίδης θερμὸν καὶ ψυχρὸν ἀρχὰς ποιεῖ, ταῦτα δὲ προσαγορεύει πῦρ καὶ γῆν: and Parmenides 112 foll. (Karsten): see too Aristotle, *de gen. et corr.* II. ix. 336ᵃ 3. The four elements of Empedokles likewise reduced themselves to two: cf. Aristotle, *metaph.* A. iv. 985ᵃ 3 οὐ μὴν χρῆται γε τέτταρσιν, ἀλλ' ὡς δυσὶν οὖσι μόνοις, πυρὶ μὲν καθ' αὑτό, τοῖς δ' ἀντικειμένοις ὡς μιᾷ φύσει, γῇ τε καὶ ἀέρι καὶ ὕδατι: and *de gen. et corr.* II. iii. 330ᵇ 20. His division, however, does not agree with that of Plato, who classes fire, air and water as forms of the same base, and places earth alone by itself.

Stallbaum.

Duo ponit primitiva rerum elementa... Ignem vero et terram illa vult esse propterea, quod rerum natura et adspectabilis debeat esse et vero etiam tractabilis. Alterum autem igne, alterum terra effici arbitratur v. Aristotel. Part. An. II. i. 2 Ignem et terram rerum generatarum principia fecerunt etiam Democritus, Anaxagoras, Parmenides de quo vid. Karsten, p. 221 sqq., 229 sq., &c. &c.

The two notes are clearly on the same lines: but the quotations from Aristotle are not the same, and though Parmenides is mentioned in both, the point about Empedocles is not noticed by Stallbaum. Stallbaum, however, refers to passages in Karsten's Parmenides (p. 221 sqq. and 229 sqq.). In Karsten, p. 221, will be found the first of the editor's quotations from Aristotle, in p. 224 the second. In p. 229 will be found the editor's remark on Empedocles. The latter passage naturally occasions a reference to a part of Karsten's Empedocles, and here, p. 342, occur the two last of the editor's quotations from Aristotle.

7. A comparison of the two editions in the earlier part of the Timaeus would produce the impression that the editor's commentary was a kind of rewriting of Stallbaum's, which would not cost much trouble. This obligation to Stallbaum is not so marked later on, where the notes become mainly a reproduction of Martin.

In the instances given there is no acknowledgment whatever, and so it is generally.

There is of course some common ground which editors are likely to traverse, and this may fairly explain a certain number of passages which have not been given above; but the bulk of the coincidences cannot be explained in this way.

That the coincidences in learned quotations are accidental will scarcely be believed by the reader who will look into the edition and see how constantly the notes repeat what is found in Stallbaum and Martin (and others), more especially when the imperfectness of the editor's knowledge of the authors quoted is taken into account. The latter point is treated of below in connection with Martin and the editor's use of 'testimonia.' See Pt. I. §§ 3 and 4; Pt. II. par. 50.

The editor is indeed forgetful, as the following instance shows:—In his note on Atlantis, 24 D (where, by the way, the statement that 'Plato is our only authority for the legend: there is no trace of confirmation from any independent source,' and others given without reference to any one, are doubtless due to the researches of Martin), there is a passage which may be put beside Jowett's note on the same subject in his introduction to the Critias.

Editor.	Jowett.
It appears to me impossible to determine whether Plato has invented the story from beginning to end:—ῥᾳδίως Αἰγυπτίους καὶ ὁπαδαποὺς ἂν ἐθέλῃ λόγους ποιεῖ—or whether it really more or less represents some Egyptian legend brought home by Solon.	Hence we may safely conclude that the entire narrative is due to the imagination of Plato, who *could easily invent 'Egyptians or anything else'* (Phaedr. 275 B), and who has used the name of Solon (of whose poem there is no trace in antiquity) and the tradition of the Egyptian priests to give verisimilitude to his story.

(The passage in italics is more accurately quoted by Jowett in his introduction to the Parmenides.)

Some other remarkable instances of forgetfulness will be given later. But in the nature of the case bad memory will not be seriously alleged as a sufficient excuse for the absence of acknowledgment to Stallbaum, especially as the editor so often remembers those notes of Stallbaum's which he thinks he can show mistaken.

§ 2.—CRITICISMS OF STALLBAUM.

8. After seeing this evidence of the usefulness of Stallbaum's commentary to the editor, it is amusing to find this judgment delivered in the Preface:—

'Ten years later came Stallbaum's edition; concerning which it were unbecoming to speak with less than the respect due to the zeal and industry of a scholar who has essayed the gigantic enterprise of editing with elaborate prolegomena and commentary the entire works of Plato, and it would be *unfair to disparage the learning which the notes display*: none the less it cannot be denied that in dealing with this dialogue *the editor seems hardly to have realised the nature of the task he has undertaken.*'

If the editor did not feel obliged to make any acknowledgment to Stallbaum, yet Stallbaum deserved to be treated by him with great consideration. But the editor seems to take every opportunity to speak slightingly of his predecessor; and we find such expressions as these: ' of Stallbaum's note the less said the better '—' extremely inaccurate '—' most erroneous '—' his [Stallbaum's] treatment of the whole subject is as confused as it can well be '—' what Stallbaum means or fails to mean it is difficult to conjecture[1].' Enough has been seen of the quality of the editor's work to make it doubtful whether these phrases are safe for him to use, and it will be seen hereafter that they are particularly unfortunate.

A nemesis attends this treatment of Stallbaum. The editor is so concerned to attack that he will contradict his own view to do it. For the same reason he criticises notes of Stallbaum's hastily read or imperfectly remembered, and so falls into mistakes which would have been avoided if he had taken another look at Stallbaum before publishing his criticism. He is unfair in other ways also, and when not unfair is often wrong himself. A considerable part of his long record of mistakes is made in this connection; and here, as indeed in places where Stallbaum is not attacked, his great superiority to the editor in scholarship becomes apparent.

Some examples will be given.

---

[1] Compare the style of these notes. In 55 C, a curious slip in which Stallbaum has followed some ancient commentators is spoken of as 'an opinion which Stallbaum welcomes with joy, saying that it "mirifice convenit" with the 360 degrees into which the circle is divided,' &c. Note on 74 B—'The expression is very obscure: and no two interpreters agree as to its meaning. Stallbaum is entirely at sea: Lindau, at *whom he scoffs*, throws out a suggestion which is much more reasonable than anything in Stallbaum's note, &c.' It will be clear that the editor had better have said nothing about scoffing. It happens also that Stallbaum's note is far more sensible than Lindau's. For the value of the editor's own note see below, paragraph 39, page 67.

9. In the two following the editor contradicts himself:—

21 A. ἀλλὰ δὴ ποῖον ἔργον τοῦτο Κριτίας οὐ λεγόμενον μέν, ὡς δὲ πραχθὲν ὄντως ὑπὸ τῆσδε τῆς πόλεως ἀρχαῖον διηγεῖτο κατὰ τὴν Σόλωνος ἀκοήν; (the story of the defeat of the invaders from Atlantis by the Athenians).

The note is—

'Stallbaum is ill-advised in adopting the interpretation of Proklos μὴ πάνυ μὲν τεθρυλημένον, γενόμενον δὲ ὅμως. The meaning is beyond question "not a mere figment of the imagination (like the commonwealth described in the *Republic*) but a history of facts that actually occurred." Cf. 26 E τό τε μὴ πλασθέντα μῦθον ἀλλ' ἀληθινὸν λόγον εἶναι πάμμεγά του.'

(1) Stallbaum is 'beyond question' right whether the Greek or the context is considered. The editor's explanation violates the known rule, set forth in the Grammars about the distinction between δέ and ἀλλά: and thus he has not noticed the difference in form between this sentence (21 A) and the one he quotes (26 E).

Stallbaum's explanation is also confirmed by the context. Cf. especially 21 D (πρᾶξιν) ἣν ἥδε ἡ πόλις ἔπραξε μέν, διὰ δὲ χρόνον καὶ φθορὰν τῶν ἐργασαμένων οὐ διήρκεσε δεῦρο ὁ λόγος, and 20 E ἔργα τῆς πόλεως ὑπὸ χρόνου καὶ φθορᾶς ἀνθρώπων ἠφανισμένα.

(2) The editor in his Translation actually renders in the 'ill-advised' manner of Stallbaum—' But what was the deed which Kritias described on the authority of Solon as actually performed of old by this city, though unrecorded in history?'

55 D. Plato says of the number of the κόσμοι:—τὸ μὲν ἀπείρους ἡγήσαιτ' ἂν ὄντως (τις) ἀπείρου τινὸς εἶναι δόγμα ὧν ἔμπειρον χρεὼν εἶναι· πότερον δὲ ἕνα ἢ πέντε αὐτοὺς ἀληθείᾳ πεφυκότας λέγειν προσήκει, μᾶλλον ἂν ταύτῃ στὰς (vv. ll. ἱστάς, πᾶς) εἰκότως διαπορήσαι.

In the note—

'ταύτῃ στάς] This is evidently the right reading. ... Stallbaum's πᾶς, which has but slight support, is quite inappropriate; "Plato could not say that it was reasonable for everyone to doubt whether there are five κόσμοι or one; it would not be reasonable in his own case, as we see in 31 B."'

(1) πᾶς is obviously not at all inappropriate. Plato thinks it absurd to suppose the number is unlimited, but that anyone might reasonably raise the question whether the number was five, since there are five regular solids. But the editor has himself spoken to this effect in the preceding note, 'Plato regards as a comparatively reasonable supposition the view that there may be five κόσμοι, because there exist in

nature five regular rectilinear solids,' and thus he really contradicts himself: though of course to criticise Stallbaum, he makes a captious refinement about the meaning of πᾶs. Quite apart from the question as to whether πᾶs is the best reading or not, it is clear that the sentence with πᾶs would only be a natural way for Plato to express what the editor supposes him to mean.

(2) However, in his later edition Stallbaum does not read πᾶs, but στάs. This is one of several proofs that the editor criticises Stallbaum's text without looking at his later edition. Moreover the edition of Stallbaum in which στάs appears is earlier than that of C. F. Hermann, whom the editor follows in reading στάs.

(3) Though the editor says 'στάs is evidently the right reading,' he does not say whether it is the reading of any MS., though it is important that this should be expressly stated. Perhaps the reason is that neither Hermann nor Bekker (the authorities he relies on, see below, par. 48) nor Stallbaum happen to say.

10. The next three instances show, beside other things, the same ignorance of Stallbaum's later edition.

In 26 B, Critias says of the story he heard as a boy, ἦν μὲν οὖν μετὰ πολλῆς ἡδονῆς καὶ παιδικῆς (v. l. παιδιᾶς) τότε ἀκουόμενα.

The note is—

'Stallbaum with very slight ms. authority reads παιδιᾶς, without noticing any other reading: apparently he failed to perceive that παιδικῆς was in agreement with ἡδονῆς.'

(1) It is characteristic of the editor's attitude that he should assume a scholar like Stallbaum could have overlooked such an obvious concord. He has 'failed to perceive' the appropriateness here of the idiom μετὰ παιδιᾶς as opposed to μετὰ σπουδῆς, which may well have influenced Stallbaum.

(2) The note betrays that the editor has not read Stallbaum's appendix which contains Bast's collection of Paris. A, in which παιδικῆς is recorded as the reading of Paris. A, with -ιᾶς written above it.

(3) In his later edition Stallbaum followed the authority of the principal MS. and read παιδικῆς.

33 A, κατανοῶν, ὡς ξυστάτῳ σώματι θερμὰ καὶ ψυχρὰ καὶ πάνθ' ὅσα δυνάμεις ἰσχυρὰς ἔχει περιιστάμενα ἔξωθεν καὶ προσπίπτοντα ἀκαίρως λύει κ.τ.λ.

App. crit.—' ξυστάτῳ dedi cum H(ermanno) e W. Wagneri conjecturâ.'

Note—

'The reading of Stallbaum and the Zurich edition ἁ ξυνιστᾷ τὰ σώματα has poor ms. authority and is weak in sense; moreover the form ξυνιστᾷ is extremely doubtful Attic. The mss. for the most part have ξυνιστὰς or ξυνιστὰν τῷ σώματι.'

(1) This is an instance of an unfairness which the editor sometimes shews, that of raising a difficulty without saying that the person criticised has raised it himself. The remark on ξυνιστᾷ is found in Stallbaum in a more valuable form. ' Pro ξυνιστᾷ etsi Atticorum usus exigit fere ξυνίστησι, tamen illam formam non dixerim cum Buttmanno Gr. Ampl. § 107 ann. 8. Matthiae Gr. § 210 ann. 1. et Poppone ad Thucyd. VIII. 64, 5. citerioris tantum Graecitatis propriam esse, &c., &c.' (It may be noted that the remark of the editor's which follows —' the MSS. for the most part, &c.,' is also from Stallbaum.)

(2) In his later edition Stallbaum reads ξυνιστάμενα.

The following betrays another serious defect in the editor's studies.

86 E, παντὶ δὲ ταῦτα ἐχθρὰ καὶ κακόν τι προσγίγνεται.

The editor reading καὶ ἄκοντι, says, ' Cornarius' correction of κακόν τι into ἄκοντι seems nearly as certain as an emendation can be; and I can only wonder at Stallbaum's defence of the old reading.'

(1) In his later edition Stallbaum reads ἄκοντι.

(2) This fact is specially noted in the critical preface to C. F. Hermann's edition (Teubner), p. xxvi, '... p. 86 E, ubi jam Stallb. egregiam Vat. o et Flor. x lectionem ἄκοντι pro κακόν τι ascivit.' This shews how little the editor has studied the apparatus criticus of the very edition on which he bases his own text.

(3) The editor's note is inaccurate, for he speaks as if the reading were only the correction of Cornarius (cf. Stallb., ' Cornarius κ. ἅ. conjectabat'): but it appears both from Stallbaum and Hermann that it is found in some MSS.

11. The next instance is due at best to inexcusable carelessness and forgetfulness.

68 B, τῇ δὲ διὰ τῆς νοτίδος αὐγῇ τοῦ πυρὸς μιγνυμένου (cor. Steph. : Vulg. μιγνυμένῃ) χρῶμα ἔναιμον παρασχόμενον (Codd. παρασχομένῃ).

App. crit.—' παρασχόμενον scripsi. παρασχομένῃ A. H(erm). S(tallb). Z.'

Note.—' Stallbaum, accepting μιγνυμένου, oddly enough retains παρασχομένῃ.'

(1) The emendation which the editor puts as if his own is in the note of Stallbaum which he has before him, and is due to Lindau, whose book he has used. 'Primum enim legendum est μιγνυμένου, quod jam Stephanus pervidit; deinde pro παρασχομένη haud dubie de conjectura Lindavii reponi opportet παρασχόμενον.' (Stallbaum goes on to suggest that τοῦ πυρὸς μιγνυμένῃ may be a gloss.)

(2) It is true that Stallbaum's text has παρασχομένη, but the note just quoted, preceded as it is by the words 'duplici utique, si quid video, opus est medicinâ ut locus in integritatem suam restituatur,' shews that he meant to read παρασχόμενον. παρασχομένη, in the text, is then a mere oversight; it has escaped correction in his later edition.

12. The foregoing recalls some other emendations in the notes in which justice is hardly done to Stallbaum.

37 B, ὅταν μὲν περὶ τὸ αἰσθητὸν γίγνηται καὶ ὁ τοῦ θατέρου κύκλος ὀρθὸς ὢν εἰς πᾶσαν αὐτὰ τὴν ψυχὴν διαγγείλῃ κ.τ.λ.

App. crit.—'αὐτὰ scripsi : αὐτοῦ A. H. S(tallb). Z.' Note—'The MS. reading αὐτοῦ is clearly wrong, though Martin defends it. Stallbaum proposes αὐτό : but as we presently have αὐτὰ referring to λογιστικόν, that is perhaps more likely to be right here.' This is not a very serious matter, but illustrates the way in which Stallbaum's notes get spoiled. The passage cited in objection to Stallbaum is one which he himself had considered : indeed it is the passage on which he bases (and rightly) his approval of the emendation of which the editor's is but a trifling and doubtful alteration. Stallbaum also had before him, though in a different form, the difficulty (if it can be called one) that in one clause αὐτό would refer to τὸ αἰσθητόν, and in the other the plural αὐτά to τὸ λογιστικόν. Again, the note inaccurately implies that the conjecture is Stallbaum's. Stallbaum says—'Scribendum haud dubie εἰς πᾶσαν αὐτὸ (sc. τὸ αἰσθητὸν) τὴν ψυχήν, quum αὐτοῦ non habeat quorsum commode referatur. Quam emendationem teste Tennemanno System. Phil. Plat. III. p. 72 a Damanno propositam unice veram esse evincunt quae deinde sequuntur : καὶ ὁ ταὐτοῦ κύκλος εὔτροχος ὢν αὐτὰ μηνύσῃ, ubi αὐτὰ item refertur ad praegressum τὸ λογιστικόν, ita quidem ut quae mente et cogitatione comprehenduntur significantur : neque enim hic αὐτὸ cum Tennemanno corrigendum esse docebunt quae ad Gorg. p. 447 A, De Rep. p. 504 D, Apol. Socr. p. 19 D, de hoc usu numeri pluralis exposuimus.' The editor's proposal to read the plural (αὐτά) in both places is the converse of Tennemann's to read the singular. Stallbaum doubtless felt αὐτό to be the more natural emendation of αὐτοῦ, and that αὐτά was not likely to have been changed from αὐτό in the second clause. It is also somewhat against the assimilation of the pronouns that while αὐτό would refer directly to τὸ αἰσθητόν, αὐτά does not refer so directly to τὸ λογιστικόν—which denotes a mental faculty and not, as the editor wrongly thinks (see par. 61, p. 114), its object—but rather to the objects of τὸ λογιστικόν. And apart from this, there are instances of harsher change from singular to plural and vice versa in the Timaeus itself, where the editor raises no difficulty, e.g. 49 B, πῶς οὖν δὴ τοῦτ᾽ αὐτὸ καὶ πῆ καὶ τί περὶ αὐτῶν εἰκότως διαπορηθέντες κ.τ.λ. (Ed. 'How then are we to deal with this point, and what is the question that we should properly raise concerning it?'); 61 A, τὰ δὲ δὴ τῶν ξυμμίκτων ἐκ γῆς τε καὶ ὕδατος σωμάτων, μέχρι περ ἂν ὕδωρ αὐτοῦ τὰ τῆς γῆς διάκενα . . . κατέχῃ.

35 A, Τῆς τε ταὐτοῦ φύσεως αὖ πέρι καὶ τῆς θατέρου. The note in the app. crit. is surprising. 'Post φύσεως delevi αὖ πέρι, quae cum consensu codicum retinent S (=Stallb.) Z; inclusit H.' Stallbaum says (app. crit.) 'Istud αὖ πέρι ejiciendum censet Davisius ad Ciceron. De Nat. Deor. L. 8 secutus auctoritatem Sexti Empir. Pyrrhon. Hypotyp. III. 24 et adv. Mathem. p. 60. Nos αὖ in ὂν commutandum, πέρι ejiciendum censemus.' Beside the unfairness both to the author of the emendation and to Stallbaum in the editor's note, its inferiority to Stallbaum's is evident. In his commentary, Stallbaum returns to the point, and it appears that Sextus Empiricus, twice quoting this passage, omits both αὖ and πέρι each time. But the editor has made no study of 'testimonia.' (Stallbaum cites Cicero's translation for his own emendation, 'quod esset ejusdem naturae et alterius'; but Cicero might have so translated without reading ὄν.)

13. In the next instance Stallbaum is not criticised, directly at least, but, as in a previous one, the editor puts forward an important suggestion as if his own, which is given by Stallbaum in a note, where he expresses another opinion which the editor himself has quoted.

38 D, σώματα δὲ αὐτῶν ἑκάστων (sc. τῶν πλανητῶν) ποιήσας ὁ θεὸς ἔθηκεν εἰς τὰς περιφοράς, ἃς ἡ θατέρου περίοδος ᾔειν . . . σελήνην μὲν εἰς τὸν περὶ γῆν πρῶτον, ἥλιον δ᾽ εἰς τὸν δεύτερον ὑπὲρ γῆς, ἑωσφόρον δὲ καὶ τὸν ἱερὸν Ἑρμοῦ λεγόμενον εἰς τοὺς (v. l. τὸν) τάχει μὲν ἰσόδρομον ἡλίῳ κύκλον ἰόντας.

The note is—

'I have with Stallbaum adopted τούς . . . It may be objected that if κύκλους is to be supplied, we have an awkward tautology in κύκλους κύκλον ἰόντας. But may we not understand πλανήτας?' This would give the impression that Stallbaum understood κύκλους, and it would certainly be inferred that it had not occurred to him to understand πλανήτας.

Stallbaum's note is—

'Observes ante omnia singularem dicendi rationem. Neque enim εἰς τὴν (sc. φοράν) corrigendum, quod vel proxima verba prohibent; sed ad εἰς τὸν intelligendum πλανήτην vel πλάνητα . . . Ne vero mireris hanc loquendi formam, in promtu sunt alia ejus exempla. Ita statim post : εἰς τοὺς τάχει—ἰόντας,—εἰληχότας, ubi Stephanus frustra conjecit εἰς τὸν ἰόντα et εἰληχότα, intell. κύκλον. Politic. 281 C, πότερον οὖν ἡμῖν ὁ περὶ τῆς ὑφαντικῆς λόγος—ἱκανῶς ἔσται διωρισμένος, ἐὰν ἄρ' αὐτὴν τῶν ἐπιμελειῶν, ὁπόσαι περὶ τὴν ἐρίαν ἐσθῆτα, εἰς τὴν καλλίστην καὶ μεγίστην πασῶν τιθῶμεν; Sophist. 235 A, εἰς γόητα μὲν δὴ καὶ μιμητὴν ἄρα θετέον αὐτόν τινα : ubi v. Heindorf . . . Legg. IX. 867 B, βέλτιστον μὴν καὶ ἀληθέστατον εἰς εἰκόνα μὲν ἄμφω θεῖναι. Infra 40 A, τίθησί τε εἰς τὴν τοῦ κρατίστου φρόνησιν : 57 E, εἰς ἀνωμαλότητα τιθῶμεν.

(1) It will be seen that the proposal to understand πλανήτας is really made by Stallbaum, which is sufficiently surprising.

(2) While the editor only puts the proposal tentatively, Stallbaum sees it is right, and gives a scholarly account of it, showing how idiomatic the construction is. It seemed worth while to quote so much of his note as given above to illustrate the valuable quality of his philological notes as compared with the editor's.

(3) From the use made of Stallbaum's edition, it is likely enough, as in another remarkable instance to be given later, that the editor owed the idea of the construction to Stallbaum, but forgot this afterwards; for it is clear from the way in which he has forgotten the important confirmation given by Stallbaum, that he could not have looked at the note for some time when he wrote his own.

14. 59 D, τὸ πυρὶ μεμιγμένον ὕδωρ, ὅσον λεπτὸν ὑγρόν τε διὰ τὴν κίνησιν καὶ τὴν ὁδόν, ἣν κυλινδούμενον ἐπὶ γῆς ὑγρὸν λέγεται, μαλακόν τε αὖ τῷ τὰς βάσεις ἧττον ἑδραίους οὔσας ἢ τὰς γῆς ὑπείκειν κ.τ.λ.

Lindau, Stallbaum, and the Zurich editors have no comma after ὁδόν. The above punctuation is Hermann's, adopted by the editor, who, as he says, mainly reproduces Hermann's text.

The note is—

'Although Stallbaum asserts that this sentence is "turpi labe contaminatus," I see no necessity for alteration: his own attempts are certainly far from fortunate. The repetition of ὑγρόν, which offends him so sorely, is, I think, due to the fact that we have, as Lindau saw, an etymology implied in the words ἦν . . . λέγεται "the mode of rolling on the earth which has in fact gained it the name of ὑγρόν": as if ὑγρὸν = ὑπὲρ γῆς ῥέον. Thus under tood, the objection to the second ὑγρόν vanishes. μαλακόκ τε is then coordinate with λεπτὸν ὑγρόν τε, and τῷ . . . ὑπείκειν with διὰ τὴν κίνησιν.'

This note is unfair to Stallbaum, and inaccurate as regards Lindau. To be intelligible it necessarily implies that Stallbaum had not seen there was an etymology in the words referred to, which would have been a bad slip: it would also give the impression that Lindau having seen the true solution which makes the objection to the second ὑγρόν vanish had felt no difficulty, and retained ὑγρόν in each place.

(1) Stallbaum was perfectly aware that there was an etymology in the words. He says ' Etenim ὑγρόν videtur significare ab ὕω dictum esse, in quo motionis notio continetur.'

(2) Lindau, on the other hand, so far from thinking that the difficulty about the repetition of ὑγρόν 'vanishes,' expresses himself like Stallbaum about it, and proposes to substitute ὑπέροον for the first ὑγρόν. Stallb.—' Quis enim ferat ita loquentem: τὸ ὕδωρ ὅσον, λεπτὸν ὑγρόν τε—ὑγρόν λέγεται?' Lindau—'ὅσον λεπτὸν ὑγρόν τε—ὑγρὸν λέγεται. Praeter verborum anacoluthiam facilem cognitu notandum videtur vitium, quod habet prius ὑγρόν, pro quo vox expectatur unde possis e more Platonis alterum derivare ὑγρόν &c.' (Stallbaum omits the second ὑγρόν, and inserts ἐστί before ἐπί.)

(3) The editor interprets according to C. F. Hermann's punctuation (to which no acknowledgment is made), and this is probably the right way; for λέγεται should be the verb of the relative clause, and Stallbaum can only avoid this construction by inserting ἐστί after κυλινδούμενον. But the editor has not seen the true difficulty at all. The question is by no means whether there is an etymology or not—all the editors have seen that, but whether ἐστί or λέγεται is to be understood after the first ὑγρόν. Stallbaum understands λέγεται. The difficulty of understanding ἐστί (as in C. F. Hermann's punctuation) is, that though the kind of ὕδωρ spoken of might be (ἐστί) ὑγρὸν διὰ τὴν κίνησιν, it could not well be said to have this quality (εἶναι ὑγρόν) διὰ τὴν ὁδὸν ἣν κυλινδούμενον κ.τ.λ., for, on the contrary, it is its quality of being ὑγρόν which causes it κυλινδεῖσθαι ἐπὶ γῆς. On the other hand, it might well be said to be *called* ὑγρόν because of the κυλινδεῖσθαι ἐπὶ γῆς.

(4) Stallbaum supposes the derivation intended to be from ὕω; and this seems possible. The editor has not noticed considerable difficulties in the one (ὑπὲρ γῆς ῥέον) which he adopts from Lindau. If the latter were right we should expect not κυλινδούμενον ἐπὶ γῆς, but ῥέον or καταρρέον instead of κυλινδούμενον, and at least ὑπέρ instead of ἐπί. Again the editor's explanation of ὑπὲρ γῆς ῥέον seems against the use of ὑπέρ with genitive; ὑπὲρ γῆς should mean ' over (i. e. " above " or " up above ") the earth,' as it does a line or two below, where hail and ice are thus distinguished—παγέν τε οὕτω τὸ μὲν ὑπὲρ γῆς μάλιστα παθὸν ταῦτα χάλαζα, τὸ δ' ἐπὶ γῆς κρύσταλλος. The editor's rendering, in his translation, of the difficult words ὁδὸν ἣν κυλινδούμενον ἐπὶ γῆς, ' its way of rolling along the ground,' seems impossible. Perhaps διὰ τὴν κίνησιν καὶ τὴν ὁδόν κ.τ.λ. means ' on account of its motion and the direction which the motion takes,' this direction being defined by κυλινδ. ἐπὶ γῆς. Compare the use of ὁδός in Plato's account of attraction, where it combines the meaning of direction and tendency to move in a direction.

It is, by the way, inadvisable to render as the editor in his translation, ' rolling *along* the ground,' as if it were κατὰ γῆν instead of ἐπὶ γῆς. With a verb of motion ἐπὶ γῆς, if not indicating direction, would mean simply ' on the earth ' as opposed to any other place. So again 80 A, ὅσα ἐπὶ γῆς φέρεται is rendered ' move *along* the ground ' by the editor; but it is opposed to ὅσα ἀφεθέντα μετέωρα φέρεται, so that ἐπὶ γῆς properly means ' on the earth ' as opposed to ' in the air.' Compare the passage quoted above where ἐπὶ γῆς is opposed to ὑπὲρ γῆς. The sense of ' direction down upon ' would suit Stallbaum's derivation.

15. A remarkable instance of unfairness is the note upon 66 A.
Τῶν δὲ αὐτῶν προλελεπτυσμένων μὲν ὑπὸ σηπεδόνος, εἰς δὲ τὰς στενὰς φλέβας ἐνδυομένων, καὶ τοῖς ἐνοῦσιν αὐτόθι μέρεσι γεώδεσι καὶ ὅσα ἀέρος ξυμμετρίαν ἔχοντα, ὥστε κινήσαντα κ.τ.λ.

The editor says ' In this portentous sentence it is quite probable that some corruption may lurk. But no emendation suggests itself of sufficient plausibility to justify its admission into the text, although I have little doubt that ἐχόντων should be read for ἔχοντα. Stallbaum's proposed alterations are the result of his not understanding the construction: ὅσα ἀέρος is parallel to τοῖς γεώδεσι, and equivalent to τοῖς ὅσα ἀέρος ἔνεστιν.'

(1) The reader would of course suppose from this that Stallbaum had seriously proposed to alter the text, whereas the editor thinks that no emendation is probable enough to be admitted. Stallbaum expresses

here the same opinion as the editor, and no more proposes a serious emendation than he does. (Restat igitur difficultas verborum. Quae quomodo tollenda sit, eo magis dubium est, quo mirabilior est codicum de his corruptelis consensio. Itaque proponere licebit conjecturam quandam nostram *sic, ut non tam quid scriptum fuerit, quam quid potuerit scriptum legi*, significemus &c.) (2) The reader would never gather that Stallbaum had even mentioned the emendation ἐχόντων; and as the editor expressly denies that Stallbaum understood the construction which would lead naturally to this emendation, it would never be supposed that Stallbaum had even thought of it, and in any case the impression would be that Stallbaum had not understood it.

In the criticism of this note in the Classical Review, I omitted the first misrepresentation altogether, and spoke only of the more important ones under the second heading, as follows: 'It may seem incredible, but it is true, that the emendation is Stallbaum's, and the construction he is supposed not to understand is the very one he gives, "Itaque legendum fortasse videbitur ἐχόντων &c." He takes ὅσα ἀέρος, exactly as the editor does, as parallel to γεώδεσι, translating the one "partibus aeriis," and the other "partibus terrenis."'

I went on to attribute the editor's error to its obvious cause, forgetfulness. He must have read the note he attacks, and must have afterwards forgotten the first part of it, for this contains the suggestion ἐχόντων &c., and indeed had very probably suggested the correction to himself originally.

I said also that in common fairness the editor before passing such a criticism should have looked again at the note which it is charitable to suppose he had not seen for some time: also that, strange as this behaviour was, there was something as strange in a similar criticism of Martin [1].

The editor has in the Classical Review for April made a determined attempt to overthrow this perfectly just criticism of himself, and that in such language, with such an imputation on my good faith, and with such misrepresentation on his own part, that I have to treat the subject again with some detail.

As I do not intend to let any of the facts escape, it will be necessary to repeat the editor's answer entire.

'Mr. Wilson discourses for three-fourths of a column upon my "unfairness" to Stallbaum, in reference to the note on 66 A; the gist of his indictment being that Stallbaum is accused by me of misunderstanding the construction, whereas he takes it as I do; and that I put forward as my own an alteration (ἐχόντων for ἔχοντα) which is

---

[1] See the end of this paragraph.

Stallbaum's. Now this time one single grain of truth may be sifted out of all this. Stallbaum's comment upon ὅσα ἀέρος is not very clear; and I was mistaken, I now think, as to the manner in which the words are intended to be taken in the earlier part of his note. So, had Mr. Wilson known how to let well alone, he might have scored a point against me, such as it is. But our critic, who in some other respects does not resemble Socrates, unfortunately does not enjoy a δαιμόνιον σημεῖον to " check him always, whatever he is doing." For he goes on, " it seems incredible, but it is true, that the emendation is Stallbaum's," i.e. ἐχόντων.

Now what are the facts? First it will be seen by any one who reads Stallbaum's note to the end that he sets aside the interpretation of ὅσα ἀέρος which I adopt, although I was wrong in believing that he never saw it. Secondly the emendation ἐχόντων is even less his than it is mine, though I am not aware that he has been charged with piracy for not disclaiming it. (I need hardly say that I have made not the slightest claim to the authorship of a correction so obvious that it must have occurred to every one who has tried to construe the sentence.) Stallbaum says indeed "legendum fortasse videbitur ἐχόντων," which, for Mr. Wilson's benefit, I will translate: "perhaps it will be thought that ἐχόντων ought to be read." But that Stallbaum does not think so is evident from the whole tenor of his note; and from the fact that in his final reconstruction of the passage (to which the criticism in my note refers) he retains ἔχοντα. The emendation in fact is Stallbaum's neither by adoption nor by origination, for it is quoted in Bekker's note. So far then from ἐχόντων being "a proposed alteration of Stallbaum's,"[1] it is a suggestion, apparently of Lindau's, which Stallbaum mentions only to set aside. If a correction for which Stallbaum is not responsible and which he deliberately rejects is Stallbaum's, then, I fear, all Mr. Wilson's statements which I quote may, on the same showing, be termed mine. ἀλλ' εὐφημεῖν χρή.

It were easy to go on almost *ad libitum* culling flowers from Mr. Wilson's Χαρίτων κᾶπος, were it worth while.'

The editor, it will be seen, cannot gainsay the most important part of my objection: he endeavours to contradict and ridicule the other part.

It will be shewn that the objection he raises is irrelevant to the real charge against him, and this would remain as serious as it was even if he were right. But it will also be shewn that he is wrong on the issue which he has chosen, and to which he attaches so much importance.

(i) In the first place, the attempt to answer my criticism depends on a grave misrepresentation of the whole point of it.

The editor gives the reader to understand that I have accused him of pirating the emendation ἐχόντων from Stallbaum (cf. e. g. ' and that I have put forward as my own an alteration which is Stallbaum's.' ' Secondly, the emendation is even less his than it is mine, though I am not aware that he has been charged with piracy for not disclaiming it. I need hardly say that I have made not the slightest claim to the authorship, &c.'). He answers, then, with emphasis that the suggestion is not really Stallbaum's, and that he (the editor) has not claimed it himself.

---

[1] The expression in quotation marks is none of mine but the editor's own.

The reader has but to look at my review to see that the charge of unfairness was not at all that the editor had 'pirated' an emendation of Stallbaum's. I did not even suspect him of it. My very point was that when he wrote his own note he did not know of the suggestion in Stallbaum, and that he ought to have known it, considering what he thought fit to say of Stallbaum's view.

I said expressly, what I believed and shall make evident below, that he had forgotten the earlier part of Stallbaum's note which contains the suggested alteration and the construction in question, and remembered only the second part of it.

The reader may judge from the style of the editor's answer what he would have said if I had been found misrepresenting his own arguments thus.

My contention was in effect this. I pointed out the scarcely credible fact that the editor gave as a correction of Stallbaum's view an emendation suggested by Stallbaum himself, and without even a hint that it was in Stallbaum; also that he presumed to attack his predecessor on the ground that he did not understand a certain construction, whereas this very construction is given by his predecessor, and is presupposed by the suggested emendation itself. The editor was of course not charged with piracy from Stallbaum, but with being so unfair and so eager to attack him that he did not take ordinary trouble to be sure his attack was justified.

Thus the editor's answer, in the form in which he presents it, is shewn to be an evasion[1] and is disposed of. But it will next be considered whether any of the matter which he uses in his answer makes a difference to the justice of the criticism passed upon him.

(ii) Suppose (what is untrue) that the editor was right in what he says of Stallbaum's rejection of ἐχόντων.

---

[1] A further misrepresentation, though it is but a minor one, must be pointed out; because by its means the editor helps the impression he seeks to give. He restates my criticism so as to put a misleading emphasis upon the point relating to the alteration of ἔχοντα into ἐχόντων and give the better introduction to his misstatement of what was said about it. He represents me as first attacking him for accusing Stallbaum of not understanding the construction, and then afterwards, as I did not know how to stop in time, 'going on' to another charge about ἐχόντων. I have quoted my own remark above, and the reader will at once see how it has been misrepresented. The two points are not separated in any such way as he implies. On the contrary both are introduced by the words 'It may seem incredible,' &c., which the editor represents as though forming a separate introduction to the matter of ἐχόντων. (My words are 'It may seem incredible but it is true that the emendation is Stallbaum's, and the construction he is supposed not to understand is the very one he gives.') The fact is the two points are inseparable as will appear directly. It is the editor's interest to separate them as much as possible, because he is forced to admit one of them entirely.

He admits that he was wrong in saying that Stallbaum's view was the result of his not understanding the construction: but he says, 'Stallbaum's comment upon ὅσα ἀέρος is not very clear,' and also tries to make light of his own unfairness. The part of Stallbaum's note which shews the construction of ὅσα ἀέρος is quite clear[1]; and would be very obvious indeed to anyone who read it with the care to be demanded from one who intended to criticise it.

On the other hand, the attempt to make light of such a fault is only a new confirmation of what has been said of the editor's spirit of unfairness to Stallbaum.

(iii) It will have become plain that it makes no difference to the validity of the charge whether the suggestion occurred independently to Stallbaum or not. It is enough that he makes it. But though the point is irrelevant, it may be shewn that the editor's own logic is fatal to his statement of it. If the 'correction is so obvious that it must have occurred to everyone who,' &c., why should it not have occurred independently to Stallbaum? And there is nothing to shew that it did not. And there is certainly no less evidence to shew that it did, than there is in the editor's own note to shew that it occurred to him independently. And here a question may be asked. If the editor really knew when he wrote his note that an emendation which he thinks so probable in this difficult text had been already suggested by Lindau, why did he not say so? It is thought a matter of courtesy if not of honour to mention such things, and it is obligatory on one who speaks so slightingly of Lindau as the editor sometimes does. A similar omission in relation to Lindau has been noticed before (par. 11).

(iv) However, the editor not only takes the untenable position, that the suggestion is not Stallbaum's, but affirms that it is in no sense Stallbaum's, for that he mentions it only to reject it.

It will be shewn that even if this were true, it could invalidate nothing essential in the charge of unfairness: and indeed it will become most probable that the editor had not even formed this opinion on Stallbaum's attitude when he wrote the note objected to.

But also this opinion which the editor tries to make so important, and puts with something more than confidence, will be proved to be wrong.

The thing on which he most insists is that I have misunderstood

---

[1] He translates in fact thus: 'Eadem haec quum antea extenuata sunt putredine et in venarum angustias influunt, atque *partibus terrenis et aeriis* ibi extantibus convenienter se habent,' &c.

the words (itaque) legendum fortasse videbitur ἐχόντων, 'which' he says 'for Mr. Wilson's benefit I will translate: "perhaps it will be thought ἐχόντων ought to be read," &c.'

When such a tone is adopted, the risk is so great that care should be taken that the argument is right. The editor in the first place has sacrificed his own point to a personality. Of course there is no difficulty about the translation. I translated as the editor does, though he seeks to give the reader the impression that I did not.

The question obviously is what meaning is to be attached to the English, which is ambiguous without a context; and here is the real difference of opinion.

But, in the second place, there is a graver matter. The reader would little suspect that the editor gets the interpretation, on which, as has been seen, he risks so much, by suppressing the continuation of the sentence he translates. He professes that Stallbaum in saying 'perhaps it will be thought that ἐχόντων ought to be read' i.e. (itaque) legendum, &c., is putting a view which he does not share at all, and indeed 'only mentions to set aside.'

The whole sentence reads thus: 'Itaque legendum fortasse videbitur ἐχόντων, *quod ipsum interpretatione nostrâ expressimus*: ita enim dativus e ξυμμετρίαν ἔχειν aptus nexusque erit.' (In the next sentence he states certain difficulties on the other hand, which will be explained below.)

Now a man does not usually adapt his own translation (translatio nostra) to a reading which (in the editor's words) 'he deliberately rejects,' or ' mentions only to set aside,' nor does Stallbaum.

The translation in question[1] is that with which Stallbaum begins his note, and it presupposes ἐχόντων as he himself says in the clause which the editor has suppressed.

The fact is that the editor, with the inaccuracy and with the incautiousness in attack which are so exemplified in his book, has misunderstood the real drift of Stallbaum's long note even now that he has read it again.

Stallbaum thinks the text corrupt, but is quite undecided what the emendation ought to be. One of the suggestions before him is ἐχόντων, which he certainly puts as a man might put what is his own, and instead of 'deliberately rejecting it,' he so far approves it that the only translation he gives of the Greek implies it. He points out that it removes certain difficulties, but is prevented by other difficulties, which he names, from adopting it as certain.

---

[1] Given above in note to p. 32.

All this will be clear, as well as the origin of the editor's mistake, from an analysis of Stallbaum's note.

Before giving any comment Stallbaum translates the first part of the passage, explaining its relation to a clause from which it is separated by an interposed sentence. Then he says that the Greek of the first part is corrupt; that there are certain difficulties; that these suggest the reading ἐχόντων; that he has actually adopted the reading himself in his translation. But he adds there are some serious objections to it.

'Verum haec principialis enuntiati pars dubium non est quin foede misereque corrupta sit. Primum enim non apparet unde dativus τοῖς ἐνοῦσιν αὐτόθι μέρεσι κ. τ. λ. pendeat, siquidem καὶ ὅσα ἀέρος ξυμμετρίαν ἔχοντα valet καὶ τοῖς ὅσα ἀέρος ξυμμετρίαν ἔχει. Itaque legendum fortasse videbitur ἐχόντων, *quod ipsum interpretatione nostrā expressimus*: ita enim dativus e ξυμμετρίαν ἔχειν aptus nexusque erit. Verum ut alias dubitationes silentio praeteream, illud certe huic rationi officit, quod ipsa sententia istud ξυμμετρίαν ἔχειν non ferre videtur.'

To get a better view of the whole difficulty he goes on to consider the remainder of the passage, which he also thinks corrupt. Then he gives what he thinks Plato really intended in the passage taken as a whole (nec dubitandum est quin sententia Platonis omnino clara sit et perspicua): but thinks it is not conveyed by the words (restat igitur difficultas verborum). In face of the consensus of the MSS. he knows of no satisfactory emendation (quae difficultas quomodo tollenda sit eo magis dubium est quo mirabilior est codicum de his corruptelis consensio), and therefore, at the end of his note gives merely his idea of the kind of thing which might have been expected—what the editor inaccurately calls 'his final reconstruction of the passage'—but by no means as a serious emendation. 'Itaque proponere licebit coniecturam quandam nostram sic, ut non tam quid scriptum fuerit, quam quid potuerit scriptum legi, significemus. Nihil igitur desideraremus, si oratio hunc in modum esset concinnata, καὶ ὅσα ἀέρος ξυμμετρίαν ἔχοντα (sc. ἐστὶ) συνιόντων, ὥστε κινήσαντα κ.τ.λ. ac deinde: νοτερὰ ἀγγεῖα ἀέρος ἀνάγκη (sc. ἐστὶ) κοῖλα περιφερῆ τε γενέσθαι κ.τ.λ.

The editor, therefore, has given in his answer quite an erroneous impression of 'the whole tenor of the note.' He thus misinterprets the meaning of 'itaque legendum fortasse, &c.' which he has translated so triumphantly. Stallbaum obviously means that something is to be said in favour of reading ἐχόντων: so much indeed that his translation is based on the alteration, though he does not see his way clear to decide for it. In fact, though it is not said in so many words, ἐχόντων is with Stallbaum a sort of minimum alteration: and though he does not adopt it, it is the nearest he comes to a real emendation.

(v) I was quite aware of the difference between the first and second parts of Stallbaum's note when I wrote my criticism. The editor, unless I misunderstand him, wishes to give the impression that I was not[1]. My very point was that he himself was not aware of it, and had only remembered the second part (see Class. Rev., March 1889, page 116, col. 1, lines 20–25). When I said that the emendation was Stallbaum's, I meant it was a proposal of his, I did not mean he thought it conclusive. Indeed in the original article, which I had to condense as being too long for the Class. Review, stood a sentence to that effect, and referring to what Stallbaum says in the second part of his note. This was suppressed as not necessary to the argument. If it had been kept it might have saved the editor from his present unfortunate mistake.

(vi) If the editor were to be taken at his word, his own admission as to ὅσα ἀέρος would involve the admission of what has been proved in the foregoing about ἐχόντων. He admits (with what grace has been seen) that the construction of ὅσα ἀέρος, which he had said Stallbaum did not understand, is 'the manner in which the words are intended to be taken in the earlier part of the note.' But the construction involves the separation of ὅσα ἀέρος from ξυμμετρίαν ἔχοντα and the reading of ἐχόντων for ἔχοντα. And thus the editor has admitted that it was 'intended in the earlier part of the note' to read ἐχόντων. He may reply, appealing to the sequel of his answer, that his expression 'intended to be taken in the earlier part of the note' was unguarded, and that he really meant 'the manner in which the words (ὅσα ἀέρος) are *not* intended to be taken; a manner, in fact, which is mentioned to be set aside.' But really his expression is accurate, and the natural way of putting what Stallbaum says.

(vii) But suppose the editor had been right in his opinion that Stallbaum 'only mentions the reading ἐχόντων to set it aside'—what difference would it make?

In the first place, if the editor really had formed this opinion on Stallbaum's attitude when he wrote his note, his case is even worse than I put it. Clearly it is more inexcusable to write a note of such

---

[1] See the second part of his reply quoted on page 30 above.

a form and tendency as above [1] described with such (supposed) knowledge than without it.

The most lenient supposition is that he had not arrived at this opinion when he wrote his book; and this seems to be the truth.

(1) If he had arrived at it he would in all probability have said not what he did say, but something like this, 'Stallbaum rejects the suggestion (or "Lindau's suggestion") $\dot{\epsilon}\chi\acute{o}\nu\tau\omega\nu$, because he did not understand how $\ddot{o}\sigma\alpha$ $\dot{\alpha}\acute{\epsilon}\rho os$ was to be taken.'

(2) There is a more cogent reason. Considering how closely the construction of $\ddot{o}\sigma\alpha$ $\dot{\alpha}\acute{\epsilon}\rho os$ is connected with the conjecture $\dot{\epsilon}\chi\acute{o}\nu\tau\omega\nu$—a connection which the editor's own criticism of Stallbaum implies —it is quite incredible that the editor should have come to believe what he now alleges about Stallbaum's view of $\dot{\epsilon}\chi\acute{o}\nu\tau\omega\nu$ and not have seen that he construes $\ddot{o}\sigma\alpha$ $\dot{\alpha}\acute{\epsilon}\rho os$ in the manner which that reading implies. The reader will see this at once if he looks at Stallbaum's note, for not only is the translation perfectly clear, but Stallbaum in pointing out difficulties in the emendation $\dot{\epsilon}\chi\acute{o}\nu\tau\omega\nu$ says nothing whatever of the construction of $\ddot{o}\sigma\alpha$ $\dot{\alpha}\acute{\epsilon}\rho os$, which would have been his greatest difficulty if he had misunderstood it.

(3) But what is really beyond doubt, is fully confirmed by the form of the editor's defence. He does not attempt to deny what I said I believed, viz. that when he attacked Stallbaum he had forgotten all about the earlier part of Stallbaum's note, which mentions the alteration $\dot{\epsilon}\chi\acute{o}\nu\tau\omega\nu$.

Thus the editor's criticism is convicted of the precise injustice with which it was charged.

The foregoing discussion may be recapitulated as follows—

The form of the editor's attempted answer has been shewn to be a grave misrepresentation of the real issue.

In the matter of it there are certain statements, in unfortunate language, accusing my arguments of mistakes which the editor seeks to make essential to the issue.

Of these statements I have shewn that even if they were true, some were irrelevant, and as to the rest that, if the editor had arrived at such opinions when he wrote, this knowledge aggravated his fault; that if he had not, he was entirely liable to the charge made; also that beyond doubt, he had not arrived at them.

But, also, I have accepted the editor's own issues in his own form, and shewn that he is wrong in all of them. One of them is not only

---

[1] Pages 28, 29.

[37]

unprovable, but his own logic makes it untenable for him. The rest have been disproved.

Thus the editor's fault has only become plainer by his effort to get out of it.

A complete vindication has been given of the original charge, that in his eagerness to attack Stallbaum, he did not take ordinary care to see that his attack was justified; and that he was liable to the accusation he presumes to bring against Grote, that of 'eagerness to convict' others 'of irrationality.'

It would not be expected that a mistake of the kind would be made more than once, but compare above, parr. 11, 12 (note on 35 A), 13; and below, par. 28.

16. The following confident and very unfortunate attack on Stallbaum is a good illustration of the inferiority of this edition to Stallbaum's in Greek scholarship.

37 A, ψυχή ... ὅταν οὐσίαν σκεδαστὴν ἔχοντός τινος ἐφάπτηται καὶ ὅταν ἀμέριστον λέγει κινουμένη διὰ πάσης ἑαυτῆς, ὅτῳ τ' ἂν τι ταὐτὸν ᾖ καὶ ὅτου ἂν ἕτερον, πρὸς ὅ τί τε μάλιστα καὶ ὅπῃ καὶ ὅπως καὶ ὁπότε ξυμβαίνει κατὰ τὰ γιγνόμενά τε πρὸς ἕκαστον ἕκαστα εἶναι καὶ πάσχειν καὶ πρὸς τὰ κατὰ ταὐτὰ ἔχοντα ἀεί.

On this passage, Stallbaum has an excellent note.

Difficiliora ad explicandum videntur quae sequuntur, &c. ... de quibus jam a veteribus multum esse dubitatum Proclus auctor est, p. 231 sq. ... ante omnia constructionis rationem exquirere juvat, quam mirari sane licet ne ab uno quidem inter tot interpretes satis perspectam esse. Est autem junctura verborum haec : κινουμένη διὰ πάσης ἑαυτῆς λέγει, πρὸς ὅ τι μάλιστα καὶ ὅπῃ καὶ ὅπως καὶ ὁπότε τοῦτο, ὅτῳ ἄν τι ταὐτὸν ᾖ καὶ ὅτου ἂν ἕτερον, ξυμβαίνει ἕκαστα εἶναι καὶ πάσχειν πρὸς ἕκαστον κατὰ τὰ γιγνόμενά τε καὶ πρὸς τὰ κατὰ ταὐτὰ ἔχοντα ἀεί. Itaque loci sententia huc fere redit: 'Anima dum isto modo vires exercens suas vel res concretas animadvertit vel res intelligibiles attingit, disquirit atque indicat id, cuicunque quid est idem et a quo diversum, ad quidnam maxime et quo modo quove tempore ad unumquodque se omnibus modis habeat omnibusque modis afficiatur, et in iis quae fiunt (h. e. in rebus corporeis vel individuis) et in illis, quae semper sibi constant.'

He then explains the latter part of the construction thus :—'ἕκαστα εἶναι καὶ πάσχειν πρὸς ἕκαστον, h. e. jegliches (veluti ταὐτὸν et ἕτερον) sein und leiden im Verhältniss zu jeglichem.'

Stallbaum deserves great credit for his scholarly elucidation of a passage previously misunderstood.

The editor writes as follows—

'Stallbaum, affirming that no one has hitherto understood this passage, takes the antecedent of ὅτῳ as the subject of ξυμβαίνει : "she declares of that wherewith anything is the same and wherefrom it is different, in relation to what &c." It may well be doubted whether he has thus improved upon his predecessors. Surely the discernment of sameness and difference is a function necessarily belonging to soul and necessarily included in the catalogue of her functions: yet Stallbaum's rendering excludes it from that catalogue. The fact that we have ὅτῳ ἂν ᾖ, not ὅτῳ ἐστί, does not really favour his view—"with whatsoever a thing may be the same, she declares it the same.' I coincide then with the other interpreters in regarding the whole sentence from ὅτῳ τ' ἂν as indirect interrogation subordinate to λέγει.'

And adds in his next note 'Lindau has justly remarked that all or nearly all Aristotle's ten categories are to be found in this sentence.' His translation is:—

And she tells that wherewith the thing is same and that wherefrom it is different, and in what relation or place or manner or time it comes to pass both in the region of the changing and in the region of the changeless that each thing affects another and is affected.

(1) The logic of the objection made to Stallbaum—'Surely the discernment, &c.' is quite extraordinary. Stallbaum's rendering of course does not exclude the discernment of sameness and difference from the soul's functions. If the soul is said to perceive the particular ways in which things are different or the same, it is necessarily implied that the soul discerns sameness and difference. Cf. a little farther on in Stallbaum's note—'anima dicitur... id agere, ut identitatis et diversitatis rationes et in ideis et in rebus individuis... conspicuas dijudicet.' Plato might indeed have expressed his meaning by saying that the soul *both* perceives sameness and difference, *and* in what ways things are the same and different, but obviously the other mode of expression is both possible and natural. Captious objections of this kind would be fatal to interpretation, especially in a Greek author, and it is amusing to observe that they are fatal to the editor's interpretation of this very passage. He wishes of course (cf. his approval of Lindau above) to include the perception of action and passivity 'in the catalogue of the soul's functions,' but the Greek as he renders it would, on his own shewing, exclude them from that catalogue; because it is not said that the soul *both* perceives activity and passivity, *and* in what ways these come to pass, but simply that it perceives in what ways activity and passivity come to pass—'in what relation or place, or manner, or time it comes to pass ... that each thing affects another and is affected.' This is a sufficient reductio ad absurdum.

(2) This mistake in logic carries with it serious mistakes in translation. The clause ὅτῳ τ' ἄν τι ταὐτὸν ᾖ καὶ ὅτου ἂν ἕτερον is made an indirect interrogative coordinate with πρὸς ὅ τί τε μάλιστα καὶ ὅπῃ

κ.τ.λ., which is impossible. Stallbaum rightly makes the clause a substantive clause and subject of εἶναι or ξυμβαίνει εἶναι.

(3) ἕκαστα is of course predicate with εἶναι to this subject, and = 'identical and different,' cf. Stallbaum's note. The editor makes ἕκαστα the subject, and thus construes εἶναι πρὸς ἕκαστον = ' to *act* upon each thing,' which again is obviously impossible.

(4) ὅπῃ is translated 'in what place,' as if it were ὅπου. This mistake, which comes from an attempt to find a place for Aristotle's category ποῦ in accordance with Lindau's comparison (see above) of the Aristotelian categories with this passage, is the less excusable, because Lindau's own note and translation (qua via) ought to have warned the editor, and because Stallbaum has said 'neque argutandum in verbis καὶ ὅπῃ καὶ ὅπως, quae interpres recentissimus parum recte accepit. Etenim ὅπῃ καὶ ὅπως dicitur ut nostrum: auf Welche Art und Weise: nihilque significat nisi quomodo, de qua loquendi forma v. ad Phaedon 78 D, &c.' The confusion of ὅπῃ and ὅπου is 'massgebend.'

17. Even if the editor's rejection of Stallbaum's claims to have discovered the true interpretation here had been justified, it was all the more necessary to acknowledge any obligation he might be under to other parts of the same note, but we find the following portion of it reproduced without comment.

Stallbaum.

πρὸς τὰ κατὰ ταὐτά] This phrase is exactly parallel to κατὰ τὰ γιγνόμενα above. The only reason for the change of preposition is the obvious lack of euphony in κατὰ τὰ κατὰ ταὐτά.

Denique verbis κατὰ τὰ γιγνόμενα respondent haec: πρὸς τὰ κατὰ ταὐτὰ ἔχοντα dei, in quibus cur non item positum sit κατά, sed potius πρός, causa in aprico est. Quis enim ferat hoc modo loquentem: κατὰ τὰ κατὰ ταὐτὰ ἔχοντα?

Similarly where the editor thought that Stallbaum had rightly claimed to have 'improved on his predecessors,' he was the more bound to say so: but in the very next note, where Stallbaum proposes also to remedy the mistake of his predecessors, the editor, without such acknowledgment, follows his interpretation and reproduces that part of his note which Stallbaum considers the key to the passage.

37 B.

λόγος δὲ ὁ κατὰ ταὐτὸν ἀληθὴς γιγνόμενος περί τε θάτερον ὂν καὶ περὶ τὸ ταὐτόν.

Stallbaum.

Haec quoque dici non potest quantum molestiae interpretibus creaverint, qui neque verba neque sententiam usquequaque recte perceperunt. Sic priora illa: λόγος

Note.	ὁ κατὰ ταὐτὸν ἀληθὴς γιγνόμενος, Ficinus perquam absurde reddidit : . . . neque felicius reddiderunt alii. Sententia autem quae esset, quantum quidem sciamus, usque ad hunc diem nemo perspexit penitus . . . Cardo rei, si quid video, versatur in eo ut istud κατὰ ταὐτόν recte accipiatur. Duplex autem suppetit ejus interpretatio. Aut enim significatur λόγος, qui pro τοῦ ταὐτοῦ ratione verus evadit ; aut κατὰ ταὐτὸν significat *pariter, pari ratione* quod fere dicitur κατὰ ταὐτά. . . . Vix est cur moneam, quid in hac [sc. priore] interpretatione offendat. . . . Itaque eo inclinat animus ut κατὰ ταὐτὸ ita dictum putemus ut alibi fere κατὰ ταὐτά, veluti supra 34 C, De Rep. 615 C, Symp. 221 D, Sophist. 253 B, Phaed. 95 B. Quod si recte statuimus ac certe usus loquendi non adversatur, sensus nascetur hic : *oratio autem, quae pariter vera evadit sive versatur in diverso sive in eodem*, &c.
'κατὰ ταὐτόν is adverbial, "equally": there is nothing in it of the technical sense of ταὐτόν.' [i.e. the sense in Stallbaum's 'prior interpretatio.']	
Translation.	
'This word of hers is true alike whether it deal with same or other.'	

(The superiority here of Stallbaum's note from a grammatical point of view is obvious.)

18. It would be well for the editor if the claims of discovery and improvement which he himself makes were as well founded as these of Stallbaum. Two instances may be subjoined here because they involve unfairness to Stallbaum [1]

41 A, Θεοὶ θεῶν, ὧν ἐγὼ δημιουργὸς πατήρ τε ἔργων, ἃ δι' ἐμοῦ γενόμενα ἄλυτα ἐμοῦ γε μὴ ἐθέλοντος· τὸ μὲν οὖν δὴ δεθὲν πᾶν λυτόν κ.τ.λ.

'It is impossible not to admire the serenity with which all the editors set a full stop after ἐθέλοντος, and then make a fresh start, as though the words from θεοὶ to ἐθέλοντος were a sentence ; as though γίγνεται stood in place of γενόμενα . . . . . I regard . . . all the words down to ἐθέλοντος as constituting an appellation.'

Now of course from this it would be supposed that Stallbaum's punctuation was due to the mistake that the editor speaks of, and that he had not seen the first clause was 'an appellation.'

But Stallbaum makes no such mistake : he does not treat the words from θεοί to ἐθέλοντος as a sentence, as this extract from his note proves. 'Dii satu divino orti, quorum opera me opificem et parentem habent, *quae, utpote a me facta, sunt indissolubilia, me quidem ita volente.*' The last clause in which the editor supposes the mistake to be made is treated exactly as the editor treats it, and the whole 'constitutes an appellation' with Stallbaum as much as with the editor.

---

[1] For another see par. 60.

As to the punctuation, the editor himself shews why Stallbaum might well retain the full stop, for just after what has been quoted above he adds—

'The difficulty then arises, however, that the particles μὲν οὖν δὴ seem to indicate the commencement of a fresh sentence. Yet the objection is not, I think, fatal: for although the words θεοί . . . ἐθέλοντος are not in form a sentence containing a statement, they do practically convey a statement; and the προσηγορία being somewhat extended, Plato proceeds as if the information implied in a description were given in the form of a direct assertion,' &c.

And thus finally the editor himself, instead of putting a comma after ἐθέλοντος, as would be expected from his note, puts a colon: a compromise which is a sufficient refutation of the charge of unintelligence which the editor practically brings against his predecessors.

It may be added that Stallbaum is not the only editor of whom the charge is untrue. The Engelmann translator renders precisely as the editor does (except that he, like Stallbaum, omits μή before ἐθέλοντος), which is not to the present purpose.

In 40 D there is a passage on the popular gods, on which the editor says, 'The irony of the passage, though it seems to have generally escaped the commentators, is very evident; more especially in the opening sentence of the next chapter. Plato had no cause for embroiling himself with the popular religion,' &c.

The irony is quite obvious and can hardly have escaped any reader, and there is no ground for supposing it has generally escaped the commentators. It has not escaped Martin or Stallbaum. Martin has no special note on the passage, but in his note on the following are these words (vol. 2, p. 138), 'Ce qu'il dit dans le *Timée* sur les dieux de la fable est trop evidemment ironique,' &c., and again (p. 146, vol. 2), 'la manière ironique dont il parle, dans le *Timée*, des dieux de la mythologie, montre suffisament, qu'il était loin de donner son adhésion aux fables d'après lesquelles les dieux auraient été les ancêtres de certaines familles d'hommes.'

Stallbaum also happens to say nothing in his note on the irony of the passage, but in his Prolegomena, p. 15, he says—

' Jam istorum deorum mentione injecta Timaeus quaedam addit de diis, qui vulgo credebantur. Quos quidem e Terra et Caelo ortos ait ita, ut origo eorum nostram superet intelligentiam. Quocirca non vult de iis exponere, sed detrectat omnem hujus rei disputationem. P. 40 D–41 A. Hoc vero sapienter ita ab eo factum esse, quis est quin statim intelligat secum reputans, vulgarem superstitionem impugnare quam periculosum fuerit !'

The last sentence is almost identical with what the editor says himself.

19. Another instance of a matter of scholarship is added: others will be found further on.

47 E—48 A. ... ἐπιδέδεικται τὰ διὰ νοῦ δεδημιουργημένα· δεῖ δὲ καὶ τὰ δι' ἀνάγκης γιγνόμενα τῷ λόγῳ παραθέσθαι. μεμιγμένη γὰρ οὖν ἡ τοῦδε τοῦ κόσμου γένεσις ἐξ ἀνάγκης τε καὶ νοῦ συστάσεως ἐγεννήθη· νοῦ δὲ ἀνάγκης ἄρχοντος τῷ πείθειν αὐτὴν τῶν γιγνομένων τὰ πλεῖστα ἐπὶ τὸ βέλτιστον ἄγειν, ταύτῃ κατὰ ταὐτά τε δι' ἀνάγκης ἡττωμένης ὑπὸ πειθοῦς ἔμφρονος οὕτω κατ' ἀρχὰς ξυνίστατο τόδε τὸ πᾶν. εἴ τις οὖν ᾗ γέγονε κατὰ ταῦτα ὄντως ἐρεῖ, μικτέον καὶ τὸ τῆς πλανωμένης εἶδος αἰτίας, ᾗ φέρειν πέφυκεν.

The last words are translated thus, 'we must add also the nature of the Errant cause, *and its moving power*,' with the note—

'Literally "how it is its nature to set in motion." The πλανωμένη αἰτία is the source of instability and uncertainty (relatively to us) in the order of things; whence Plato terms it the moving influence. What Stallbaum means or fails to mean by his rendering "ea ratione, qua ipsius natura fert," it is difficult to conjecture.'

It was unlucky for the editor that he did not conjecture what Stallbaum meant. His own explanation is obviously wrong. The meaning is, 'must be mingled in the way which suits its nature,' and so far Stallbaum is right. Cf. also Lindau, 'adjicienda ea quoque [causa], quae necessitate sive lege naturae continetur, *quatenus natura ejus fert.*'

But whether the meaning comes from the sense of 'enduring' or 'tending' in φέρειν is perhaps doubtful.

20. The next passage shews how little care the editor takes to see that his criticism of Stallbaum is just.

In the passage on the creation of human souls (41 D, E) these are represented as first sent to the *fixed stars*; afterwards they are to be sent to the earth and *planets* and there united with bodily forms. The latter stage is called in this passage πρώτη γένεσις, and there can be little difficulty in seeing that it is so. The editor says, 'Stallbaum is obviously wrong in understanding by πρώτη γένεσις the distribution among the stars.' The passage of Stallbaum referred to is 'Est autem prima haec generatio haud dubie illa ipsa animarum cum sideribus conjunctio, quam summus ipse deus fecisse narratur.' The editor no doubt understood 'sideribus' here to mean the fixed stars; but the very next words of Stallbaum should have prevented the mistake— 'id quod apparet e verbis p. 42 B, unde etiam *quaenam astra* intelligantur facile perspicias.' The passage which Stallbaum here refers to (42 B) is ἔσπειρε τοὺς μὲν εἰς γῆν, τοὺς δ' εἰς σελήνην, τοὺς δ' εἰς τὰ ἄλλα ὅσα ὄργανα χρόνου—the sowing of the souls in the earth and planets. Thus, of course, Stallbaum meant by 'sidera' and 'astra' the planets, and therefore is right about the πρώτη γένεσις.

21. The next are examples of criticism of Stallbaum in matters relating to Greek philosophy.

In Plato's theory of vision the editor has some criticisms of Stallbaum which betray, especially in one place, imperfect acquaintance with original authorities.

On 45 C is the following note:—

'It is plain too that Plato's theory is peculiar to himself and quite diverse from the Empedoklean (or Demokritean) doctrine of effluences, with which Stallbaum confuses it; although the two theories have some points in common, as appears from the statement of Aristotle *de sensu* 437ᵇ. 11 foll. Empedokles, as Aristotle informs us, wavered in his explanation, sometimes adopting the ἀπορροαί aforesaid, sometimes comparing the eye to a lantern, sending forth its visual ray through the humours and membranes which correspond to the frame of the lantern. But as propounded in the passage quoted by Aristotle (302-310 Karsten), this notion amounts merely to a metaphor or analogy and is not worked up into a physical theory: it agrees however with Plato in taking fire for the active force of the eye.'

The criticism is not new. The essence of it is given already by Cousin (p. 349 note): 'Stallbaum est beaucoup plus fondé à rapporter cette opinion à Empédocle. Toutefois un examen attentif pourrait conduire à un résultat différent. Empédocle, dit Aristote, explique la vision tantôt par une lumière qui sort des yeux, tantôt par des effluxes venant des objets (*de sensu*, c. 3). Or Plato n'adopte ni l'une ni l'autre de ces explications, il les réunit.'

The editor has overstated this point with habitual exaggeration, as is clear from his own note. The 'two theories' instead of being 'quite diverse,' agree in a very remarkable feature, viz. the doctrine that in sight light (or 'fire') proceeds from the eye towards the object. This is an essential, and justifies the classification of the two theories together; and they are thus considered cognate by Aristotle in the familiar passage (De Sensu) and by Theophrastus. The editor supplies evidence himself, when referring to the doctrine of Empedocles, as expressed in the verses quoted by Aristotle. He says 'it agrees however with Plato in taking fire for the active force of the eye,' yet he argues with singular perversity that 'as propounded in the passage quoted by Aristotle the notion amounts merely to a metaphor or analogy, and is not worked into a physical theory.' In the well-known verses the eye is compared to a lantern emitting light through its transparent sides, but to explain a doctrine by help of a metaphor is not to make the doctrine itself 'amount to a metaphor': the metaphor and the doctrine are distinguished clearly enough in the verses. Aristotle himself (De Sensu, l. c.) represents Empedocles as holding like Plato that light was emitted from the eye. But, as will be seen hereafter, the editor seems imperfectly acquainted with the De Sensu, and even with this chapter, though he quotes it (after his predecessors).

The difference however on which the editor seems to lay most stress appears to be that there is not in Empedocles a cooperation between light from the eye and an emanation from the object (as in Plato) arguing from the words of Aristotle, ὅτε μὲν οὖν οὕτως ὁρᾶν φησίν· ὅτε δὲ ταῖς ἀπορροίαις, that the doctrine of emanation from the object was an alternative to that which represented light as coming from the eye, and that in the latter case there was no action of the external light. Stallbaum holds that there was cooperation of the emanation from the object in the latter case. Here he has the support of Ueberweg and Zeller. It may be wondered whether the editor can have given any careful study to the latter's note on the subject. It seems clear that he cannot have read the important passage on the subject in Theophrastus through, though he gives a stock quotation from the beginning of it in another note. It is this passage of Theophrastus (De Sensibus ii. and iii.) which gives considerable evidence in favour of Stallbaum's view, and no one can presume to pronounce either way without having considered it.

Of the superficial nature of the editor's acquaintance with Theophrastus De Sensibus there is very amusing evidence in another note where the same subject turns up. On 67 C, φλόγα τῶν σωμάτων ἑκάστων ἀπορρέουσαν ὄψει ξύμμετρα μόρια ἔχουσαν he writes 'Stallbaum says Plato is following Empedocles, but this is incorrect: see Theophrastos *de sensu*, § 7, Ἐμπεδοκλῆς δὲ περὶ ἁπασῶν ὁμοίως λέγει καί φησι τῷ ἐναρμόττειν εἰς τοὺς πόρους τοὺς ἑκάστης αἰσθάνεσθαι.' (This is the quotation above referred to.) The affinity of Plato and Empedocles here will strike anyone from a mere comparison of what the editor himself quotes from Theophrastus and the words above quoted from the Timaeus (67 C). Not only so, but unluckily for the editor the statement of Theophrastus which he gives as evidence *against* the affinity of the two theories, is repeated in another part of the same treatise, and made by Theophrastus himself *evidence for their affinity*, and with reference to this very passage of the Timaeus—περὶ δὲ χρωμάτων σχεδὸν ὁμοίως Ἐμπεδοκλεῖ λέγει· τὸ γὰρ σύμμετρα ἔχειν μόρια τῇ ὄψει τὸ τοῖς πόροις ἐναρμόττειν ἐστίν.'

In this connection the editor has himself made a 'confusion' between two philosophic theories. In the note above quoted he says 'Plato's theory is quite diverse from the Empedoklean (*or Demokritean*) doctrine of effluences, with which Stallbaum confuses it.' Again in 67 D, 'It must be remembered that Plato's conception differs from the *Demokritean* or Empedoklean effluences, inasmuch as he does not hold that any image of the object is thrown off.'

Thus the editor supposes that the 'emanations' of Empedocles were images thrown off from the object like those of Democritus. There is no evidence whatever in the fragments of Empedocles of this, nor does there appear to be any in Aristotle or Plato, or any competent authority. A confusion might easily spring up about it later, and there is a passage in the Placita Philosophorum (quoted by Sturz, p. 416[1]) where it seems to be found. But it may be doubted whether the editor's opinion is based on the passage, for he does not seem aware even of the necessity of producing support for it.

34 B, ψυχὴν δὲ εἰς τὸ μέσον αὐτοῦ θεὶς διὰ παντός τε ἔτεινε καὶ ἔτι ἔξωθεν τὸ σῶμα αὐτῇ περιεκάλυψε ταύτῃ.

In his note the editor says—

'In the words that follow, ἔξωθεν τὸ σῶμα αὐτῇ περιεκάλυψε ταύτῃ, Stallbaum (who seems throughout to regard Plato as incapable of originating any idea for himself) will have it that he is following Philolaos. Now the Pythagorean πνεῦμα ἄπειρον, the existence of which is peremptorily denied by Plato in 33 C, has not a trace of community with the Platonic world-soul: nor is there any reasonable evidence that Philolaos or any other Pythagorean conceived such a soul.'

Here, as too often, the editor is trying to make Stallbaum, who has entirely the advantage of his critic in all matters of learning and accuracy, look merely foolish. Stallbaum's remark is a very sensible one, and in agreement with perhaps the best authority on such subjects in his time—Boeckh. The editor puts his remark in quite a false light and misses the true criticism of it; and the true criticism is not in the least to Stallbaum's discredit, because it depends on the result of more modern researches. The note would give the impression that Stallbaum connected this passage of the Timaeus with passages which represent the world-soul in the special form of the πνεῦμα ἄπειρον, but

---

[1] Stallbaum refers to Sturz here but not for this purpose.

he does nothing of the kind. Again, the note conceals from the reader that there are passages in the fragment of Philolaus (so called) remarkably like this in the Timaeus, and that Stallbaum referred to these. He says 'Enimvero sequutus ille est Philolaum, de quo Athenagoras Legat. p. Christ. 6, p. 25 ed. Oxon (ap. Boeckh p. 151) καὶ Φιλόλαος δὲ ὥσπερ ἐν φρουρᾷ πάντα ὑπὸ τοῦ θεοῦ περιειλῆφθαι λέγων καὶ τὸ ἕνα εἶναι καὶ τὸ ἀνωτέρω τῆς ὕλης δεικνύει. Idem apud Stobaeum Eclogg. Phys. p. 426, ed. Heer. καὶ τὸ μὲν ἀμετάβολον ἀπὸ τᾶς τὸ ὅλον περιεχούσας ψυχᾶς μέχρι σελάνας περαιοῦται &c., &c.' These passages are given by Boeckh (Philolaus pp. 151 and 167) who says (p. 107) 'das eine ist beiden' [sc. the Timaeus and the doctrines of Philolaus] gemein dass die Weltseele im Timäos von der Mitte ausgeht, und wiederum das ganze Weltall in sie eingewickelt ist, Philolaos aber das Centralfeur eben auch als den Hauptsitz der Seele oder des Göttlichen ansieht, und mit der Seele das All umfasst darstellt. P. 167, 'Noch wird aber bestimmt, dass der erste von der das All umfassenden Seele aus anfange, welche nehmlich von der Hestia an durch den Kosmos durchgedehnt und um denselben, wie im Platonischen Timäos, herumgewickelt ist . . . : übereinstimmend mit der Vorstellung, welche Cicero (N. D. I. 11) dem Pythagoras beilegt (Deum, die Weltseele) animum esse per naturam rerum omnem intentum et commeantem, und mit der Philolaischen, dass Gott das Weltall wie in Gefangenschaft zusammenhalte.'

The true criticism of Stallbaum is of course that the passages which he (with Boeckh) refers to are likely to be or to be derived from forgeries influenced partly by the Timaeus itself. See Zeller, Phil. d. Gr. I. 385; and I. 341, where Zeller speaks of his difference from Boeckh on these subjects.

22. The following note on the same page may be added as an illustration of the same tone in the treatment of Stallbaum.

34 C, ἀλλά πως ἡμεῖς πολὺ μετέχοντες τοῦ προστυχόντος τε καὶ εἰκῇ κ.τ.λ.

The note on this is as follows:—

Cf. *Philebus* 28 D τὴν τοῦ ἀλόγου καὶ εἰκῇ δύναμιν. Stallbaum has the following curious remark: 'egregie convenit cum iis quae Legum libro x. 904 A disputantur, ubi animam indelebilem quidem esse docetur, nec vero aeternam.' This were 'inconstantia Platonis' with a vengeance: fortunately nothing of the kind is taught in the passage cited. The words are ἀνώλεθρον δὲ ὂν γενόμενον [τὸ γενόμενον Herm.] ἀλλ' οὐκ αἰώνιον, ὥσπερ οἱ κατὰ νόμον ὄντες θεοί. Plato here plainly denies eternity, not to soul, but to the ξύστασις of soul and body, which is ἀνώλεθρος, since such a mode of existence must subsist perpetually, but not αἰώνιος, since it belongs to γένεσις.

It is not clear what is exactly meant by saying ' This were " inconstantia Platonis " with a vengeance,' but it looks as if the editor had not understood Stallbaum's 'curious remark' : which, by the way, is not made *à propos* of the words with which the editor here connects it, and is perfectly sensible where it really does occur. It looks also as if he had not read Stallbaum's note on the passage of the Laws to which he refers—

'Quod corpus et animus hominis dicitur ἀνώλεθρον μέν, ἀλλ' οὐκ αἰώνιόν τι esse pertinet hoc sine dubio eo, quod vis et natura utriusque, quia non est constans, perpetua et sempiterna, sed obnoxia mutationibus, αἰώνιος judicari non potest; sed quoniam neutrum, nec corpus nec animus prorsus interit aut extinguitur, ac mutatur tantum ... idem merito censetur ἀνώλεθρον'—

where Stallbaum quotes very appositely among other passages to illustrate this Tim. 41 A sqq., 69 C, D, 72 D.

Perhaps, however, the editor's whole objection is contained in his remark that Plato in the Laws is not speaking of the soul by itself, but of the complex of soul and body. The contemptuous tone of this ('fortunately nothing of the kind,' &c.) is very unfortunate for himself. There is no evidence whatever in the passage that Plato is speaking of the complex of soul and body, as opposed to either : on the contrary, there is evidence that he is not, as is seen in the words which immediately follow what the editor has quoted—ἀνώλεθρον δὲ ὂν γενόμενον ἀλλ' οὐκ αἰώνιον ψυχὴν καὶ σῶμα, καθάπερ οἱ κατὰ νόμον ὄντες θεοί—γένεσις γὰρ οὐκ ἄν ποτε ἦν ἀπολομένου τούτοιν θατέρου. The editor has omitted the last clause.

Boeckh interprets the passage as Stallbaum does—'Die Seele hingegen ist geworden, nebst dem Körper zwar unvertilgbar, aber nicht ewig.'

§ 3.—Obligations to Martin and some others.

23. The relation of the Commentary to that of Martin, the editor from whom most has been borrowed, will now be considered.

The greater part of the Timaeus is taken up with questions not properly philosophic, but rather scientific, including matter pertaining to mathematics, astronomy, physical science, and biology; some psychology being associated with the latter. Far the greater part of the notes of any importance on these subjects seems to be not much more than a rewriting of Martin, whose work suffers in the process, with additions from Boeckh, and occasionally from Stallbaum. Reference is made not unfrequently to Martin, but the nature and amount of what is silently reproduced cannot be fairly covered by the mere general acknowledgment which the editor makes in his preface, 'The debt owed to Martin by any subsequent editor must needs be very great.' The reader would certainly often think the editor was speaking in his own person when he appears to be reproducing material supplied by others. The instances are numerous. A few specimens will be given. It is of course understood in all of them that no acknowledgment whatever is made. The sense of Martin's notes with his references, is generally reproduced, though sometimes they seem almost translated.

24.   68 C.

Martin.

πυρροῦ δὲ μέλανι πράσιον] This seems an exceedingly odd combination. πράσιον is bright green, or leek-colour; and a mixture of chestnut and black appears very little likely to produce it.

Aristotle more correctly classes green along with red and violet, as a simple colour: see *Meteorologica* III. ii. 372ᵃ 5 [which is then fully quoted].

According to Democritus πράσιον is ἐκ πορφυροῦ καὶ τῆς ἰσάτιδος, ἢ ἐκ χλωροῦ καὶ πορφυροειδοῦς: combinations which seem hardly better calculated than Plato's for producing the desired result.

Je rends par *vert-tendre* le mot πράσινον, qui signifie la couleur du *vert-de-gris*, πράσιον, ou des feuilles du poireau, πράσον. Platon prétend que cette couleur résulte du mélange du roux et du noir: est-ce bien *vraisemblable ?*

Aristote déclare, au contraire, que cette même couleur, qui est le vert de l'arc-en-ciel, est une couleur simple. [Météorol. III. 2, p. 372, col. 1, Bekker.]¹

Dans toute cette théorie des couleurs, Platon parait suivre en partie Empédocle les Pythagoriciens et Démocrite [V. le traité *Des op. des philos.* I. 15 et Théophraste, cité dans les notes 126 et 128.]

The editor's quotation of Democritus is from the part of Theophrastus which Martin refers to.

25.   54 E.

Martin.

It is notable that Plato uses six of the primary scalenes to compose his equilateral triangle when he could have done t equally well with two. The reason is probably this: the sides of the primary triangles mark the lines along which the equilaterals are broken up in case of dissolution. Now had Plato formed his equi-

De là on doit conclure que de même le triangle equilatéral ABC peut être considéré comme composé de deux triangles rectangles scalènes, par exemple AEB et AEC, semblables aux six dont il vient d'être question et jouissant par conséquent des trois mêmes propriétés. Mais c'est à la division en six triangles que Platon

---

¹ The references in square brackets are given by Martin as foot-notes.

lateral of two scalenes only, it would have been left in doubt whether the triangle ABC would be broken up along the line AD, or along BE, or CF. But if they are composed of six, the lines along which dissolution takes place is positively determined; since there is only one way in which six can be joined so as to form one equilateral. . . . Also by taking one-sixth of the equilateral, instead of one-half, we get the smallest element possible for our primal base.

s'arrête, parcequ'elle ne peut s'opérer que d'une seule manière, tandis qu'il y a trois manières d'opérer la division en deux triangles.

Et parcequ'il veut arriver aux éléments les plus simples.

(D, E, F are feet of perpendiculars from vertices on sides.)

The point to notice here is that Martin's view is peculiar. The obvious reason why Plato divides the equilateral triangle into six of the right-angled triangles instead of two, is that the former division is symmetrical and the latter is not. Martin misses this simple explanation, and gives rather a cumbrous one, and this is reproduced by the editor.

26. 36 C, ταύτην οὖν τὴν ξύστασιν πᾶσαν διπλῆν κατὰ μῆκος σχίσας μέσην πρὸς μέσην ἑκατέραν ἀλλήλαις οἷον χῖ προσβαλὼν κατέκαμψεν, εἰς ἓν κύκλῳ ξυνάψας αὐταῖς τε καὶ ἀλλήλαις ἐν τῷ καταντικρὺ τῆς προσβολῆς κ.τ.λ.

Martin.

We are to conceive the soul, after having been duly blended and having received her mathematical ratios as extended like a horizontal band: then the creator cleaves it lengthwise, and lays the two strips across each other in the shape of the letter X (i. e. at an acute angle) and so that the two centres coincide: next he bends them both round till the ends meet, so that each becomes a circle touching the other at a point in their circumferences opposite to the original point of contact. Thus we have two circles bisecting each other and inclined at an acute angle. The obliquity of the inclination is insisted on, because, as we shall presently see, the two circles represent respectively (amongst other things) the equator and the ecliptic.

Platon ajoute que les parties de l'âme du monde ayant été disposées en une longue bande, Dieu, l'artisan suprême, ὁ δημιουργός, coupa cette bande en deux suivant la longueur, et croisa les deux parties l'une sur l'autre en la forme d'un X, c'est à dire non à angle droit, et qu'ensuite il les courba toutes deux en cercle, unissant les extrémités, et appliquant celles de l'une sur celles de l'autre au point opposé à la première intersection des deux bandes, c'est à dire qu'il leur donna la forme de deux grands cercles d'une sphère se coupant en deux points opposés, mais non perpendiculaires l'un sur l'autre. Tels sont l'équateur et l'écliptique.

It may be argued fairly in such cases as this one that a certain amount of coincidence is only natural. But then there is so much of this kind of thing, and the English is nearly a translation of the French. The coincidence about the acute angle is not unimportant. So far from the obliquity being 'insisted on,' there is not a word about it in the text here. Though of course Plato's circles are obliquely inclined (cf. 39 A, three pages further on), it does not follow that he compared the X for anything more than the crossing of the lines, especially as the angle between them does not seem to have always been oblique. In the older uncial (to judge from Gardthausen) the angle is as nearly as possible a right angle. Martin may have got his view from Proclus, to whom he here refers.

The following is given merely as an amusing variant of a note of Martin's.

60 D, τὸ μὲν ἐλαίου καὶ γῆς καθαρτικὸν γένος λίτρον.

Martin.

M. Lindau entend que le nitre purifie l'huile et la terre, en formant, par sa combinaison avec la première, le savon, qui sert à nettoyer, et par sa combinaison avec la seconde, le verre, corps pur et brillant. Mais cette explication me semble forcée.

Lindau, imputing to Plato, 'brevitatem prope similem Thucydidis,' somehow extracts from the words the manufacture of soap and of glass: but such more than Pythian tenebricosity of diction, I think, even Thucydides would shrink from.

27. There is a certain difficulty about the composition of corpuscles from the elementary triangles, which Martin notices, and of which he offers a solution. On the passage 57 C, in which it is said that the elementary triangles differ in size, Martin says:—

'Pour concilier ce passage avec celui où il a été dit que les éléments de la pyramide, de l'octaèdre et de l'icosaèdre étant les mêmes, celui de ces trois corps qui a le plus d'éléments est nécessairement le plus grand, il suffit de supposer que les grandeurs des éléments ne peuvent varier que dans certaines limites, de sorte qu'aucune pyramide ne soit plus grande qu'un octaèdre et qu'aucun octaèdre ne soit plus grand qu'un icosaèdre.

The corresponding note of the editor is as follows:—' It is obvious that the variations in the size of the triangles must be confined within definite limits, for the largest pyramid is always smaller than the smallest octahedron, and the largest octahedron than the smallest icosahedron.'

(1) It is clear that Martin should have had the credit of noticing the difficulty, and, if his solution is adopted, of solving it. Zeller, in mentioning it, does not omit to couple Martin's name with it.

(2) The editor has spoiled Martin's note, which he has obviously reproduced, for that is accurate, and shews how the difficulty really

arises—'les éléments ... *étant les mêmes*, celui de ces trois corps qui a le plus d'éléments est nécessairement le plus grand '—the editor's note does not.

(3) The omission is serious, for the statement omitted (*étant les mêmes*) shews that the solution has not the 'obvious' character the editor would give to it.

The elementary atom of fire, the pyramid, is not merely said by Plato to be least of all, but is said to be ἐλαφρότατον, because it is ἐξ ὀλιγίστων ξυνεστὸς τῶν αὐτῶν μερῶν, which presupposes the size of the elemental triangles *not* to vary. And this shews that Martin can hardly be right. The more natural account is that we have here merely one of those inconsistencies in detail, overlooked by Plato, which are to be found in the Timaeus. There are more serious ones than these, which the editor himself is obliged to give up.

28. But the most remarkable reproduction of a special view (and a mistaken one) of Martin's is found in the note on 41 D.

We have already seen a piece of unfairness and carelessness in the editor's criticism of Stallbaum, which, it might be thought, could scarcely be paralleled. The editor proposed as against Stallbaum an emendation which Stallbaum himself proposes, though with reserve: he accuses Stallbaum of 'not understanding the construction,' which Stallbaum himself gives. But there is a parallel here quite as surprising in a criticism of Martin, and one which shews clearly that the opinion expressed in the former case that the editor probably learned originally from Stallbaum the view he maintains against him, and afterwards forgot the obligation, was by no means groundless.

In Timaeus 41 D the Creator is represented as dividing the substance compounded to make souls from into as many souls as there are stars. These souls are sent to the stars (each of which has already a soul of its own) to learn the laws of the Universe. Afterwards they are sown in the earth and planets, there to be born as men. One would suppose the reader of Plato's text would take these souls sent to the stars to be identical with the individual souls born afterwards with human bodies; and so Zeller understands it. But Martin has a peculiar theory, shared by the editor, that the souls sent to the stars are not the individual souls, but large portions of soul substance, so to speak, out of which, when sown in the earth and planets, are formed the greater multiplicity of human souls. This view is repeated point for point by the editor.

What the δημουργὸς did I conceive to be this. Having completed the admixture of soul he divided the whole into portions, assigning one portion to each star.

These portions, be it understood, are not particular souls nor aggregates of particular souls: they are divisions of the whole quantity of soul, which is not as yet differentiated into particular souls.

It is hardly necessary to observe that these ψυχαὶ ἰσάριθμοι τοῖς ἄστροις are quite distinct from the souls of the stars themselves.

Next the δημουργὸς explains to these still undifferentiated souls the laws of nature.

Martin II. p. 151.

Il faut bien se garder de confondre ces âmes dont une a été confiée à chacune des planètes ... soit avec les âmes des hommes et des animaux, formées en grand nombre de diverses parties de ces grandes âmes....

... soit avec les âmes de ces astres.

C'est à ces grandes âmes confiées aux astres, c'est à ces vastes dépôts de substance incorporelle et intelligente, que Dieu révèle ses desseins.

Martin's idea of the relation of these larger souls ('divisions of the whole quantity of the soul not differentiated,' &c.—'ces vastes dépôts de substance incorporelle,' &c.) to the particular souls is the same as the editor's, viz. that the latter are contained potentially in the former. Besides what has been quoted compare the following:—'Cependant, après cet exposé des décrets divins, pour dire que Dieu sema ces âmes dans les astres, Platon se sert du masculin : *c'est que dans chacune d'elles il considère déjà par avance les hommes qui devaient en être formés.*' But to our astonishment a little later in his note above quoted, the editor adds the following (the italics are not in the original) :—

Martin's interpretation appears to me *wholly unplatonic*, indeed *unintelligible*. He regards the ψυχαὶ ἰσάριθμοι as distinct from the soul that was afterwards to inform mortal bodies. 'C'est à ces grandes âmes confiées aux astres, c'est à ces vastes dépôts de substance incorporelle et intelligente, que Dieu révèle ses desseins.' This he himself most justly terms an 'étrange doctrine,' and certainly it is not Plato's.

Certainly the doctrine is not Plato's, but certainly it is the doctrine which the editor supposes to be Plato's. Thus the view which he himself maintains he rejects decisively when presented as Martin's. This is even worse than the former instance in the editor's attack on Stallbaum, and it may be doubted whether even in the editor's own writings anything more extraordinary can be found.

The comparison of the notes which are above put side by side leads inevitably to the conclusion that not only does the editor agree on the essential point (for there is a difference, of which, however, the editor is entirely unconscious) with Martin, but that his note is a reproduction of Martin's. If this is so, we can only offer the same explanation as in the other instance, that the editor in any case forgot where his own view came from, and either had not looked at Martin's note at all for some time when he printed, or else, if he looked at it again, misread it somehow, perhaps from that attitude towards other commentators which has been remarked before[1]. His quotation of a bit of Martin's note is hard to explain on any hypothesis; but a rather startling instance of misrepresentation of what the editor had before his eyes will be given later[2]

But there remains a very amusing, and, to a certain extent, confirmatory circumstance. Martin's view, which at first looks so odd, is but the necessary result of a mere mistake of interpretation made by Martin which the editor has not detected.

Martin apparently did not observe that the stars to which the souls were first to be sent were the fixed stars: he thinks they are the planets. Consequently for him τὸ πᾶν διεῖλε ψυχὰς ἰσαρίθμους τοῖς ἄστροις would mean that the whole substance of soul was divided into as many souls as there are *planets*, and as the number of these is only seven (or at most eight, if for this purpose the earth is added), whereas the souls which are to spring from them are so numerous, nothing remains but to suppose that each of the original souls gives birth to a large number.

But while it is thus in a way reasonable for Martin to hold this view, it is quite unreasonable for the editor, since he does not make the mistake[3] on which it depends. This confirms the suspicion derived from other evidence that it was first suggested to him by Martin's note.

The reason why the editor did not see Martin's original mistake is no doubt that he did not see that in the words 'C'est à ces grandes âmes confiées aux astres, &c.,' Martin means by 'astres' the planets, as is proved by the context. Just so he failed to remark that Stallbaum used 'astra' for planets, and, as we have seen, criticised him wrongly in consequence.

29. But attention must be directed to another kind of use of Martin's notes. There are, especially in the latter part of the book, a considerable number of learned notes with quotations from Aristotle, Theophrastus, Hippocrates, Galen, &c., without acknowledgment to

---

[1] Par. 15, fin.
[2] Par. 70.
[3] He rightly distinguishes the two stages, (1) the distribution of the souls among the fixed stars to learn the laws of the universe, (2) the sowing of them in the planets.

anyone. They are largely made up of the abundant learning in Martin's Commentary. This is not perhaps obvious on a mere cursory inspection, because Martin as a rule gives the sense of the passages without the Greek, and puts the references in footnotes, while the editor often writes out the Greek, and generally changes the form of the reference. The latter procedure is right enough, for though it is still usual to quote Hippocrates by the pages of Foësius as Martin does, it is perhaps more convenient to refer to the pages of Kühn. The same holds of the substitution of Kühn's pages for those of the Basle edition in Galen. The changes are easy to make, for Kühn gives the other forms of reference in his edition. The following instance of confusion seems to betray the source of his quotations. In a note by the editor on 70 A there is a reference to Galen, De Plac. [i.e. De Plac. Hippocr. et Plat.] II. 292. The full reference would be Bk. III. Kühn V. p. 292, which might, according to a method of the editor's, be abbreviated, III. 292. But II. has been substituted for III. Now Martin in his note refers to 'Galien, *Des op. d'Hippocr. et de Plat.* Liv. 2, t. 1, p. 265, l. 28 et suiv.,' a context which contains what the editor refers to. This is according to the volume and page of the Basle edition, but Martin has by mistake written Liv. 2 instead of Liv. 3, and the mistake in the editor's reference is exactly similar.

The changes prove that the editor has been industrious in looking out the passages for himself, of which there is enough evidence otherwise. But it will be clear that the labour of producing learned notes has been wonderfully shortened: and it is only reasonable that those who did the original work should have the credit of it. For anything the editor says, the reader would suppose that he is giving his own, and the impression is not weakened by the interpolation of remarks on the authors or passages quoted, the value of which will be presently illustrated.

A few typical instances of different kinds will suffice. It will be understood, as before, that only those reproductions of Martin are given in which there is no acknowledgment.

30.

70 A.

Martin.

II. 297, n. 6.

διάφραγμα] The word, which has since become specially appropriated to the midriff, is used in a general sense by Plato for a fence or partition [i.e. in this passage]:

Cette expression d'abord métaphorique, devint plus tard technique. V. Platon *Timée* 70 a et 84 d; Aristote, *Des part. des Anim.* III. 10, p. 672, col. 2, l. 20 ... Ce qu'Aristote

[55]

Aristotle applies it to the cartilaginous wall dividing the nostrils, *historia animalium* I. xi. 492 ᵇ. 16.

The midriff he often calls διάζωμα.

Mart:n.

appelle διάφραγμα, c'est la *cloison* du nez. V. *Hist. des Anim.* I. 11 (9), p. 492, col. 2, l. 16, Bekker.

II. 297, n. 5.
diaphragme ... διάζωμα). V. ... Aristote *Des part. des Anim.* III. 10, p. 672, col. 2; III. 14, p. 674, col. 1, l. 9; *Hist. des Anim.* I. 17 (14), p. 496, col. 2.

65 C.

ἐν τοῖς πρόσθεν ἀπελίπομεν] The reference would seem to be to the enumeration of χυμοί in 60 A. Plato's statement is quoted by Theophrastos *de causis plantarum* VI. iᵃ.: to the list of χυμοί given by Plato in the present passage he adds λιπαρός.

Further on he gives the views of Demokritos, who referred differences of taste to differences in the shape of the atoms: cf. *de sensu* §§ 65–69 ᵇ.

ᶜ Opinions not dissimilar to Plato's are ascribed to Alkmaion, and to Diogenes of Apollonia, by pseudo-Plutarch *de placitis philosophorum* IV. 18 ᵈ.

ᶜ Cette explication des saveurs parait, suivant la remarque de M. Cousin, avoir été empruntée en partie à Alcméon, à Diogène d'Apollonie et à Démocrite.

Footnote.

V. Théophraste, *De causis plant.* VI. 1 ᵃ: *De la sens.*, § 65–67 et 89 ᵇ, et le traité *Des op. des philos.* IV. 18 ᵈ.

Here (65 C) the editor gets all the material out of the sources given him by Martin, which he has studied for himself.

31. The next is a typical instance of the way in which the notes are often put together.

70 C, Plato says that the lungs receive drink as well as breath—τό τε πνεῦμα καὶ τὸ πόμα δεχομένη—on which there is the following note:—

In this curious error Plato is at one with all, or nearly all, the best medical science of his day. Plutarch, *de Stoicorum repugnantiis* XXIX, says: Πλάτων μὲν ἔχει τῶν ἰατρῶν τοὺς ἐνδοξοτάτους μαρτυροῦντας Ἱπποκράτην, Φιλιστίωνα, Διώξιππον τὸν Ἱπποκρατεῖον· καὶ τῶν ποιητῶν Εὐριπίδην, Ἀλκαῖον Εὔπολιν Ἐρατοσθένην, λέγοντας ὅτι τὸ ποτὸν διὰ τοῦ πνεύμονος διέξεισι.

It is remarkable that Galen also held this view: cf. *de plac. Hipp. et Plat.* VIII. 719 ἀλλὰ εἰ καὶ ζῷον, ὅ τι ἂν ἐθελήσῃς διψῆσαι ποιήσεις, ὡς κεχρωσμένον ὕδωρ ὑπομεῖναι

Martin.

Plutarque [Des Contradictions des Stoïciens, c. 29] voulant la défendre contre Erasistrate et Chrysippe, invoque, outre l'autorité des poètes, celle d'Hippocrate et des médecins Dioxippe et Philistion de Locres, dont l'opinion, &c.

Galien lui-même [Des op. d'Hippocr. et de Plat. liv. 8, fin t. 1, p. 329, l. 36 et suiv.] dit que si l'on fait avaler à un animal un liquide coloré d'azur ou de

πιεῖν, εἰ δοίης εἴτε κυανῷ χρώματι χρώσας εἴτε μίλτῳ, εἶτα εὐθέως σφάξας ἀνατέμοις, εὑρήσεις κεχρωσμένον τὸν πνεύμονα. δῆλον οὖν ἐστὶν ὅτι φέρεταί τι τοῦ πόματος εἰς αὐτόν.
Galen's observation is, I believe, correct, though his inference is not so.

Aristotle, on the contrary, was aware that no fluid passes down the windpipe to the lungs: see *historia animalium*, I. xvi. 495[b]. 16 ἡ μὲν οὖν ἀρτηρία τοῦτον ἔχει τὸν τρόπον, καὶ δέχεται μόνον τὸ πνεῦμα καὶ ἀφ᾽ ησιν, ἄλλο δ᾽ οὔθεν οὔτε ξηρὸν οὐθ᾽ ὑγρόν, ἢ πόνον παρέχει ἕως ἂν ἐκβήξῃ τὸ κατελθόν. See too *de partibus animalium*, III. iii. 664[b]. 9, where he gives divers demonstrations that the hypothesis is untenable.

It is also denied by the writer of Book IV of the Hippokratean treatise *de morbis*, vol. II. pp. 373, 374, Kühn; but affirmed by the author of *de ossium natura*, a work of uncertain date, vol. I. p. 515, Kühn.

Galen, de plac. VIII. 715, points out that Plato conceives only a part of the fluid to pass down the trachea: οὐκ ἀθρόον οὐδὲ διὰ μέσης τῆς εὐρυχωρίας τοῦ ὀργάνου φερόμενον, ἀλλὰ περὶ τὸν χιτῶνα αὐτοῦ δροσοειδῶς καταρρέον.

Martin.

minium, et qu'on l'ouvre immédiatement après, on voit le poumon coloré, et il en conclut qu'*une partie* du liquide se rend directement dans le poumon.

Cette erreur, parfaitement réfutée par Aristote [Hist. des Anim. I. 16 (13), p. 495[b]. 1. 14-19 des parties des animaux III. 3, p. 654 (should be 664) col. 2. l. 9-19,

et par l'auteur, probablement antérieur [Littré, Œuvres d'Hipp. t. 1, Int. 373-379] du traité hippocratique *Des Maladies* [Sect. 5, p. 513-514 Foës], avait cependant été reproduite par l'auteur plus récent [Littré, Œuvres d'Hipp. Int. p. 382] du traité *Du Cœur* auquel sans doute Galien l'a empruntée.

Daremberg Frag. d. Com. d. Gal. p. 48.

Il parait d'après d'autres passages du Timée, que suivant Platon ce n'était pas toute la boisson, mais seulement une partie qui se rendait dans le poumon. Galien (de Dogm. Hippocr. Pl. VIII. 9, t. V. p. 714) dit, &c.

This note is obviously, with some slight exceptions to be noticed presently, made out of Martin's—who for his part acknowledges his obligations to others. It is evident that the passages referred to by Martin have been read in the original, except perhaps, as will appear, that from the De Corde.

One remark and two passages are not in Martin.

The remark, 'Galen's observation is, I believe, correct,' is characteristic. In a scientific matter the mere expression of personal belief without grounds is hardly valuable.

Probably the inspiration is not far to seek. There is in Daremberg's edition of Galen on the ~~Timaeus~~ a note which the editor, to judge by the end of his note, seems to have had before him [1]. In this Daremberg says—

---

[1] Another use of this Commentary will be pointed out later in Section 5.

'Je dois dire cependant, à la défense des anciens, que cette erreur a pour origine, ou du moins pour confirmation, une expérience physiologique, qui devait certainement conduire à quelque fausse interprétation des physiologistes qui n'avaient aucune idée de la circulation; cette expérience, signalée pour la première fois par le traité *de Corde*, reproduite depuis par Galien comme un argument péremptoire, consistait à faire boire à un animal un liquide coloré et à l'ouvrir immédiatement après; on trouvait alors la trachée et les bronches toutes de la même couleur.'

A biologist would have told the editor that what Galen describes (' Galen's observation ') is impossible. Now, as Martin says, Galen's remark probably originated somehow from the De Corde. But the experiment described there (Kühn I. 485) is a reality. It is not said there that the *lungs* will be found coloured if the animal is dissected, but that if the animal's throat is cut while it is drinking the *trachea* (λαιμός here) will be found to be coloured. In fact, a little fluid gets into it: and I am told that this would be especially the case in a pig, the animal mentioned in the De Corde. Galen, then, has somehow altered the true account.

It is clear also that Daremberg's remarks refer properly to the *De Corde*, and that he inaccurately speaks as if Galen had merely repeated what is there described. This is probably the origin of the editor's mistake.

Of the two passages not in Martin's note, one is in the note of Daremberg just mentioned.

The other (De Oss. Nat.) replaces rather unluckily, as has been seen, Martin's reference to the De Corde. The De Oss. Nat. is associated with the De Corde in the part of Littré to which Martin refers in a footnote. However the editor came by his citation, it cannot evidence much knowledge of the subject, for it is accompanied by one of those unfortunate remarks which are the snare of those who make up notes of the kind. The editor may have seen in the part of Littré just referred to that several treatises, including a *part*—the significance of this will appear in a moment—of the De Oss. Nat. were not earlier than Aristotle, or he may have seen that the De Oss. Nat. is not included in the list of treatises that have any claim to genuineness, and thought it safe to speak of ' the author of *de ossium natura*, a work of uncertain date.' But the De Oss. Nat. cannot be said to have an ' author,' or a ' date,' or even to be a ' work.'

It has been established beyond controversy (vid. Littré) that it is a collection of extracts made from different books upon the veins—so that the collection has not even the right title—by some unknown hand. This is not a doubtful matter like, for instance, a theory of the composition of the Homeric poems: the evidence is complete. For instance, Aristotle himself quotes the second and third of the five extracts which compose the De Oss. Nat., and tells us the names of their authors (Hist. An. 511ᵇ 24, 512ᵇ 13). The one he assigns to Syennesis the Cyprian, and the other to Polybus. This is of course absolute demonstration. The latter comes indeed from the treatise περὶ φύσιος ἀνθρώπου, where it will be found (Kühn I. 364). The fourth extract is from Hippocrates Epidemics, bk. II. The fifth extract is referred to by Galen as belonging to an Appendix to the treatise called μοχλικός (τὰ προσκείμενα τῷ μοχλικῷ). The authorship of the first extract is unknown to Littré.

What the editor happens to quote is from the fifth extract.

32. If anything can heighten the effect of the editor's mistakes, it is generally his own defence of them.

After quoting, with an unimportant omission, the criticism upon himself in the 'Classical Review' ending with this passage:—

> Now the *De Oss. Nat.* cannot be said[1] to have an author or a date. It is established that it consists of five extracts from different books, some at least by different authors, on the subject of the veins (not the bones) collected by some unknown hand. Two of them are quoted by Aristotle himself, who gives their authors.

he replies:—

> I am sorry to make so long a quotation, but less would hardly serve. The passage I have omitted from the above is simply the citation from my note. In this the reader will doubtless expect to find, first, that the *de ossium natura* is assigned to some definite author of a definite period subsequent to Aristotle; secondly (thanks to the adroit parenthetical innuendo) that it is said to be concerned with the bones. What he actually will find is this: 'It [Plato's theory of fluid passing through the lungs] is denied by the writer of book IV. of the Hippocratean treatise *de morbis*, vol. II. pp. 373, 374, Kühn: but affirmed by the author of *de ossium natura*, a work of uncertain date, vol. I. p. 515, Kühn.' And this is all. Now, assuming the correctness of all Mr. Wilson says, are we expected, in a passing mention of a treatise (or compilation) of the most uncertain character, to interpolate an irrelevant disquisition upon its structure and origin? And are we forbidden to describe the *Nicomachean Ethics*, for example, as a 'work'?

This shews that the editor did not even understand the nature of his mistake when it was pointed out to him. Of course 'the reader would not expect to find' from my criticism what the editor says he would expect, but the sort of thing which the editor says he really would find. The unluckiness of the reference to the 'Nicomachean Ethics' is obvious. But the most amusing thing is the question, 'Are we ex-

---

[1] The editor has omitted by mistake the words 'to be a "work," or'.

pected, in a passing mention of a treatise (or a compilation) of the most uncertain [!] character, to interpolate an irrelevant disquisition upon its structure and origin?' It is precisely because the editor quite unnecessarily 'interpolated' a remark on the date and 'the author' that he got into trouble.

As I have elsewhere pointed out, his mistake is like that of a foreigner who reading Wordsworth's ode in a selection, should say that the immortality of the soul ' is affirmed by the author of ' the Golden Treasury of Lyric Verse ' a work of uncertain date.'

The editor prefaces the part of his reply just examined with the words ' A perhaps yet more instructive example of Mr. Wilson's style is this.'

33. Here may be added an instance of a composite note where the obligation is mainly to Zeller.

58 A, ἡ τοῦ παντὸς περίοδος, ἐπειδὴ συμπεριέλαβε τὰ γένη κυκλοτερὴς οὖσα καὶ πρὸς αὐτὴν πεφυκυῖα βούλεσθαι ξυνιέναι, σφίγγει πάντα καὶ κενὴν χώραν οὐδεμίαν ἐᾷ λείπεσθαι. διὸ δὴ πῦρ μὲν εἰς ἅπαντα διελήλυθε μάλιστα, ἀὴρ δὲ δεύτερον, ὡς λεπτότητι δεύτερον ἔφυ, καὶ τἆλλα ταύτῃ· τὰ γὰρ ἐκ μεγίστων μερῶν γεγονότα μεγίστην κενότητα ἐν τῇ ξυστάσει παραλέλοιπε, τὰ δὲ σμικρότατα ἐλαχίστην.

1.

μεγίστην κενότητα] This expression shews plainly enough that Plato was well aware of the fact which Aristotle urges as a flaw in his theory, namely that it is impossible for all his figures to fill up space with entire continuity. In the structure of air and water there must be minute interstices of void;

2.

there must also be a certain amount of void for the reason that, the universe being a sphere it is impossible for rectilinear figures exactly to fill it up.

3.

But, it is to be observed, Plato's theory does not demand that void shall be absolutely excluded from his system, but only that there shall be no vacant space large

Zeller, Phil. d. Gr. II. i. 679.
. . . . Für Plato ergiebt sich freilich aus dieser Behauptung eine doppelte Schwierigkeit. Für's erste nämlich füllen seine vier Elementarkörper keinen Raum so vollständig aus, dass keine Zwischenräume entstehen (ARIST. de Coelo III. 8. Anf.),

auch abgesehen davon, dass sich überhaupt keine Kugel durch geradlinige Figuren ausfüllen lässt; und sodann müsste bei der Auflösung eines Elementarkörpers in seine Dreiecke jedesmal ein leerer Raum entstehen, da zwischen diesen nichts war (MARTIN, II. 255 f.)

Plato muss diese Schwierigkeiten entweder unbeachtet gelassen haben, was in Betreff der ersten freilich bei einem solchen Mathematiker auffallend wäre,

oder er will den leeren Raum nicht schlechthin läugnen, sondern nur behaupten, dass kein Raum leer bliebe, der überhaupt von einem Körper eingenommen werden kann.

enough to contain the smallest existing corpuscle of matter.

4.
The larger corpuscles have larger interstices between them than the smaller. So long however as these interstices are not large enough to afford entrance to the smallest particle of any element, the effect is the same as of a solid mass without any cavities; but when once they are large enough to contain any particle πίλησις instantly forces one into the vacancy.

5.
This is all Plato means by κενὴν χώραν οὐδεμίαν ἐᾷ λείπεσθαι; he denies void as a mechanical principle, but not its existence altogether in the nature of things.

6.
Beside the atomists, the existence of void was affirmed by the Pythagoreans; see above, 33 C, and Aristotle, *physica* IV. vi. 213^b 22: it was denied by the Eleatics, by Empedokles, by Anaxagoras, and by Aristotle: see *physica* IV. vii.

Martin, II. 255.
Les Pythagoriciens et les Atomistes [v. Arist. *Phys.* IV. 6. &c.] avaient admis l'existence du vide; Empédocle et Anaxagore l'avaient niée.... Aristote lui-même nie le vide encore plus fortement que Platon [*Phys.* IV. 6–9].

Zeller, l. c.
Schon Empedokles und Anaxagoras hatten nach dem Vorgang der Eleaten den leeren Raum geläugnet.

Martin's note here is very like Zeller's, but the point reproduced in the second of the paragraphs into which the editor's note is divided above, does not seem to be in Martin.

The correspondence of thought and language in the notes which are put side by side tells its own story. But there is one point which may be specially noticed. The expression 'geradlinige Figuren' is peculiarly appropriate in Zeller, because, as his next sentence shows, he supposes the elementary atoms may be resolved into their elementary triangles. The editor, however, who has gone quite wrong on this subject, and treats Aristotle with contempt for taking a view which is clearly right, denies that triangles can be elements and only admits resolution into solid bodies. For him then the expression 'rectilinear figure' is neither appropriate nor natural.

The fourth paragraph is merely an interpretation of the text on Zeller's principle.

The fifth seems to be quite *de suo*. What can be meant by the dark saying that 'Plato denies void as a mechanical principle, but not its existence altogether in the nature of things'?

The sixth is nearly a translation of Martin, adding 'the Eleatics' which is given in Zeller.

The editor's compilation, as is usual, is inferior to Martin's note on the scientific point, but this may be left to the discussion of his scientific notes in general.

§ 4.—Acquaintance with Ancient Authors quoted.

34. Instances of the foregoing kind might be greatly multiplied, as any reader will discover who will take trouble enough: but it is more important here to shew how the impression they inevitably make is confirmed by the nature of the editor's acquaintance with the books he quotes, outside the parts which happen to be quoted by his predecessors.

We have already had an illustration in the case of the medical writers whom he so often quotes after his predecessors.

As to Galen's writings, there is one use at least which the editor should have made of them if he had worked at them on his own account. The treatise De Placitis Hippocratis et Platonis, quoted sometimes by the editor (after his authorities), contains, as its title might suggest, a considerable number of quotations from Plato's dialogues, including the Timaeus. These should be read to see if they throw any light on the readings in the text. It must be doubted whether the editor has done this. In two places (58 C, 83 B) he says that Galen confirms the text, but gives no reference. In the second of these the information is supplied by Martin, who also gives no reference, and in the first by Stallbaum, whose reference agrees with none of the three usual methods, and is really to the Aldine folio. On the other hand, in 70 A τὴν δὲ δὴ καρδίαν ἅμμα τῶν φλεβῶν κ.τ.λ. there is a question about the reading, for which two passages of the De Plac. Hipp. et Plat. ought to be cited, for Galen quotes it twice, and both passages in Kühn's[1] text have a variant on ἅμμα, bk. III, Kühn V. 292 τὴν δὲ καρδίαν ἅμα τῶν φλεβῶν καὶ πηγὴν τοῦ περιφερομένου κ.τ.λ.: bk. VI, V. 581 τὴν δὲ δὴ καρδίαν ἅμα τῶν φλεβῶν πηγὴν καὶ τοῦ περιφερομένου κ.τ.λ. In the latter the position of καί is of course interesting.

The editor refers to the first place in Galen (bk. III.)—'Galen quotes this passage'—and has evidently looked at it. The passage is in a

---

[1] Lindau indeed says, 'τὴν δὲ καρδίαν ἅμμα τῶν φλεβῶν καὶ πηγήν. Sic Galenus cum optimis codd. pro vulgate ἅμα.' But according to Müller no MS. of Galen reads ἅμμα, and no edition. I do not know what authority Kühn had for the position of καί in the second passage. The Aldine has ἅμα in both places and καί before πηγήν.

context of Galen referred to by Martin here, not however with a view to the reading. The editor says nothing of its bearing on the reading. He does not refer to the other and more interesting passage in Galen (bk. VI.) at all.

Further, the editor writes 'Stallbaum's ἀρχὴν ἅμα is comparatively feeble. It is true that Aristotle *de juventute* iii. 468^b 31 has ἡ δὲ καρδία ὅτι ἐστὶν ἀρχὴ τῶν φλεβῶν :' [quoted by Martin in a previous note] 'but that is no evidence that Plato wrote ἀρχὴν here.' The criticism of Stallbaum is trivial; the reading would be very apt, and is found in three inferior MSS.[1] (in two apparently a correction), and it is therefore very important to quote a passage from the same book of Galen, where he refers to this passage of the Timaeus, and connects with it statements about the heart being ἀρχὴ τῶν φλεβῶν. Kühn V. 573 ὡς ἐσφάλησαν οἱ καὶ τὴν καρδίαν ἀρχὴν εἰπόντες εἶναι τῶν φλεβῶν ἐπιδέδεικται. εἴπερ γὰρ αἵματός τινος εὐθὺς δήπου καὶ φλεβῶν ἐνόμισαν, ὥσπερ μὴ καὶ τῶν ἀρτηριῶν ἐχουσῶν αἷμα λεπτομερέστατον καὶ θερμότατον. ὡς οὖν ἀρτηριῶν, οὕτως καὶ τοῦ πνευματώδους τε καὶ τοῦ ζέοντος αἵματος ἀρχή τε καὶ πηγὴ τοῖς ζῴοις ἐστὶν ἡ καρδία, καὶ διὰ τοῦτο καὶ τὸ θυμοειδὲς ἐνδείκνυται τῆς ψυχῆς ἐν αὐτῇ κατῳκῆσθαι (as here in the Timaeus). ταῦτ' ἄρα καὶ ὁ Πλάτων τὴν καρδίαν ἔλεγεν πηγὴν τοῦ περιφερομένου κατὰ πάντα μέλη σφοδρῶς αἵματος οὐ ταὐτὸν γάρ ἐστιν ἢ πηγὴν αἵματος ἁπλῶς εἰπεῖν ἢ προσθεῖναι τοῦ περιφερομένου σφοδρῶς κ.τ.λ. which certainly seems to indicate that Galen did not read ἀρχὴν ἅμα τῶν φλεβῶν : for he seems really trying to shew that it does not follow that because Plato said the heart was πηγή of one kind of blood that it was therefore ἀρχὴ τῶν φλεβῶν. Now on the one hand the editor omits all reference to this important passage in his note, on the other hand, in his next note he does quote a part of it on account of the doctrine contained in it : but it never occurs to him to use it as evidence of the reading. The fact is, that in this next note he is merely repeating (without acknowledgment) something which Martin says on Galen's misunderstanding of Plato's doctrine : and Martin says nothing about the reading in connection with it. This is significant enough.

35. But illustrations may now be given which relate to books better known and more in the ordinary course.

An editor of the Timaeus ought to have a fair acquaintance with certain treatises of Aristotle, especially the De Anima and the De Sensu, and the Parva Naturalia generally : and he ought to know the frag-

---

[1] The editor says nothing of this, but mentions ἀρχὴν ἅμα in his app. crit. merely as Stallbaum's reading.

ment De Sensibus, by Theophrastus, which is of no great length. These are often quoted by Martin and Stallbaum and (after them) by the editor. Of the nature of his knowledge of Theophrastus we have given evidence relative to an attack on Stallbaum. Another indication is to be found in his note on 67 B φωνὴν θῶμεν τὴν δι' ὤτων ὑπ' ἀέρος ἐγκεφάλου τε καὶ αἵματος μέχρι ψυχῆς πληγὴν διαδιδομένην, where the editor governs the genitives ἐγκεφάλου and αἵματος by πληγήν not by διά. Whether this construction is right or not, he gives an unsound reason for it. But apparently the editor is unaware that it is confirmed by Theophrastus in two different passages, one near the beginning of the De Sensibus, and one near the end. In § 6 and § 85 Plato's definition of sound is given as πληγὴν ὑπ' ἀέρος ἐγκεφάλου καὶ αἵματος δι' ὤτων μέχρι ψυχῆς (without διαδιδομένην).

This, by the way, also illustrates the editor's acquaintance with Pseudo-Plutarch de Placitis Philosophorum, quoted often enough by him, after his predecessors. In this treatise, IV. 19, Plato's definition is repeated in such a way as to shew that the writer supposed ἐγκεφάλου καὶ αἵματος governed by διά—πληγὴν ὑπ' ἀέρος δι' ὤτων καὶ ἐγκεφάλου καὶ αἵματος μέχρι ψυχῆς διαδιδομένην—the same reading is found in Stobaeus' excerpt from the Placita (or the source of the Placita). If the editor had read Theophrastus de Sensibus and the Placita on his own account, he could hardly have passed this over. He quotes the latter treatise on 82 A after Martin (without acknowledgment as usual), but instead of giving the reference as he found it in Martin (Plut. de Plac. V. 30) he prefers to quote the part of Stobaeus in which it is also found ('Stobaeus florilegium 100 ... and again 101'). The form of the quotation would hardly be natural to a reader of Stobaeus. '100' should be 100,25 (i. e. tit. 100, lemm. 25), and '101' should be 101, 2. The 100th title contains about 7 octavo pages (Gaisford), and contains 28 lemmas, of which the one quoted is the 25th; title 101 contains 16 pages and 30 lemmas. Diels prints the excerpt from Stobaeus parallel with the text of the Placita, and the headline of his page has simply 'Flor. t. 101, 100'; but of course the accurate reference is given below in the Apparatus Criticus, where the editor might have found it.

36. The editor's statements about the authors whom he quotes are not trustworthy, even in matters of no great difficulty, as illustrated by the note upon the same treatise of Theophrastus.

On the doctrine expressed in 57 A that like cannot affect like he says, 'This view was universally held with the sole exception of Demokritos: cf. Arist. de Gen. et Corr. I. vii.' After quoting this passage at some length, he adds 'Theophrastos however considers that the view of Demokritos is uncertain; see *de sensu* § 49.' (The passages quoted from Aristotle and Theophrastus are the two which Zeller gives in his note on this same subject.) It will be found that Theophrastus does not thus differ from Aristotle, and that he does not say that Democritus' view was uncertain on the question of action; on the contrary, he represents Democritus as committed to the opinion that only like can act on like, and uses almost exactly the same words as Aristotle, ἀδύνατον δέ, φησί, τὰ μὴ ταὐτὰ πάσχειν, ἀλλὰ κἂν ἕτερα ὄντα ποιῇ οὐχ ᾗ ἕτερα ἀλλ' ᾗ ταὐτόν τι ὑπάρχει (cf. Arist. 323ᵇ. 12–14). Theophrastus does express uncertainty upon a different matter, viz. whether in the theory of Democritus sense-perception took place through a relation of opposites or similars. The editor seems to have been misled by misunderstanding the drift of the passage. All it comes to is that while Democritus treated of the particular senses, he left no definite statement on the question as to whether sensation in general was effected by a relation of opposites or not. Δημόκριτος δὲ περὶ μὲν αἰσθήσεως οὐ διορίζει πότερα τοῖς ἐναντίοις ἢ τοῖς ὁμοίοις ἐστίν . . . περὶ ἑκάστης δ' ἤδη αὐτῶν ἐν μέρει περᾶται λέγειν. Theophrastus gives reasons why the relation might be one or the other, and the 'aporia' is clearly his and not that of Democritus.

37. As to Aristotle's treatise De Sensu, the editor quotes it after his authorities. We have had an instance already in his note on 45 D, where he refers to a well-known passage given in Stallbaum's note, from De Sensu, chap. 2. If the editor had read thirty lines further in this chapter he would have found a passage which would have saved one of his numerous mistakes of translation. In Timaeus 64 D, Plato speaking of the vision says—τὴν ὄψιν . . . ἣ δὴ σῶμα ἐν τοῖς πρόσθεν ἐρρήθη καθ' ἡμέραν ξυμφυὲς ἡμῶν γίγνεσθαι. He thinks vision effected by a stream of light (ὄψεως ῥεῦμα) proceeding from the eye, forming a sort of material body (σῶμα), which is an organ of sense, and in a way part of the human body like any other organ of sense. In this passage then σῶμα ξυμφυὲς ἡμῶν means 'a material body *adhering to* us.' The editor translates 'a material body *cognate with* ourselves,' and has this note, 'Stallbaum is perhaps right in reading ἡμῖν. But as ξυγγενὴς is several times followed by the genitive . . . it seems possible that ξυμφυὴς might have the same construction. ξύμφυτος seems to have the same construction in *Philebus* 51 D.' Now in the part of the De Sensu referred to is a passage on the very subject, which makes the meaning of ξυμφυής clear and the true construction of the genitive—ἄλογον δ' ὅλως τὸ ἐξιόντι τινὶ τὴν ὄψιν ὁρᾶν, καὶ ἀποτείνεσθαι μέχρι τῶν ἄστρων, ἢ μέχρι τινὸς ἐξιοῦσαν συμφύεσθαι, καθάπερ λέγουσί τινες· τούτου μὲν γὰρ βέλτιον τὸ ἐν ἀρχῇ συμφύεσθαι τοῦ ὄμματος κ.τ.λ. And apart from this even, if the author had had a tolerable acquaintance with the De Anima (so necessary for the student of the Timaeus) he must have remembered (for the interpretation) ἀκοῇ δὲ συμφυὴς ἀήρ (Torstrik, MSS. ἀκοή ... ἀερί) in De An. II. viii.

Again in a note on Plato's theory of smell (66 D) we are informed that Aristotle makes air or water the medium of smell, for which De An. II. ix. is quoted. Though in the next sentence the author quotes from De Sensu, chap. v. (quoted in Stallbaum's note) he is unaware that in this very chapter the account given in the De Anima is refined upon, and the medium of smell is more precisely determined as something common to both air and water, viz. τὸ ὑγρόν.

38. The notes upon Plato's theory of respiration illustrate the editor's knowledge of other parts of the Parva Naturalia, which he quotes like his predecessors, and also the inaccuracy with which he reads the book he is editing. The Aristotelian treatise De Respiratione is one of those which an editor of the Timaeus ought to know. In Tim. 70 C Plato describes the lungs as devised to cool the heat of the heart. One of the agencies by which the lungs effect this is the respiration of air. Now this is the very function assigned by Aristotle in the De Resp. to the lungs—they cool the animal heat and especially the heart, the centre of it. The editor, however, in his note on 70 C says nothing of this important and essential agreement, but merely points out a difference, for which he quotes De Part. An., not mentioning the De Resp.: 'he (Plato) is also of course quite wrong in calling them (the lungs) ἄναιμον. His view is impugned by Aristotle on grounds of comparative anatomy, de Part. Animal. III. vi. 669ᵃ 18, Τὸ δὲ πρὸς τὴν ἄλσιν εἶναι τὸν πλεύμονα τῆς καρδίας οὐκ εἴρηται καλῶς: further on, 669ᵇ. 8, he says ὅλως μὲν οὖν ὁ πλεύμων ἐστὶν ἀναπνοῆς χάριν: but he does not seem to have had a very clear idea of the function performed by the lungs.' The last sentence is remarkable, as well as the absence of reference to the De Respiratione. But we seem to find the explanation in the corresponding note of Martin, where nothing is said of the De Resp. or of the affinity between Aristotle and Plato, but we find the following 'Aristote reconnaît qu'il a du sang dans le poumon, sinon de tous les animaux, du moins de l'homme et de tous les vivipares. V. *Des part. des anim.*, III. 7. 669ª 24, 669ᵇ 12,' which seems to account for the limitation of the editor's quotations.

Of course if in writing this note he as yet only had before him the passage from the De Part. An., it is not hard to understand why he should say Aristotle had not a very clear idea of the functions of the lungs; yet if he had read the preceding part of the chapter he might have found something more to say about Aristotle's view than merely that he thought the lungs were ἀναπνοῆς χάριν.

Further on, Martin in his note on the circulation of the blood (77 E) does quote the De Respiratione, mentioning Aristotle's conception of a cooling function for the lungs: and now we find the editor on the same passage quoting from the De Respiratione and from the same context: and it is a mark of the editor's imperfect assimilation of Martin that the passage does not suggest to him the necessity of improving his former note. In quoting it he makes some fresh mistakes:—' It will be seen that Plato conceives respiration solely as subsidiary to digestion: an opinion which is perhaps peculiar to him alone among ancient thinkers: the ordinary view being that its function was to regulate the temperature of the body, as thought Aristotle cf. *de resp.* XVI. 478ª 28 καταψύξεως μὲν οὖν ὅλως ἡ τῶν ζῴων δεῖται φύσις, διὰ τὴν ἐν.τῇ καρδίᾳ τῆς ψυχῆς ἐμπύρωσιν. ταύτην δὲ ποιεῖται διὰ τῆς ἀναπνοῆς.' All these statements are incorrect. Plato did not think respiration 'solely subsidiary to digestion,' for as we have seen in the passage (just considered) where the lungs are first spoken of, it is said they were made to cool the heart by respiration of air and absorption of moisture, so that the spirited element residing in it might be better controlled by reason. And this function of respiration is the only one spoken of at first by Plato. Again, it is not true that Plato was alone so far as he made respiration subsidiary to digestion, nor that Aristotle differed from him in not connecting it with the digestion. According to the De Respiratione the purpose of respiration of air is to preserve the central fire; for otherwise it would consume itself away (μάρανσις). The purpose of the central fire is to digest the food. Hence the ultimate object of respiration is digestion. Anyone who had given even a cursory reading to the De Respiratione ought to have known this. The mistake is the less excusable because the same doctrine is stated at length in other parts of the Parva Naturalia, which also are quoted from by the editor (after his authorities).

39. One other proof will be added, though more could be given, of the nature of the editor's acquaintance with this part of Aristotle (i.e. the De Anima and the Parva Naturalia). 74 A, Plato describes the purpose for which God made joints in the backbone—ἐμποιῶν ἄρθρα, τῇ θατέρου προσχρώμενος ἐν αὐτοῖς ὡς μέσῃ ἐνισταμένῃ δυνάμει, κινήσεως καὶ κάμψεως ἕνεκα. On τῇ θατέρου προσχρώμενος the editor says 'This expression is very obscure,' and after a supercilious and unfortunate attack on Stallbaum and remarks on different interpretations, adds 'Dr. Jackson has suggested to me an interpretation which is certainly much more natural, and, I think, right. We know that θάτερον expresses plurality. Plato then, when he says that the gods used ἡ θατέρου δύναμις ... simply signifies that by means of joints they divided the bones into a number of parts, κάμψεως καὶ κινήσεως ἕνεκα. ὡς μέσῃ I take to mean between the bones—the joints represent the principle of θάτερον, as being the cause of division and plurality.' The editor can scarcely have known the important passage in the De Anima on the joints (III. x. 8) τὸ κινοῦν ὀργανικῶς ὅπου ἀρχὴ καὶ τελευτὴ τὸ αὐτό, οἷον ὁ γιγγλυμός· ἐνταῦθα γὰρ τὸ κυρτὸν καὶ κοῖλον τὸ μὲν τελευτὴ τὸ δ' ἀρχή· διὸ τὸ μὲν ἠρεμεῖ τὸ δὲ κινεῖται, λόγῳ μὲν ἕτερα ὄντα, μεγέθει δ' ἀχώριστα· πάντα γὰρ ὤσει καὶ ἕλξει κινεῖται. διὸ δεῖ ὥσπερ ἐν κύκλῳ μένειν τι, καὶ ἐντεῦθεν ἄρχεσθαι τὴν κίνησιν (433^b 21–27).

It is more likely that Plato is thinking of some such principle than merely of 'the division of the bones into a number of parts.' And in any case the passage ought to have been quoted and its bearing on the passage of the Timaeus considered.

40. The Ethics of Aristotle is a book very commonly read, but one must doubt whether the author has more than a superficial knowledge of it. On 71 B he quotes a very familiar passage from the first book at suspicious length; on the other hand he makes a grave omission in quoting from the tenth book in his note on 64 C. Here he summarises Aristotle's objections to the Platonic theory of pleasure and only quotes from chap. 3 of bk. X. He seems to be entirely unconscious of the long and important argument against making pleasure a κίνησις (or γένεσις) which is found in chap. 4: which could not be overlooked by anyone who knew the book even tolerably. If the editor looked at the context he perhaps was misled by the circumstance that the polemic seems to end with the end of the third chapter (τὰ μὲν οὖν λεγόμενα περὶ τῆς ἡδονῆς καὶ λύπης ἱκανῶς εἰρήσθω), and the fourth chapter opens as if the polemic was over and the subject was to be treated constructively (τί δ' ἐστὶν ἢ ποῖόν τι καταφανέστερον γένοιτ' ἂν ἀπ' ἀρχῆς ἀναλαβοῦσιν) though in the second section of it Aristotle renews his objection to Plato. But one might almost suspect that the third chapter itself is not known at first hand, for the editor omits the argument in the early sections of it directed against an important and essential feature of the Platonic theory of pleasure in the Philebus to which the editor is referring—the doctrine that pleasure is ἄπειρον. The difference which these omissions make to the validity of the confident criticism of Aristotle is rather serious. The editor's criticisms of Aristotle are generally unfortunate. They may be spoken of later on.

§ 5.—Obligations to Daremberg.

41. This part of the subject may be closed by an examination of the editor's commentary on Plato's theory of respiration, which has the look of a genuine piece of work.

Some remarks were made on this in the Classical Review for March, 1889 (p. 116), and they are given here in full together with the editor's reply, to shew how he has tried to mislead by imperfect quotation.

The criticism was as follows:—

In one place, Plato's theory of respiration, the editor gives the reader the impression that he has done a piece of original and meritorious research, by using the Greek of a commentary (Galen's) only known in 'a defective Latin translation' when Martin wrote. *All that he gets out of the Greek is equally clear in the Latin which is not here defective.* All that he rightly gets out of it, and even the illustrative woodcut (a little altered) is already given in the note and translation of the edition used (Daremberg's), to which no acknowledgment is made. *We can hardly think the editor has read the Latin: his mistake about it may come from a remark of Daremberg's.*

The editor's reply (Classical Review, April, 1889, p. 181) is as follows:—

Mr. Wilson (who seems exasperated because I have used the original text, rather than a Latin translation, of a passage in Galen explanatory of 78 B. foll.) has these observations: 'In one place, Plato's theory of respiration, the editor gives the reader the impression that he has done a piece of original and meritorious research by using the Greek of a commentary (Galen's) only known in "a defective Latin translation" when Martin wrote...... All that he rightly gets out of it, and even the illustrative woodcut (a little altered), is already given in the note and translation of the edition used (Daremberg's), to which no acknowledgment is made.'

Now my note runs thus: 'An important light is thrown upon it by a fragment of

Galen's treatise on the *Timaeus*, which deals with this passage. This fragment was found by M. Daremberg in the Paris library and published by him in 1848. On Galen's commentary the ensuing explanation is based.'

Thus, it seems, I claim originality by avowing my interpretation to be derived from a document which has been public property for forty years; while I endeavour to conceal my obligation by naming the man who brought that document to light.

The editor's pretence that I found fault with him because he went to an original source can hardly have been believed by his readers even if they did not look back to see what I really said. But he tried to give colour to the perversion by omitting the two sentences in my criticism printed above in italics. When these are restored it will be seen, of course, that he was criticised for professing to give information about a Latin commentary which he appeared never to have read. It was also suggested that the incorrect information he gave, the nature of which will appear further on, came at second-hand from Daremberg. By omitting all reference to the real charge, while professing to answer, the editor has virtually confessed that it is justified.

42. In the other part of his reply—'thus it seems I claim originality,' &c.—he puts forward with an air of injured innocence an evasion which could not mislead any one who attended even to that part of my remarks which the editor has quoted. Of course he was not accused of wrongfully claiming originality because his interpretation was really derived from Galen's Greek (which is 'the document which has been public property for forty years'), nor of concealing such an obligation to Daremberg as that which he speaks of.

The editor knew well that the question of 'originality' had nothing whatever to do with either of these points. He knew that what he had concealed was the fact that Daremberg had not only 'brought the document to light,' but had written a commentary also, the material of which down to the woodcut reappears in his own note.

Here again the editor, by ignoring the true and obvious issue, has virtually confessed that he cannot answer.

It is amusing to see how he betrays himself in a footnote. The issue which he so entirely puts out of the text of his reply has got into the note, for he forgetfully answers one of the points of it 'My woodcut, as it happens, was not taken from Daremberg.'

The editor has made his self-condemnation still more apparent by another piece of imperfect quotation. The part of his own note which he quotes in reply happens to contain one of the misleading statements referred to in the parts of my criticism which he suppresses. He actually omits this, and that without even a mark of lacuna.

He says :—

> Now my note runs thus : 'An important light is thrown upon it by a fragment of Galen's treatise on the *Timaeus*, which deals with this passage. This fragment was found by M. Daremberg in the Paris library and published by him in 1848. On Galen's commentary the ensuing explanation is based.'

But the note really runs thus :—

> An important light however is thrown upon it by a fragment of Galen's treatise on the *Timaeus*, which deals with this passage. This fragment, *which was previously known only in an imperfect Latin translation*, was found by M. Daremberg in the Paris library and published by him in 1848. On Galen's commentary the ensuing explanation is based.

It will be seen that the editor in quoting himself has left out the clause in italics.

43. The editor's tacit admissions are conclusive enough, but the best way to make the matter clear, and to shew the misleading character of his book will be to relate how the criticism passed on this part of it in the Classical Review originated.

In Timaeus, p. 78, Plato compares the respiratory apparatus to a fish-trap or weel (κύρτος) of basket work, and there is some difficulty about his exact meaning. The outer part of the apparatus is about conterminous with the outer surface of the body (or rather 'the trunk,' as Martin says). There are two inner portions corresponding to a certain inner part of the fish-trap, and called ἐγκύρτια : one of these is in the chest, the other in the belly. These and the external case are made of air. Fire also enters in some way into the composition of the network (πλέγμα, πλόκανον). One of the ἐγκύρτια opens into the gullet, the other into the windpipe and nostrils. Their termination represents the open end of the fish-trap.

The editor, as we have seen, says that 'an important light is thrown' on the passage 'by a fragment of Galen's treatise on the *Timaeus*.' He then gives an explanation which, he says, is 'based on Galen's commentary.' This explanation corrects Martin's in several important points. The editor attributes Martin's supposed mistakes to the fact that he had only the Latin version before him—he says, in fact, that previous to Daremberg's discovery, Galen's commentary had been 'known only in an imperfect Latin translation' and that

'Martin's interpretation . . . would probably have been modified had the commentary of Galen in the original been before him.'

Now I had not myself ever been interested in this part of the Timaeus, and had given no special attention to it. I had never seen either the Greek original of Galen's commentary or the Latin version of it.

I was led consequently by the editor's note, as any one else would who relied on it alone, to suppose that the part of the Latin translation of Galen which related to this passage was fragmentary, or at least so defective that it did not give the same help as the original Greek; also that the editor's interpretation founded on Galen was new.

Up to this point in his book, there had seemed to be nothing of any importance which could be honestly praised. The work, though pretentious, was nearly all second-hand and inaccurate, and the editor's treatment of the predecessors to whom he was so indebted seemed to deserve severe blame. But here at last there seemed to be something sound and valuable which the editor might justly call his own; and though in looking at the Greek commentary discovered since Martin wrote, he had only done what could not be omitted in a serious edition, I intended in my review to give him full credit for what he had done, to point out that his study of an original source had been rewarded by a discovery about the true meaning of Plato, and that he had thus made a real and meritorious contribution to the subject.

But before writing the commendation it struck me that though the editor was partly right where he differed from Martin, there was an important point in which Martin seemed to be right. As the editor professed to be here following Galen, I naturally turned to the Greek of Galen, and, in an evil hour for the editor, went on to compare the Latin version with it.

To my surprise I found I had been entirely misled by the editor in points where I had not entertained a suspicion about his trustworthiness. I found that the Latin was not for the editor's purposes 'imperfect,' that it was quite clear and gave as much 'light' as the Greek, and that there was no ground for the assertion that Martin would probably have written differently if he had had the Greek before him. It was obviously untrue that the discovery of the Greek could have had the important effect attributed to it by the editor.

But I found also that what one would suppose from the editor's manner to be an original theory of the Timaeus passage based on

Galen's had every bit of it been worked out before by Daremberg, so that the editor instead of being first in the field was again repeating what had been done long ago by a modern predecessor, and that without acknowledgment, although his own study of Galen's commentary had necessarily been made in his predecessor's book.

The only mention the editor makes of Daremberg is in the passage he quotes in his defence—'This fragment was found by M. Daremberg in the Paris library and published by him in 1848,'—from which of course I supposed that Daremberg had merely 'published' the Greek, and never suspected he had added a translation of it, with notes, and that interpretation of the Timaeus passage which was before me in the editor's own book.

These discoveries made me understand why such a book could at first seem to contain a fair amount of commentary that could be praised, for without a careful checking of the notes a reviewer would be often liable to the kind of mistake into which I had nearly been led.

44. A comparison will now be given of the Latin version of Galen's commentary with the Greek, to shew that in those points where the editor's (or Daremberg's) interpretation of the Timaeus passage differs from Martin's, the Latin version gives exactly as much help as the Greek.

(i) In 78 C Plato writes τὸ μὲν τῶν ἐγκυρτίων εἰς τὸ στόμα μεθῆκε· διπλοῦ δ' ὄντος αὐτοῦ κατὰ μὲν τὰς ἀρτηρίας εἰς τὸν πλεύμονα καθῆκε θάτερον, τὸ δ'. εἰς τὴν κοιλίαν ... τὸ δ' ἕτερον σχίσας κ.τ.λ.

Martin makes τὸ μὲν τῶν ἐγκυρτίων 'one of the two ἐγκύρτια;' misled probably by the apparent opposition of τὸ δ' ἕτερον σχίσας, it should be 'the two ἐγκύρτια together,' or 'the complex of the ἐγκύρτια.' The editor's note is—'Galen warns us against taking this "one of the ἐγκύρτια," in which case, as he justly remarks, Plato would have gone on "τὸ δὲ εἰς τόδε τι τοῦ σώματος[1]." He understands πλόκανον, in which he is probably right[2].'

Galen's Greek is οὐ τοῦτό φησιν ὅτι τὸ μὲν ἕτερον τῶν ἐγκυρτίων εἰς τὸ στόμα καθῆκεν· εἴρηκε γὰρ ἂν ἐφεξῆς,—'τὸ δ' ἕτερον εἰς τόδε τι τοῦ σώματος'—ἀλλ' ἐπὶ τὸ[ν] πλόκανον ἀναφέρων εἶπεν, ὡς εἶναι τὸν ὅλον λόγον αὐτοῦ τοιοῦτον, ὡς εἶπον· πλοκάνων τριῶν, ἑνὸς μὲν τοῦ μεγάλου κύρτου, δυοῖν δὲ τῶν οἷον ἐγκυρτίων, τὸ μὲν τῶν ἐγκυρτίων πλόκανον εἰς στόμα τε μεθῆκε κ.τ.λ.

---

[1] Inaccurate. Galen says τὸ δ' ἕτερον εἰς τόδε τι.
[2] For the editor's own mistake here see below, par. 54.

The Latin is—Non hoc dicit, quod alteram nassularum in os demisit, nam deinceps utique dixisset, alteram vero in hanc corporis partem demisit: sed ad tricam referens dixit, ut tota ejus oratio talis, ut dixi, sit. Tres cum sint tricae, una quidem, quae magna nassa est, duae vero reliquae, quae veluti nassulae sunt; nassularum quidem tricam in os trajecit, &c.

(Nassa is in the Latin version the equivalent of κύρτος, nassula of ἐγκύρτιον.) It is obvious that the Latin is as clear and direct as the Greek is.

(ii) A part of this same mistake of Martin's about τὸ τῶν ἐγκυρτίων seems to be, as Daremberg pointed out, his rendering of ὧν θάτερον αὖ πάλιν διέπλεξε δίκρουν, dont il fit encore l'un double; he takes δίκρουν as he takes διπλοῦ 78 C, to mean that one of the two ἐγκύρτια was double, whereas δίκρουν refers merely to the forked entrance of one ἐγκύρτιον. This mistake is really corrected by the parts of Galen, whether in Latin or Greek, just quoted, but Galen has another passage on it.

The editor's note may be put side by side with Daremberg's.

Editor.	Daremberg.
διέπλεξε δίκρουν] The ἐγκύρτιον occupying the cavity of the thorax he constructed with a double outlet, one by the larynx through the mouth, the other through the nostrils.	l'une (de petites nasses) . . . dans le poumon . . . la première nasse est fourchue et les deux branches partant d'un tronc commun . . . sont figurées l'une par la bouche, l'autre par les fosses nasales.

(The editor does not here refer expressly to Galen.)

The Greek of the Commentary on ὧν θάτερον αὖ διέπλεξε δίκρουν has τὴν γὰρ τῆς τραχείας γινομένην ἀναπνοὴν δίκρουν ἔφη ὑπάρχειν, εἶπε δὲ τοῦτο διὰ τὸ τὴν μὲν ἀναπνοὴν ἡμῖν γένεσθαι διά τε τῆς ῥινὸς καὶ τοῦ στόματος κ.τ.λ.

The corresponding Latin is equally plain.

'Respirationem enim asperae arteriae bicornem esse dixit. Hoc autem dixit, proptereà, quòd respiratio nobis per nares, et os fit, &c.

A little below, the Latin translation has for the words τὰ δύο πέρατα [margin κέρατα, which Daremberg substitutes] τό τε διὰ τῆς ῥινὸς καὶ τὸ διὰ τοῦ στόματος, duo illa extrema, tum quod per os pervenit, omitting to render τὸ διὰ τοῦ στόματος: but this could cause no difficulty since the phrase has occurred, as we see, above and is rightly rendered; the unanswered 'tum' shews the lacuna at once.

(iii) The other point on which the editor would correct Martin by the help of Galen concerns the relation of the ἐγκύρτια to the κύρτος.

'Martin,' says the editor, 'conceives the κύρτος to consist of two baskets, one fitting into the other; but Galen says it is ἁπλοῦν. The ἐγκύρτιον ... is explained by Stallbaum (whom Liddell and Scott follow) to mean the entrance or neck of the κύρτος. But on this point Galen is explicit; he says it is ὅμοιον μὲν τῷ μεγάλῳ, μικρὸν δέ. We must therefore conceive the ἐγκύρτια to be two smaller κύρτοι similar to the larger, contained within it and opening into its neck.'

Galen's words are νενοημένου σοι τοῦ τῶν ἁλιέων κύρτου, ὅπερ ἐστὶ πλέγμα ἁπλοῦν, νόησον ἐν αὐτῷ περιεχόμενον ὅμοιον μὲν τῷ μεγάλῳ, μικρὸν δέ, οἷον ἐκεῖνο κύρτον.

The Latin is—

Excogitatâ abs te piscatorum nassâ, quod certe est rete simplex, in ipsâ (sc. nassâ) alteram nassam excogitato, magnae quidem assimilem, parvam tamen contineri.

Here again, all that the editor (after Daremberg) gets [1] out of the Greek can be got with equal ease from the Latin, which faithfully represents the original.

These seem to be all the points in which Martin's interpretation might be supposed capable of correction from Galen's Greek, and it is obvious that the conclusions might have been got from the Latin with equal ease.

To illustrate further the adequacy of the Latin here, another note will be given where the editor agrees with Martin.

Editor (on 78 B).	Martin.
διετείνατο οἷον σχοίνους] Here Plato has departed somewhat from the analogy of the fishing-trap. The σχοῖνοι of course represent the arteries and veins which permeate the structure of the body.	Galien fait observer que ces joncs n'existent point dans les nasses véritables, mais que Platon les a imaginées pour représenter les vaisseaux sanguins, par lesquels la chaleur animale se répand dans tout le corps.

(The editor does not expressly say that Galen is his authority for his first sentence.)

Galen's commentary.	Latin version.
τούτου τὸ ἀνάλογον οὐκέτι κατὰ τοὺς τῶν ἁλιέων ἔστι κύρτους· ἀπὸ τῶν ἐγκυρτίων γὰρ πρὸς τὸ τοῦ περιέχοντος κύκλου πλέγμα	non amplius in piscatorum nassis reperitur quod huic proportione respondeat: neque enim in nassulis ad continentis cir-

[1] It will be seen hereafter that the view thus derived from Galen is untenable.

Galen's commentary.	Latin version.
σχοῖνος οὐδεμία διήκει, κενοῦ τοῦ μεταξὺ παντὸς ὄντος· ἐν ἡμῖν δὲ διήκουσιν ἔκ τε τῆς κοιλίας καὶ τοῦ πνεύμονος εἰς ἅπαν τὸ σῶμα μέχρι τῶν ἐσχάτων αὐτοῦ περάτων ἐκτὸς ἀρτηρίαι καὶ φλέβες, ἃς εἰκάζει σχοίνοις ἀπὸ τῶν ἐγκυρτίων ἐπὶ τὸν κύρτον ἐκτεινομέναις.	culi rete funis ullus pervenit, quum tota illa intercapedo vacua sit: in nobis autem ex ventre, et ex pulmone in totum corpus ad extremos usque fines foràs pertingunt venae, et arteriae, quas funibus, qui a nassulis ad nassam, extenduntur, assimilat.

Here again the Latin is as useful as the Greek, as is shewn by Martin's note, which is derived from the Latin alone.

45. From this comparison it became clear to me that the editor's statements about the Latin version proved that he had not examined it for himself, and I was curious to know how he came by what he said of it. Seeing that there was so much of his note in Daremberg, I looked in Daremberg's preface, where I found the following (the italics are mine). 'Du reste, la traduction latine obscure, difficile à lire et souvent inexacte, a jusqu'à présent rendu peu de services à ceux qui se sont occupés du Timée de Platon; beaucoup même paraissent avoir ignoré son existence, ou du moins ont dédaigné de la consulter. Si la publication d'un texte inédit excite toujours un véritable intérêt, lors même qu'on possède une traduction latine, cet intérêt augmente encore quand cette traduction est *très défectueuse* et par conséquent peu utile.' A little further on he says of the Greek, 'Ce commentaire *jette un jour tout nouveau* sur le texte de Platon' (cf. the editor's 'An important light is thrown upon it,' &c.)

After this there remained no doubt as to the origin of the editor's mistake. Galen's commentary includes a good deal more than the interpretation of this particular page of the Timaeus. Daremberg's criticism could only be true of the Latin version as a whole, and not of this part. And it will be found in his notes that while he says the preceding paragraph of the commentary is 'traduit dans Gadaldinus [1] d'une façon très obscure et parfois inexacte,' the differences to which he calls attention in the part of the Latin version with which we are concerned are of scarcely any significance, and have no bearing whatever on the points at issue. On the other hand he notes two places where the Latin is better or clearer than the Greek of his manuscript: and, what is sufficiently decisive, when he criticises Martin he does not say Martin had got wrong because he had only the Latin translation of Galen, on the contrary, he will really be found to imply that the Latin ought to have put the commentators

---

[1] The author of the Latin version.

right, and attributes Martin's mistake only to inattention or the influence of his predecessors. He points out that Gadaldinus translates the passage of the Timaeus, τὸ μὲν τῶν ἐγκυρτίων εἰς τὸ στόμα μεθῆκε κ.τ.λ., wrongly, although he translates Galen's explanation of it rightly.

'Gadaldinus a traduit le texte en litige par : *Alteram quidem nassularum in os demisit*, etc. Cependant le Commentaire de Galien qui vient immédiatement après commence par ces mots : *Non hoc dicit quod alteram nassularum in os demisit*. Est-il donc étonnant, après de telles fautes, que les traducteurs qui n'ont pas eu recours au Commentaire de Galien se soient complètement égarés et donnent un sens impossible ?— Quant à M. Martin, l'autorité de ses devanciers ou quelque pré-occupation lui ont fait perdre de vue le véritable sens si clair, et qui rende un compte si exact de la description de Platon.'

Those remarks, however, in Daremberg's preface, quoted further back, from which the editor appears to have drawn, might mislead, especially as he adds in the same context that Galen's commentary 'donne une explication nette et lumineuse de la théorie des *Nasses* (fish-trap).' But the wrong impression would be at once corrected by reading the Latin. The editor's mischance is of a kind which often befalls those who depend as he does on others.

46. As regards his fairness to Daremberg—the editor, as already observed, ignores the true issue in his reply, but yet answers a single point of it in a note—' my woodcut, as it happens, was not taken from Daremberg.' What the denial exactly means must be uncertain when the peculiarities of the editor's mode of replying are remembered[1], but its value is not exactly increased by what follows—' but there could hardly be much difference between two diagrams illustrative of this passage.' In the essential points which concern the construction of the fish-weel and Plato's idea of the respiratory apparatus, there is all the difference between Daremberg's diagram and one which would correspond to Martin's view. The editor's diagram and explanation agree with Daremberg's in all that is characteristic and essential in the criticism of Martin and the interpretation of Plato. The differences (admitted in my Review, q. v.) are immaterial, the ἐγκύρτια being represented by Daremberg rather as they would be placed in the fish-trap, by the editor rather in the position of the corresponding parts of the human body, and the top of the diagram being a little altered (for the worse). And it must be remembered that this diagram and explanation of Daremberg's were before the

[1] Compare also below, Part IV.

editor from the first, for they occur in the edition in which he first made his acquaintance with the Galen to which they relate—the only edition there is.

Apart from the general agreement, the following coincidence in a special point will be evidence enough of the editor's use of this work of Daremberg's about which he is so silent in his note.

Plato says that the outer casing (κύτος) of the respiratory network (πλόκανον) and the two bag-like ἐγκύρτια within it, are made of air, but that what he calls τὰ ἔνδον τοῦ πλοκάνου ἅπαντα is made of fire. About the latter Daremberg has a view, not found in that form in Galen. He supposes that the κύρτος or outer weel—for he thinks that the ἐγκύρτια are only two smaller weels inside it—is composed of two folds or layers (feuillets, a term to which nothing answers in Plato or Galen), the inner one of fire, the outer of air, the latter being, he thinks, the κύτος.

This peculiar, and, as will be seen afterwards, mistaken interpretation reappears in the editor's note in almost the same phrases.

Daremberg, p. 49.	Editor.	
On se représentera la grande nasse [i.e. the κύρτος] constituée, pour ainsi dire, par deux feuillets superposés; l'un aérien, qui forme l'enveloppe externe, ce que Platon appelle le κύτος, l'autre intérieur igné ... Le κύτος répond à la peau et à la couche d'air ambiant le plus immédiatement en contact avec la peau:	... we shall find that the κύρτος or large πλέγμα consists of two layers, one of fire, one of air. The outer layer (τὸ κύτος) is the stratum of air in contact with all the outer surface of the body.	Martin, vol. 2, p. 336. — la couche d'air en contact immédiat avec la surface interne et externe du corps humain ... * *
le feuillet profond est la représentation des chairs traversées par les vaisseaux sanguins ...	The inner layer (τὰ ἔνδον τοῦ πλοκάνου) is the vital heat contained in the blood and pervading all the substance of the body between the skin and the cavity within.	la chaleur animale contenue dans les chairs où sont le sang et les veines * * la substance même du corps. * *
Quant aux petites nasses [i.e. the ἐγκύρτια] elles sont tout d'air ... Les petites nasses sont l'une les poumons et l'autre l'estomac, ou plutôt l'ensemble des organes alimentaires.	The two ἐγκύρτια, which are formed entirely of air, represent respectively the thoracic and abdominal cavities of the body.	... les parois des paniers intérieurs, c'est à dire la cavité du ventre et de la poitrine.

And yet in spite of this, and in spite of what has been seen as to the origin of his statements about the Latin version, the editor in his reply risked the attempt to persuade his readers that his obligation to Daremberg was discharged by merely mentioning the fact that Daremberg had discovered the Greek of Galen's Commentary.

The quotations from Martin above are merely added to shew that the editor, though sometimes closely following Daremberg, expresses himself in phrases of Martin's. One of these quotations however leads us to another circumstance, which bears out the impression already sufficiently established about the unsoundness and the dependent character of the editor's notes on this passage. Daremberg has another peculiar view about the κύρτος, which he derived from Galen. Galen held that the external envelope or κύτος consisted first of the skin, and secondly of a certain part of the external air which surrounds the body, which he seems to have supposed adhered to the skin: this is the couche d'air which the editor translates by 'stratum.' Daremberg does not explain this view or its origin in this particular note (n. 64, p. 49), but it is in consequence of it that he says, 'Le κύτος répond à la peau et à la couche d'air,' &c. He explains more particularly further on (n. 75, p. 50).

It will be seen that the editor omits the words 'à la peau,' and expresses himself like Martin. Now it is difficult to believe, if he understood the special significance of Daremberg's phraseology (which, as just observed, does not come out till a later note of Daremberg's), and varied it with full consciousness, that he would say nothing about it; for it is not only an important point, but one which is expressly put forward by Galen, whose Commentary the editor professes to follow as being so excellent. It is difficult to believe that the editor had read the Galen so far.

47. There is another rather unfortunate piece of unacknowledged borrowing in this same note. It is said that the fish-trap 'seems to have had a narrow funnel-shaped neck through which the fish entered, but was unable to return, *owing to the points of the reeds being set against it.*' There is nothing about such a hindrance in Plato, Galen, or Daremberg. It is clearly got from Martin (p. 335, vol. ii.): 'Il (le poisson ne) pouvait ressortir par le même chemin, parce que le trou était entouré de pointes convergentes dirigées vers le fond de la nasse.' The amusing thing is that, while this suits well such a weel as Martin describes, it will not suit at all the editor's idea of a weel—an awkward confusion. This is part and parcel of a mistake made about the ἐγκύρτιον, which leads the editor in the next paragraph of his note[1]

[1] Quoted above, p. 74.

to an erroneous criticism of Liddell and Scott. The precise nature of this confusion and mistake must be postponed to the account of the intrinsic value of the scientific notes in the edition, as this is rather the place to discuss obligations to others. It is enough to say here that it will be shewn hereafter that whereas the editor, following the lines of Daremberg and Galen, contends that Martin's whole notion of a fish weel ($κύρτος$) and the $ἐγκύρτιον$ is wrong, Martin is quite right. It is the editor who, in following Galen or Daremberg, has gone wrong: his trap would never catch a fish. It will be shewn also that Galen's Commentary, supposed to have thrown so much light on Plato's text, is wrong on the essential point, because Galen misunderstood the construction of a fish-weel himself, and that, as a further complication, an erroneous inference has been drawn by the editor from what Galen says about the $κύρτος$ being $ἁπλοῦς$. The erroneous nature of the view about 'the layer of fire' repeated from Daremberg will also be explained: it has involved the editor in a mistranslation of 78 D.

In fact, the appearance of originality and discovery which the editor contrives to give his notes here is not their only defect. He seems to be wrong on every point in which he differs from Martin, with one exception—the meaning given to $τὸ\ μὲν\ τῶν\ ἐγκυρτίων$ (see above). The right meaning however of this expression is not only to be found in Daremberg, but was given ten years before Daremberg's discovery of the Greek Commentary by Stallbaum himself, but with such a difference from the editor as we have learned to expect. The editor repeating the right meaning makes a serious mistake about the way it comes out of the Greek: Stallbaum explains the idiom rightly. (Cf. below, par. 54.)

PART II.

TEXT AND APPARATUS CRITICUS.

48. The following account of the text and apparatus criticus of this edition is given at the end of the Introduction :—

> It remains to say a few words about the text. In this edition I have rather closely adhered to the text of C. F. Hermann, which on the whole presents most faithfully the readings of the oldest and best manuscript, Codex Parisiensis A. The authority of this ninth century MS. is such that recent editors have frequently accepted its readings in defiance of a *consensus* among the remainder; an example which I have in general followed. In departing from Hermann I have usually had some manuscript support on which to rely, and sometimes that of A itself: but in a very few cases (about six or seven, I believe, in all) I have introduced emendations, or at least alterations, of my own; none of which are very important. In order that the reader may have no trouble in checking the text here presented to him, I have added brief critical notes in Latin, wherein are recorded the readings of the Paris manuscript (quoted on Bekker's testimony), of C. F. Hermann, of Stallbaum, and of the Zürich edition by Baiter Orelli and Winckelmann, wherever these differed from my own. These authorities are denoted respectively by A, H, S, and Z. The readings of other manuscripts have not been cited. Fortunately the text of the *Timaeus* is for the most part in a fairly satisfactory condition.

In an edition of this kind something more is needed to satisfy modern requirements. But we shall only ask how far the editor has carried out his own scheme.

There are two collations of Paris A, by two great scholars, Bast and Bekker. They differ not unfrequently. They were made many years ago, and, considering their difference, for an edition which is to follow this MS. in the main, a new collation should have been made, if not of the whole, at least of the places where Bast and Bekker differ. If this were not undertaken, at least there should have been a full account of both collations.

The editor has not collated the Paris MS. But, what is extraordinary, he does not seem even to have seen Bast's collation. He does not even give accurately the collation he professes to follow— Bekker's. Although 'he has adhered rather closely to the text of C.

F. Hermann,' he has taken no trouble to study Hermann's apparatus criticus, though he has used it here and there; and the consequences are serious. The variations of the other editions are not given accurately; and, in short, the apparatus criticus is entirely untrustworthy and of no use. A few specimens may be given of the mistakes.

49. In 23 D and 23 E the editor reads πολιτῶν without variant. Both Bekker and Bast give πολιτειῶν in both places as the reading of Paris A.

25 E he reads οὕς without variant. According to both Bekker and Bast, Paris A reads ὥς with οὕς written over it.

So again 25 C fin., where Bekker and some others have ἐλθούσης, ἐπελθούσης is given as if read by A. According to Bekker, whom the editor professes to follow, ἐπελθούσης is by the later hand in A.

The following are among the instances which shew unacquaintance with Bast. 17 C κατὰ φύσιν δὴ δόντες, from A is given διδόντες as variant for δόντες (only), whence A would read δὴ διδόντες. From Bast it appears that A reads κατὰ φύσιν διδόντες, where διδόντες is variant for δὴ δόντες, γε δή being written above the line. Bekker gives διδόντες as if variant of δόντες, but adds the superscript γε δή.

24 D, ὑπερβεβηκότες, ὑπερβεβληκότες is given merely as the reading of C. F. Hermann (Teubner), but according to Bast it is the reading of A. The editor, who seems to have used Hermann's preface sometimes (cf. his note on μηχανώμενοι 18 C), might have inferred the truth from it ('a plurimis optimisque libris oblatum'), if, indeed, he looked at this part of the preface, though this may be doubted, as Hermann also gives good reason for preferring ὑπερβεβληκότες. More evidence may be found in Liddell and Scott, though they read -βεβηκότες.

23 A, ἢ κατ' ἄλλον τόπον ὧν ἀκοὴν ἴσμεν. The editor is alone in reading ἀκοήν for ἀκοῇ. He says 'ἀκοὴν dedi ex A.' The adoption of ἀκοήν here is mere perversity. In 23 C we find ὁπόσων ὑπὸ τὸν οὐρανὸν ἡμεῖς ἀκοὴν παρεδεξάμεθα (not appealed to by the editor); but ἀκοῇ ἴσμεν is a fixed phrase, with a special meaning (appropriate here) which makes the combination εἰδέναι ἀκοήν extremely improbable. Hence of course Bekker (from whom the editor gets A's variant), Stallbaum, Hermann, and the Zurich editors all read ἀκοῇ. Now it appears from Bast that the reading of A is not ἀκοήν, but ἀκοῆν́ (sic).

In 19 A the editor reads μεταλλάττειν. His note is simply 'μεταλλάττειν: διαλλάττειν A,' giving no MS. authority for μεταλλάττειν, and merely implying, according to his notation, that μεταλλάττειν is the reading of Hermann, Stallbaum, and the Zürich editors. μεταλλάττειν is however, according to Bast, an alternative reading in A, μετ being written over the first two letters of διαλλάττειν.

Another instance of unacquaintance with Bast, which is also another instance of the editor's neglect of the adnotatio critica of the editor whose text he professes to follow mainly, is in 20 A. Here ἱκανῆς is read in the text, and the only variant given is 'ἱκανήν H.' This means that Hermann reads in his text ἱκανήν, and A reads ἱκανῆς. But Bast gives ἱκανήν as the reading of A, and Hermann in his preface actually quotes it from Bast, in a form which might have directed the editor where to look for Bast's collation—'Bastius apud Stallb. enotavit.' Add to these the instances given in par. 10, and in par. 50. The above are all from the first ten pages of the text.

Towards the end of the book (91 C) there is a note in which Bast is quoted as differing from Bekker. 'ξυνδυάζοντες scripsi ex Hermanni conjecturâ. ξυνδιαγαγόντες H, et teste Bastio, A; Bekkerus autem ξυναγαγόντες in A legisse videtur. ἐξαγαγόντες SZ. καταδρέψαντες : κᾆτα δρέψαντες ASZ.' Where S = Stallbaum, Z = the Zürich edition. The proof of the editor's unacquaintance with Bast is so clear that it is hardly possible he is quoting Bast at first-hand. Besides if he were, he would be aware that in A ἀπο is written over the κατα of καταδρέψαντες, and that Bast gives ὄν as the reading of A for ἐν at the beginning of the same page. One must suspect that the editor's note was made up from the following by Hermann in the Teubner text. 'Nec p. 91 C cautius agi posse putavi quam si cum Stallb. hujus [i. e. Cod. Par.] lectiones ξυνδιαγαγόντες (hanc enim *Bastius testatur*; Bekk. et Schneiderus ξυναγαγόντες) et καταδρέψαντες pro ἐξαγαγόντες et κᾆτα δρέψαντες amplecterer, quanquam haud scio an priori loco aptius ξυνδυάζοντες conjecerim.'

Bast's collation is given at the end of Stallbaum's edition, and it was difficult indeed to avoid knowing that it was there. Stallbaum directs attention to it on his title page: 'Accessit varietas lectionis praestantissimi Codicis Parisini accuratissime enotata.'

The critical preface of the familiar Zürich edition, an edition to which the editor often refers, has this footnote on the first page, 'Variae lectiones a Bastio collectae et a Baehrio, viro clarissimo, cum Stallbaumio communicatae insunt editioni Gothanae, p. 443-490.'

The following are instances of inaccuracy in the record of differences from other editions. These also are in the first ten pages of the text.

17 D, the editor reads with Hermann καὶ φύσει, without noting that the Zürich edition has ἅτε φύσει, Stallbaum's first edition ἅτε φύσει,

and his second ἅτε καὶ φύσει (a reading which has MS. authority), though Hermann calls attention to the reading of both editions here in his preface.

19 A, ὡς ἀπολειπόμενον—it is not noted that Stallbaum and the Zürich editors omit ὡς, with MS. authority, as appears from Stallbaum's note and Hermann's preface.

25 D, παρ' ὑμῖν—it is not noted that the Zürich edition and Stallbaum's later edition have παρ' ὑμῶν.

Ignorance of Hermann's preface is shewn in the above, other instances of it are given in par. 10, and par. 61, p. 156.

In the case of Stallbaum we find an amusing mistake parallel to that about Bast. The editor seems quite unaware that Stallbaum edited the text again in the Tauchnitz series: and thus, as already seen, he attacks Stallbaum sometimes for not adopting readings which he did adopt even before the publication of the edition of C. F. Hermann, on which the editor mainly relies.

Compare above par. 9 (note on 55 D), par. 10, and below par. 50, 61 (note on 47 C).

Of the emendations some have been spoken of already; others are discussed in Part III.

But, as we have also seen, the editor does not represent accurately in his app. crit. the edition of Stallbaum which he had before him.

50. After this inaccuracy even in elementary matters, it is not surprising to find that the editor seems to have made scarcely any use for himself of the ancient 'testimonia.' We have already spoken of his use of Galen. What he quotes of Proclus is generally referred to by his predecessors, and while sometimes they are followed, as already observed, in referring to what is comparatively useless, sometimes no knowledge is shewn of important things which they have not noticed. It is by no means denied that he has read some of Proclus for himself, but there is no evidence of a systematic study of Proclus for textual purposes.

For instance, it is true that he gives what one may venture to think an excellent emendation from Proclus in 40 D, but Lindau had already specially noted the variant. On the other hand, on 40 C (ἐπανακυκλήσεις καὶ προσχωρήσεις) he writes, 'If Proklos is to be trusted however, it means the retardation of one heavenly body in relation to another, as προσχώρησις means the gaining by one upon another. For προσχωῥήσεις it is probable that we ought to read προχωρήσεις, which is given by one ms.' This corresponds to just as much of Proclus as Stallbaum quotes in his note. In that the reading is προσχώρησις, and it would be inferred from the editor's note that Proclus read προσχώρησις, and that the only evidence for προχώρησις in the Timaeus was in a Timaeus MS.[1] But in Proclus' commentary a few pages beyond what Stallbaum quotes, Plato's text is quoted with προχωρήσεις, and no variant is recorded by Schneider. (In the lemma Schneider reads προσχώρησις, and mentions a variant προχώρησις.)

In 25 D pains are taken to defend the reading βραχέος against βαθέος. The latter being the reading of the text of Paris A, it is important to note that Proclus has βραχέος both in the lemma and in the commentary. The editor says nothing of this, nor of the fact that Chalcidius' rendering supports βαθέος: but then Stallbaum has not mentioned these things. The editor does not cite for βραχέος the marginal reading of Paris A, καταβραχέος (instead of κάρτα βαθέος), but then this is not given in Bekker, but by Bast.

The short treatise entitled Τιμαίῳ τῷ Λοκρῷ περὶ ψυχᾶς κόσμω καὶ φύσιος is an ancient 'testimonium' of first-rate importance, and very accessible, for it is printed after the Timaeus in the Zürich edition and the Tauchnitz edition, and in the same volume of Stallbaum's commentary as the Timaeus.

A note on 35 A proves how little attention has been given to it.

'In the phrase ἀεὶ κάτα ταὐτὰ ἐχούσης οὐσίας Dr. Jackson has with some probability suggested that for οὐσίας we should read φύσεως: there is certainly an awkwardness in the use of οὐσίας, when we have the word directly afterwards in so very peculiar and technical a sense.'

The difficulty is no doubt a real one, but it is clear that it cuts both ways; for it makes it unlikely that φύσεως should be corrupted into οὐσίας without any trace of the true reading, especially as φύσεως comes in the next clause—τῆς τε ταυτοῦ φύσεως καὶ τῆς θατέρου.

Now the treatise attributed (falsely of course) to Timaeus Locrus has ἔκ τε τᾶς ἀμερίστω μορφᾶς καὶ τᾶς μεριστᾶς οὐσίας corresponding to τῆς ἀμερίστου ... οὐσίας καὶ τῆς ... μεριστῆς: and it was important to mention this.

It may be added that οὐσία is confirmed by Proclus both in lemma and commentary, by the translation of Chalcidius and by his commentary. Cicero simply has 'ex ea materia' in his translation.

---

[1] Stallbaum proposes in his note to read προχωρήσεις. In his app. crit. he says 'προχωρήσεις Vat. Θ. pr., et Proclus.'

One of the results of modern criticism has been to give great value to the commentary of Chalcidius as a 'testimonium.' The editor does not seem to be aware of this. Chalcidius is not even mentioned in the preface where ancient commentary is spoken of, and no use seems to have been made of him.

Two instances of neglect of Chalcidius have been given. In one of them (25 D) the editor objects to the reading (βαθέος) of Paris A that it is 'pointless.' He has not understood what the sense of the passage with this reading would be. The translation of Chalcidius explains it[1]. The following is a significant instance. In 47 C the editor prefers the reading φωνῇ to φωνῆς as against Stallbaum and Hermann, and proposes to omit the words πρὸς ἀκοήν. If he had known that Chalcidius read φωνῇ and did not translate πρὸς ἀκοήν, he could hardly have omitted to mention such confirmation even if he did not know its value. This is another instance of ignorance of Stallbaum's later edition, for there the reading is φωνῇ.

Again, the editor does not mention that his view of the meaning of ἐναντία in 50 A is confirmed by Chalcidius.

As to Cicero's translation, the editor quotes it occasionally where his predecessors have quoted it. In 38 C, however, he notices that Cicero does not render the words πρὸς γένεσιν χρόνου, which other editors seem to have overlooked. But in a more important place, 40 D, he reads οὐ before δυναμένοις with C. F. Hermann as against Stallbaum, with the remark that the negative rests on the authority of A alone. But the negative is rendered by Cicero. Here again there is a mistake about Stallbaum, who in his later edition reads οὐ δυναμένοις, and another instance of ignorance of Hermann's Apparatus Criticus, in which Stallbaum's later reading is mentioned.

See also above, par. 12, the note on 35 A.

---

[1] See below, par. 61, note on 24 E.

PART III.

INTERPRETATION OF THE LANGUAGE.

51. In the interpretation of the Greek text there is a want of scientific acquaintance with Greek idiom in general, and with the peculiarities of the style of Plato: for on the one hand, the editor has not made sufficient use of the standard grammars, and on the other, he has clearly not studied Riddell's Digest of Platonic Idioms, the 'sine qua non' of a modern edition. In consequence he not only fails to render some idioms correctly, but is found rather naïvely defending a sufficiently known construction, or objecting to a reading or to an interpretation some peculiarity in the language which is in its favour. Beside this there are a number of errors of interpretation which do not turn on grammatical points, and the translation said to be given with a view to relieving the notes sometimes contradicts them. Instances have occurred incidental to other matters; others will now be given, and those which are more or less grammatical may be considered first.

52. Of mistakes in single words the following may be noticed.

In 41 C the Creator is made to say to the created gods that he will begin the creation of the soul by making the divine part himself, and that he will leave the rest of it to them, σπείρας (sc. τὸ θεῖον) καὶ ὑπαρξάμενος ἐγὼ παραδώσω· τὸ δὲ λοιπὸν ὑμεῖς, ἀθανάτῳ θνητὸν προσυφαίνοντες. Here of course ὑπαρξάμενος means 'having made beginning,' as opposed to τὸ λοιπόν. The editor translates 'this, I, having sown and *provided* it': and says quaintly in his note, 'This transitive use of the verb is not quoted in Liddell and Scott.' ὑπάρχειν in its familiar sense of 'to be ready,' has nearly the meaning of 'being provided,' but that cannot yield a middle form with the meaning 'to provide.' Or possibly the editor was influenced by a misunderstanding of the active and passive uses quoted by Liddell and Scott (sub voce A 4), ὑπάρχειν εὐεργεσίας and εὐεργεσίαι ὑπηργμέναι, et sim., which need no comment. The lexicon does interpret the present passage, and interprets it rightly.

The next instances are of mistakes in the force of tenses, made in the interest of the editor's views on philosophical points.

38 B, χρόνος δ' οὖν μετ' οὐρανοῦ γέγονεν, ἵνα ἅμα γεννηθέντες ἅμα καὶ λυθῶσιν ἄν ποτε λύσις τις αὐτῶν γίγνηται. The editor who, like others before him, contends that Plato does not seriously mean there was a beginning of time or of the universe, says—'μετ' οὐρανοῦ γέγονεν] "has come into being in our story " as the tense denotes.' The tense of course cannot as such denote this, as is seen at once from the passage where the creation of the world is first asserted, 28 B, ὁ δὴ πᾶς οὐρανὸς ... σκεπτέον ... πότερον ἦν ἀεί, γενέσεως ἀρχὴν ἔχων οὐδεμίαν, ἢ γέγονεν ἀπ' ἀρχῆς τινὸς ἀρξάμενος. γέγονεν· ὁρατὸς γὰρ ἁπτός τέ ἐστι ... πάντα δὲ τὰ τοιαῦτα αἰσθητά, τὰ δ' αἰσθητά ... γιγνόμενα καὶ γεννητὰ ἐφάνη, where γέγονε cannot mean 'has come into being in our story.' But it is not necessary to go beyond the present passage, for it is rather obvious that ἵνα ἅμα γεννηθέντες κ.τ.λ. is put as a reason for a fact, and not to explain a mere convenience of expression or representation. The same is clear from the next sentence, ἐξ οὖν λόγου καὶ διανοίας θεοῦ τοιαύτης πρὸς χρόνου γένεσιν .. ἥλιος καὶ σελήνη κ.τ.λ. .... γέγονε. Even if the whole be allegorical, it would be a mere confusion of ideas to suppose that the tense of γέγονε could indicate this. The circumstances of the allegorical are represented as if they really happened. The mistake is not original : for the note appears to be an unacknowledged reproduction of Lindau, 'μετ' οὐρανοῦ γέγονεν, i. e. τῷ λόγῳ ἡμῶν. Aliter enim hoc verbi tempore scriptor uti non potuit.'

42 D–E. The Creator is represented as ceasing from his activity as creator after he had made the divine part of the human soul, and committing the task of creating all that remained to the other gods— τοῖς νέοις παρέδωκε θεοῖς : and then comes the following, 42 E, καὶ ὁ μὲν δὴ ἅπαντα ταῦτα διατάξας ἔμενεν ἐν τῷ ἑαυτοῦ κατὰ τρόπον ἤθει· μένοντος δὲ νοήσαντες οἱ παῖδες τὴν τοῦ πατρὸς διάταξιν ἐπείθοντο αὐτῇ καὶ λαβόντες ἀθάνατον ἀρχὴν θνητοῦ ζῴου κ.τ.λ. (these gods are then represented as beginning their part in the creation). We must here give the whole of the note ; it is a foretaste of the author's interpretation of the philosophical parts of the dialogue.

ἔμενεν ἐν τῷ ἑαυτοῦ. This phrase is significant. Plato does not say that the δημιουργὸς *returned* to his own ἦθος, but that he was 'abiding therein.' The imperfect expresses that not only after he had given these instructions but previously also, he was abiding.

The eternal essence, while manifesting itself in multiplicity, still abides in unity. The process of thought-evolution does not affect the nature of thought as it is in itself: thought while many and manifold is one and simple still.' (The translation has 'God was abiding after the manner of his own nature.')

It is a pity that all this philosophy should be occasioned by a mistake as to a tense. The text is an instance of a well-known usage, discussed in the grammars. In narration an imperfect is sometimes introduced after an aorist with nearly the meaning of an aorist, but to describe the beginning of an activity or state, and often can be rendered by 'proceeded to.' Here, after the aorist διατάξας, we have such an imperfect ἔμενε, which represents the entrance upon a state after the action of the aorist participle, not one which existed before and during that action. Had Plato intended the latter he would have written διατάσσων. Thus Plato does exactly mean that 'the δημιουργὸς *returned* to his own ἦθος,' and the translation should be 'after ordaining all this, he abode in his own accustomed nature.' But, as in the other passage, the immediate context ought to have made mistake impossible. μένοντος δὲ νοήσαντες οἱ παῖδες τὴν τοῦ πατρὸς διάταξιν κ.τ.λ. (see above). Here μένοντος refers back to ἔμενε as the point at which the activity of the inferior gods begins; and in the editor's interpretation it would be flat and meaningless, though standing in an emphatic position.

As often happens with the editor, the mistake is not even original. It is in Martin, who, however, only thinks this interpretation a possible one, and does not decide, much less base so much upon it.

Il y a dans la phrase grecque une ambiguité que je conserve en la traduisant. Cette phrase peut signifier soit que Dieu, tout en agissant pour produire le monde, restait cependant toujours dans le même état, soit qu'il restait dans son état accoutumé après en être sorti un instant pour former le monde. Dans ce dernier sens, les mots μένοντος δὲ signifieraient que les dieux, voyant que Dieu avait terminé son œuvre, commencèrent celle qu'il leur avait prescrite. Proclus parait opter pour le premier sens, tout en essayant de le combiner avec le second.

As akin to this we may add the explanation of λόγος in 51 C, though not a grammatical mistake. Plato asks whether the particulars perceived by the senses are the only reality, and whether it is a mistake to say that the ideas are real, so that 'fire in general' as apart from particulars is a mere phrase—ἀλλὰ μάτην ἑκάστοτε εἶναί τί φαμεν εἶδος ἑκάστου νοητόν, τὸ δὲ οὐδὲν ἄρ' ἦν πλὴν λόγος. Stallbaum rightly renders 'vana oratio,' but the editor thinks he finds something deeper. 'By λόγος Plato means a mental concept, or universal: the question is in fact between Socraticism and Platonism; that is to say, between conceptualism and idealism.' Of course λόγος is here in its familiar opposition to reality, the philosophic distinction attributed to Plato exists merely in the editor's imagination.

It may be here also noted that the translation misses the idiom—ἄρ' ἦν—the imperfect after a number of present tenses, and with ἄρα, 'but we talk idly when we speak of an intelligible idea as actually existent, whereas it was nothing but a conception'—it should be 'whereas it turns out to have been all the while nothing but a phrase.'

In 48 D an impossible force is given to the adverb ἔμπροσθεν. πειράσομαι μηδενὸς ἧττον εἰκότα, μᾶλλον δέ, καὶ ἔμπροσθεν ἀπ' ἀρχῆς περὶ ἑκάστων καὶ ξυμπάντων λέγειν. This very difficult passage has been discussed by C. F. Hermann[1], and here again the editor seems unaware of the view held by the scholar whose text he chiefly follows. His own note is, 'Stallbaum, who joins μᾶλλον δὲ with what follows, proposes to read κατὰ τὰ ἔμπροσθεν. But no change is necessary. ἔμπροσθεν means "where we were before," viz. at the starting-point of the inquiry. I think Martin is justified in his rendering "revenant sur mes pas jusqu'au commencement."' The translation has 'I will strive to give an explanation which is no less probable than another, but more so; returning back to describe from the beginning each and all things.' This is a somewhat complicated error. In the first place, if ἔμπροσθεν could mean 'where we were before,' that cannot of itself denote so determinate a point as the beginning of the enquiry. Perhaps the editor really meant that ἀπ' ἀρχῆς was an epexegesis of it. But ἔμπροσθεν can no more mean 'where we were before' than πάλαι could mean 'where we were long ago.' Thirdly, the editor does not observe that he is not even translating ἔμπροσθεν by 'where we were before,' for he does not take ἔμπροσθεν ... λέγειν = 'to describe everything where we were before,' which would make no sense, and certainly not the sense he requires.

He is putting still more into ἔμπροσθεν, for the sense he gives the passage can only be got by taking ἔμπροσθεν ... λέγειν as equivalent to 'to describe everything *beginning* from where we were before, viz. at the beginning.' The editor's own remark on Lindau's suggestion [2] ('which is not Greek, as I think') is a just criticism of his own.

[1] Jen. Literaturzeitung 1842 N^r. 32, referred to in the Engelmann edition where the reference (N^r. 31) is incorrect.

[2] Lindau suggests μᾶλλον ἢ κατ' ἔμπροσθεν. κατ' ἔμπροσθεν does not seem to be found, but it seems in itself nearly as possible a formation as κατόπισθεν or καθύπερθεν and so hardly deserves the sneer.

There is another matter in the earlier part of the same sentence. The rendering 'the *value* of a probable account' is given for τὴν τῶν εἰκότων λόγων δύναμιν, which is of course only a periphrasis for τοὺς εἰκότας λόγους.

53. Next will be given some mistakes or inaccuracies in the rendering of prepositions.

20 B, ξυνωμολογήσατ' οὖν κοινῇ σκεψάμενοι πρὸς ὑμᾶς αὐτοὺς εἰς νῦν ἀνταποδώσειν μοι τὰ τῶν λόγων ξένια. 'Accordingly you consulted together and agreed to entertain me at this time with a return " feast of reason."' εἰς with adverbial expressions of time has for one of its meanings (like the German 'bis') the designation of the time 'by which' something is to happen: as here, where εἰς νῦν means '*by* today,' as the context shews. (The context also shews that in all probability σκεψάμενοι is wrongly taken and that it should be taken as part of the object clause after ξυνωμολογήσατε—'you agreed that when you had considered the matter in concert,' &c.)

25 E, οὐκ ἀπὸ σκόπου is rendered 'unerringly.' The phrase, as is well known, means 'to the purpose'—'à propos.'

24 B. The Egyptian priest says of the laws of his country τὸ δ' αὖ περὶ τῆς φρονήσεως, ὁρᾷς που τὸν νόμον τῇδε ὅσην ἐπιμέλειαν ἐποιήσατο εὐθὺς κατ' ἀρχὰς περί τε τὸν κόσμον ἅπαντα κ.τ.λ. This is rendered, 'Again as regards knowledge you see *how careful* our law *is in its first principles*, investigating the laws of nature,' &c. εὐθὺς κατ' ἀρχάς is of course 'at the very outset,' and ἐπιμέλειαν ἐποιήσατο must be joined with περί τε τὸν κόσμον κ.τ.λ.

παρά is rendered wrongly in 53 B. τὸ δὲ ᾗ δυνατὸν ὡς κάλλιστα ἄριστά τε ἐξ οὐχ οὕτως ἐχόντων τὸν θεὸν αὐτὰ ξυνιστάναι, παρὰ πάντα ἡμῖν ὡς ἀεὶ τοῦτο λεγόμενον ὑπαρχέτω, 'And that God formed them to be most fair and perfect, not having been so heretofore, must *above all things be the foundation whereon our account is for ever based.*'

The last clause (παρὰ πάντα κ.τ.λ.) simply means that Plato lays down the principle once for all that God made the best he could out of matter, and that this (without further express repetition) is to be taken as always understood throughout (παρά) the whole account of creation which follows. The editor beside misconstruing παρά seems to have missed the sense altogether. One must wonder how he takes the words. It should be observed that in the first clause, the editor omits ἢ δυνατόν altogether from his translation; these words are very important, for, as will appear, they are a serious difficulty (among many similar ones) in the way of the views the editor adopts on Plato's philosophy.

54. In the use of the article there are inaccuracies.

In 78 C, for which see above (par. 44), τὸ τῶν ἐγκυρτίων stands, as Galen says, for 'the whole apparatus of the ἐγκύρτια,' not 'for one of the ἐγκύρτια.' The editor, after saying 'Galen warns us against taking this "one of the ἐγκύρτια,"' continues, 'He understands πλόκανον, in which he is probably right.' Of course πλόκανον is not to be understood. We have simply the well-known idiomatic periphrasis with the neuter article. τὸ τῶν ἐγκυρτίων is well rendered by Martin 'l'ensemble des petites nasses.' There are any number of instances of this idiom in Plato: cf. just below, 79 C, τὸ τῶν στηθῶν. Stallbaum, as would be expected of such a scholar, gives the right account, 'τὸ τῶν ἐγκυρτίων per periphrasin dictum pro τὰ ἐγκύρτια.' Galen explains τὸ τῶν ἐγκυρτίων by τὸ τῶν ἐγκυρτίων πλόκανον in the passage which has been quoted above, par. 44, p. 72; but it does not follow that he made the mistake of thinking that πλόκανον was actually to be supplied in Plato's Greek.

60 D, the ordinary reading is γίγνεται τὸ μέλαν χρῶμα ἔχον λίθος. The editor reads ἔχων with A, and translates 'a certain stone of a black colour,' with the note 'the vulgate ἔχον cannot be construed at all: ἔχων is supported by A, but the article is not wanted with μέλαν χρῶμα.' Objecting to Hermann's emendation and that in the Engelmann edition, he finally proposes that ἔχων should be kept and ὁ inserted thus—ὁ τὸ μέλαν χρῶμα ἔχων λίθος. He does not seem to realise the necessity of explaining what this would mean for the neuter article could not stand at all before μέλαν χρῶμα if 'a stone of a black colour' was all that was meant, it could only stand with some exceptional significance such as 'the black colour we have been speaking of' or 'the well-known black colour.'

A possible emendation seems to be to read ὁ for τό. (Just above the vulgate appears to have had before Stallbaum τῷ γένει for ᾧ γένει.)

51 A, τῶν πάντων ἀεί τε ὄντων. To Stallbaum's proposal to omit τε is objected, 'Plato would probably have written πάντων τῶν ἀεὶ ὄντων.' On the contrary the position of the article in τῶν πάντων ἀεὶ ὄντων is

not only parallel to a known usage in Attic prose found in the plural as well as the singular, but also suits Plato's usage of the article and his general tendency to hyperbaton. Riddell quotes τὸ θνητὸν πᾶν ζῷον Laws 732 E and Phaedo 100 A τῶν ἄλλων ἁπάντων ὄντων. (In the latter place a later hand has added in one MS.—not the best— ἁπάντων τῶν ὄντων.) Compare also τὰ ἀμφότερα στοιχεῖα Theaetetus 203 C (cit. Kühn.), and τὰ πάντα (στοιχεῖα). The position of πᾶς would seem in the passage before us to give an emphasis which exactly suits the sense. The editor with his usual inconsistency finally suggests that perhaps ἀεί ποτε ὄντων should be read, producing the exact order which he makes an objection to Stallbaum. Before getting to this however he says ' I think the text may be defended as it stands, ἀεί τε ὄντων being added to explain what is meant by τῶν πάντων—all things, that is, all eternal existences.' This is rather a priori scholarship. The grammars, according to which the use of τε to connect single notions is not common, do not seem to give instances where it adds an equivalent or explanatory notion, as καί often does; and we doubt altogether the possibility of its introducing the limitation of a previous notion— as it would in the editor's explanation. In any case the editor is unconscious that he is assuming a construction, which, in his own language, ' sorely needs defence.' A parallel to τῶν πάντων ἀεί τε ὄντων—' all things, that is all eternal existences,' would be οὐδὲν χρήσιμόν τε ἐπράχθη, 'nothing, that is nothing useful was effected,' which is impossible. Or (a nearer parallel) οἱ πάντες μισθωτοί τε ἔφυγον— ' all the soldiers, that is the mercenary part of them, fled.'

It may be suggested that the original was possibly τῶν πάντων νοητῶν ἀεί τε ὄντων, comparing 37 A τῶν νοητῶν ἀεί τε ὄντων. Homœoteleuton would account for the loss of νοητῶν. The proposal to write νοητῶν instead of πάντων mentioned by the editor comes doubtless from the note to the Engelmann translation.

55. Passing to the construction of clauses we may quote the following as an instance of inaccurate vindication of the obvious.

40 C (of the planets, their conjunctions, occultations, &c.), μεθ' οὕστινάς τε ἐπίπροσθεν ἀλλήλοις ἡμῖν τε κατὰ χρόνους οὕστινας ἕκαστοι κατακαλύπτονται καὶ πάλιν ἀναφαινόμενοι φόβους καὶ σημεῖα τῶν μετὰ ταῦτα γενησομένων τοῖς οὐ δυναμένοις λογίζεσθαι πέμπουσι.

This sentence is certainly complex and involved, but I see no sufficient reason for meddling with the text. The chief causes of offence are (1) the repeated interrogative μεθ' οὕστινας—οὕστινας, (2) the position of τε after ἡμῖν. Stallbaum would read κατὰ χρόνους τινάς. I think, however, that the MS. reading may be defended as a double indirect interrogative: a construction which, though by far less common than the double direct interrogative, is yet quite a good one; cf. Soph. Antig. 1341 οὐδ' ἔχω ὅπα πρὸς πότερον ἴδω. The literal rendering of the clause will then be 'behind what stars at what times they pass before one another and are now severally hidden from us, now again reappearing,' &c. The τε after ἡμῖν really belongs to κατακρύπτονται and is answered by the following καί, quasi ἡμῖν ... κατακρύπτονταί τε καὶ ἀναφαινόμενοι ... πέμπουσι. For the irregular position of τε compare Thuk. iv. 115 οἱ δὲ Ἀθηναῖοι ἠμύναντό τε ἐκ φαύλου τειχίσματος καὶ ἀπ' οἰκιῶν ἐπάλξεις ἐχουσῶν. And instances might be multiplied.

The editor evidently thinks he is doing something new in recognising this construction and in applying it to this passage. If so he is mistaken in both points. The passage is translated as a case of the double indirect interrogative in Professor Jowett's translation, with which the editor tells us he is acquainted, and in the Engelmann translation which he has used only in the preceding page. In a note to the latter, however, Stallbaum's emendation is preferred. The construction itself does not need defence, it is recognised in Grammars; and as to its rarity, it is familiar and common enough with ὅσος and οἷος and their combinations. The illustration which the editor gives is unfortunate, because it is at least doubtful; it is probably not a double indirect interrogative at all, but a confusion of constructions suited to the ἦθος of the speech in which it occurs. The constructions which appear to be combined are οὐδ' ἔχω ὅπα ἴδω and οὐδ' ἔχω πρὸς πότερον ἴδω.

The editor fails to remark on the unusual order of the words, which may have kept Stallbaum from thinking of the double indirect interrogative, and induced the Engelmann editor, though translating the text with a double interrogative, to prefer Stallbaum's emendation; κατὰ χρόνους οὕστινας would naturally begin the clause to which it belongs and precede ἡμῖν τε.

As for the second 'chief cause of offence,' it would be surprising to find that anyone thought the position of τε 'a cause of offence,' and was tempted thereby to 'meddle with the text.' There are in Plato some sufficiently bold 'trajections' of τε, but here Stallbaum (who is in general careful in his commentaries on Plato's dialogues to note the position of τε) remarks, 'Nam quod τε post ἡμῖν interpositum est, ita quidem ut sequenti καὶ respondeat, id nullam molestiam afferet iis qui voculam ad totam hanc ῥῆσιν pertinere reputaverint.' The 'irregular position' of τε follows one of the regular rules, viz. that when two clauses are joined by τε—καί, τε may follow the first word in the first clause, the two clauses being considered as wholes. Here we have two clauses with two finite verbs, κατακαλύπτονται and πέμπουσι, and ἡμῖν is the first word in the first clause : it is therefore inadequate to represent it as properly belonging to κατακ. and irregularly detached from it. The position of ἡμῖν itself in relation to the clauses (apart from the position of οὕστινας) conforms to a known rule, Kühner § 520, A. 5, b.

The case is really simpler than the instance given from Thucydides; though the two are akin, the editor does not note the distinction. His note is otherwise crude; he merely leaves the position of τε as an irregularity in both passages, not explaining it—which is like the old-fashioned way of thinking it enough to call a changed construction an anacoluthon. In fact it is rather characteristic of the editor to give grammatical notes which are useless to the average scholar, and which supply inaccurate or imperfect information to the student who needs a note, instead of referring him to some grammar where the subject is adequately discussed, or to a note by some critical authority. There are excellent notes by Stallbaum on τε in various Platonic dialogues, as well as by Kühner, who refers to him. The editor passes a much more noteworthy case of τε in 65 D without any remark (but then there is none in Stallbaum) τὰ δὲ τούτων τε ῥυπτικὰ καὶ πᾶν τὸ περὶ τὴν γλῶτταν ἀποπλύνοντα. The editor joins τὰ τούτων, like Martin, the Engelmann editor, and Jowett.

With the foregoing defence of the double interrogative may be associated another note, on the same passage, of a like naïveté. For the ordinary τοῖς δυναμένοις the editor reads τοῖς οὐ δυναμένοις with Hermann and Paris A. The negative seems to give a good sense, and grammatically it would be an instance of a very familiar idiom. But the editor after explaining the sense, gravely stands on his defence for the grammar. ' If it be objected that the negative ought to be μή, I should reply that this is one of many cases where the negative coheres so closely with the participle as practically to form one word : cf. Isok. *de pace* § 13.... There νοῦν οὐκ ἔχοντας = ἀνοήτους, as here οὐ δυναμένοις = ἀδυνατοῦσιν.' The supposed objector would really be in such an elementary stage as to require more help than the editor gives him, and he might even be misled into supposing that the usage was only with participles, for the editor only speaks of participles and quotes a passage where οὐ is similarly joined with a participle.

56. On the other hand through unacquaintance with a known idiom, the editor believes himself to be restoring Plato's words in 86 C—τὸ δὲ σπέρμα ὅτῳ πολὺ καὶ ῥυῶδες περὶ τὸν μυελὸν γίγνεται καὶ καθαπερεὶ δένδρον πολυκαρπότερον τοῦ ξυμμέτρου πεφυκὸς ᾖ. All the MSS. appear to read γίγνεται. Stallbaum says on πεφυκὸς ᾖ 'Continuavit enim scriptor verborum constructionem perinde ac si praecessisset ὅτῳ ἂν πολὺ γίγνηται, h. e. ἐάν τινι γιγνήται, neque alia est haec structurae mutatio, quam si post εἰ et indicativum deinde ἐάν cum conjunctivo infertur. ... Ne vero omissione particulae ἂν offendaris, Menon p. 92 E, ὅτῳ ... ἐντύχῃ ... Alcib. I. 134 E, ᾧ γὰρ ἐξουσία ᾖ,' and also quotes Laws 737 B and Matthiae Gk. Gr. The editor conjectures γίγνηται, and prints it in his text with the note—'I believe this slight alteration restores Plato's sentence. *The vulgate* γίγνεται καὶ *cannot possibly stand.* ... Of the omission of ἂν with the relative instances are to be found in Attic prose: see Thucyd. IV. xvii. 2, οὗ μὲν βραχεῖς ἀρκῶσι, μὴ πολλοῖς χρῆσθαι. And above in 57 B we have the very similar construction πρὶν ... ἐκφύγῃ; and so, Laws 873 A, πρὶν ... κομίσῃ.'

The vulgate (i. e. the reading of all the MSS. and editions) certainly can stand, and there is no reason for 'meddling with the text.' The editor must be unaware that the combination in the same sentence of the indicative and the subjunctive with the relative is recognised in the grammars. Madvig quotes Dem. 22. 22, αἰτία ἐστίν, ὅταν τις ψιλῷ χρησάμενος λόγῳ μὴ παράσχηται πίστιν, ὧν λέγει, ἔλεγχας δέ, ὅταν, ὧν ἂν εἴπῃ τις, καὶ τἀληθὲς ὁμοῦ δείξῃ: Kühner quotes Isaeus 3. 60 ὅσοι μὲν καταλίπωσι ... ὅσοι δὲ ... εἰσποιοῦνται. A passage of Thucydides from which Kühner quotes only a relative clause with a subjunctive without ἄν, contains also one with the indicative—a well known place, IV. xviii. 4, σωφρόνων δὲ ἀνδρῶν οἵτινες τἀγαθὰ ἐς ἀμφίβολον ἀσφαλῶς ἔθεντο ... τόν τε πόλεμον νομίσωσι κ.τ.λ. Poppo quotes besides Thucyd. II. 44, 1, IV. 92, 1, Xen.[1] Anab. I. 9, 27, and Dem. c. Theocr. § 63, ὁπόσοι ... ἢ νῦν εἰσὶν ἐν τῷ δεσμωτηρίῳ, ἢ τὸ λοιπὸν κατατεθῶσι. The superiority of Stallbaum's note is obvious.

The rest also of the editor's note on the omission of ἄν is crude and inadequate, considering what has been written on the subject. There are important notes by Stallbaum, referred to by Kühner, on Laws 920 D and other passages, which should have been made use of, or referred to (supposing the editor knew them), if he handles the subject at all. The quotations Stallbaum gives on the present passage are much needed in the editor's note—instances of the relative with

---

[1] The passage from Xenophon is a real instance—the indicative with relative in one clause, and the optative (without ἄν) with relative in the other, for the latter is oratio obliqua for the relative with subjunctive and ἄν.

subjunctive and without ἄν from Plato's own text[1]. The instance he has taken from another author is not exactly happy, Thuc. IV. xvii. 2. The passage in full is ἐπιχώριον ὃν ἡμῖν, οὗ μὲν βραχεῖς ἀρκῶσι, μὴ πολλοῖς χρῆσθαι, πλείοσι δέ, ἐν ᾧ ἂν καιρὸς ᾖ διδάσκοντάς τι τῶν προὔργου λόγοις τὸ δέον πράσσειν. It will be observed that there are two subjunctive relative clauses, the first without and the second with ἄν. It may therefore well be contended that this is not a case of the simple omission of ἄν which it is intended to illustrate, but that it belongs to a special class of passages distinguished in grammars and in Stallbaum's note on Laws 920 D, where the ἄν of one clause seems in a way to do duty for both. When two or more clauses which should have ἄν are connected by coordinate conjunctions, it is the rule to put ἄν only once. It is true that it is generally in the first clause, but Kühner points out that sometimes it is the second clause which has the ἄν, though this is rare. (Riddell gives instances in Plato of ἄν understood from the previous clause. Stallbaum in his note on the Laws gives instances from Plato in which the clauses are not even coordinate ones.) The passage from Thucydides, therefore, is at least a disputable one, and the editor might have found much better in a grammar.

57. 24 B, ἔτι δὲ ἡ τῆς ὁπλίσεως αὐτῶν σχέσις ἀσπίδων καὶ δοράτων, is rendered 'furthermore *there is* the fashion of their arming with spears and shields,' but it should be, 'their fashion of arming is with spears and shields.' Stallbaum rightly says 'cohaerent enim verba sic: ἔτι δ' ἡ σχέσις αὐτῶν τῆς ὁπλίσεως ἐστὶ σχέσις ἀσπίδων καὶ δοράτων.' Jowett also translates rightly.

59 E, τὰ δὲ δὴ πλεῖστα ὑδάτων εἴδη κ.τ.λ. . . . ξύμπαν μὲν τὸ γένος κ.τ.λ. . . . χύμοι λεγόμενοι. Here the rendering 'are called by the class-name of saps,' does not fulfil the promise in the preface, that the translation is to save some notes by shewing how the editor thinks the Greek should be taken, for it misses the idiom, and proceeds as if λεγόμενοι (with εἰσί understood) were made equivalent to λέγονται. A more accurate rendering would be 'are, taking the class as a whole, saps, so-called,' i. e. 'the so-called saps.'

The grammatical note in 41 A, a passage already referred to, shews

---

[1] The passages with πρίν given by the editor (Tim. 57 B, Laws 872 A) are those which Stallbaum associates with the present passage in a note referred to in his commentary on the first of them (Timaeus 57 B).

rather a confusion of ideas, θεοὶ θεῶν, ὧν ἐγὼ δημιουργὸς πατήρ τε ἔργων, ἃ δι' ἐμοῦ γενόμενα ἄλυτα ἐμοῦ γε μὴ ἐθέλοντος· τὸ μὲν οὖν δὴ δεθὲν πᾶν λυτόν κ.τ.λ. (see above, par. 18).

ὧν ἐγὼ δημιουργὸς πατήρ τε ἔργων] These words are almost as much debated as the preceding. (1) The clause may be taken in apposition with θεοί: sc. ἔργα, ὧν ἐγὼ δημιουργὸς πατήρ τε: (2) ὧν may be governed by ἔργων, as Stallbaum takes it: (3) or by δημιουργός. It can hardly be doubted that the interpretation is to be preferred which best lends itself to the majestic flow of Plato's rhythm; and on that ground I should give the preference to the last, making ὧν masculine: 'whose maker am I and father of works which through me coming into being &c.' The construction will thus really follow the same principle as the familiar idiom whereby a demonstrative is substituted for the relative in the second member of a relative clause: as for instance in *Euthydemus* 301 E ταῦτα ἡγεῖ σὰ εἶναι, ὧν ἂν ἄρξῃς καὶ ἐξῇ σοι αὐτοῖς χρῆσθαι ὅ τι ἂν βούλῃ.

It is difficult to see what the editor can have been thinking of, for of course there is nothing analogous to a 'demonstrative substituted for a relative in the second member,' nor does his rendering throw light on his explanation.

Perhaps the true explanation of the construction may simply be that ἔργων ἃ δι' ἐμοῦ κ.τ.λ. is related to πατήρ like an adjective, and then the whole expression πατὴρ ἔργων ἃ κ.τ.λ. is coordinate with δημιουργός, and, like it, governs ὧν.

58. Instances might be multiplied, but we will turn to usages more specially Platonic.

If the editor had studied Riddell he would have known how common hyperbaton is in Plato. As it is he constantly gets wrong in passages where it occurs.

19 C, ἡδέως γὰρ ἄν του λόγῳ διεξιόντος ἀκούσαιμ' ἄν, ἄθλους οὓς πόλις ἀθλεῖ, τούτους αὐτὴν ἀγωνιζομένην πρὸς πόλεις ἄλλας πρεπόντως, εἴς τε πόλεμον ἀφικομένην, καὶ ἐν τῷ πολεμεῖν τὰ προσήκοντα ἀποδιδοῦσαν τῇ παιδείᾳ κ.τ.λ. This is rendered 'I would fain listen to one who depicted her engaged in a becoming manner with other countries in those struggles which cities must undergo, *and* going to war, *and* when at war shewing a result worthy of her training,' &c.

Paris A has εἴς γε πόλεμον. τε read by Hermann is really Bekker's conjecture. The editor who follows Hermann gives τε without saying where it comes from, and without understanding its construction, as his translation shews. The τε='both' and is of course correlative to the καί before ἐν τῷ πολεμεῖν; it is best construed as if after πρεπόντως; it does not coordinate ἀφικομένην with ἀγωνιζομένην as the editor supposes. The reason of its apparent displacement is simple. πρεπόντως is to apply to two cases, the manner in which the state enters on a war, and its manner of prosecuting it. Thus the two clauses follow πρεπόντως quite naturally, τε coming after the first word of the first—εἰς πόλεμον ἀφικομένην, and καί introducing the second clause, which should strictly have been of some such form as ἐν τῷ πολέμῳ ἀγωνιζομένην, but the idea of πρεπόντως instead of being understood, is expressed over again in a different form, and thus a word like ἀγωνιζομένην with πρεπόντως understood is replaced by the phrase τὰ προσήκοντα ἀποδιδοῦσαν τῇ παιδείᾳ. It may be noticed, as we are on this passage, that the translation also misses the sense of ἄθλους οὓς πόλις ἀθλεῖ, which is not 'those struggles which a city *must* undergo,' but 'national contests,' as opposed to the more usual and proper sense of ἄθλοι which has occurred just above, 'contests of individuals.' And there again in the latter place the translation is wrong, καί τι τῶν τοῖς σώμασι δοκούντων προσήκειν κατὰ τὴν ἀγωνίαν ἀθλοῦντα, '*putting into active exercise* the qualities which seemed to belong to their form;' this loses the point, for κατὰ τὴν ἀγωνίαν ἀθλοῦντα (of the individual creature) corresponds to ἄθλους, οὓς πόλις ἀθλεῖ, τούτους αὐτὴν ἀγωνιζομένην.

There is a precisely similar placing of τε in 23 C, where the editor fails again—ἦν γὰρ ... ἡ νῦν 'Αθηναίων οὖσα πόλις ἀρίστη πρός τε τὸν πόλεμον καὶ κατὰ πάντα εὐνομωτάτη διαφερόντως. The translation has 'was foremost both in war *and in all besides*, and her laws were exceedingly righteous above all cities.' The editor appears to construe as if putting a comma between πάντα and εὐνομωτάτη; in any case he mistakes the true construction and gives a wrong sense. The explanation is quite the same in principle as in 19 C; ἀρίστη belongs to both the expressions joined by τε and καί, viz. πρὸς πόλεμον and κατὰ πάντα εὐνομωτάτη κ.τ.λ., only the latter has been varied from its strictly grammatical form, which might be, e. g. κατὰ πάντα τὰ περὶ τὴν πολιτείαν or κατὰ πᾶσαν εὐνομίαν. 'Exceedingly righteous' gives a wrong turn to εὐνομωτάτη which rather means 'with the most orderly constitution.'

19 E, τὸ δὲ τῶν σοφιστῶν γένος ... φοβοῦμαι ... μή πως ... ἄστοχον ἅμα φιλοσόφων ἀνδρῶν ᾖ καὶ πολιτικῶν. Stallbaum is surely right in joining ἅμα φιλοσόφων καὶ πολιτικῶν, 'men who are at once philosophers and statesmen.' This is required by the general sense. Compare also just below, γένος ... ἅμα ἀμφοτέρων (i. e. both philosophy and statesmanship) φύσει μετέχον. The editor misled by the

order of the words renders 'I am afraid . . . they may somehow fall short in their conception of philosophers and statesmen,' thus entirely losing the point of the passage. The position of ἢ comes under the section of Riddell's chapter on hyperbaton entitled 'grammatical governments intermingled by hyperbaton.' He gives (for place of a verb) πρὸς τί τοῦτ' εἶπες βλέψας; compare also below, 23 C, ἐξ ὧν . . . ἡ πόλις ἐστι τὰ νῦν ὑμῶν; 78 C; τὰ μὲν οὖν ἔνδον ἐκ πυρὸς συνεστήσατο τοῦ πλοκάνου ἄπαντα. The position of ἀνδρῶν is not a difficult hyperbaton.

With this may be associated the note upon 67 B, already mentioned in another connection. The Greek is ὅλως μὲν οὖν φωνὴν θῶμεν τὴν δι' ὤτων ὑπ' ἀέρος ἐγκεφάλου τε καὶ αἵματος μέχρι ψυχῆς πληγὴν διαδιδομένην. In his note the editor governs ἐγκεφάλου and αἵματος by πληγήν and says 'the construction of all these genitives is a little puzzling. Stallbaum constructs ἐγκεφάλου τε καὶ αἵματος with διά, but the interposition of ὑπ' ἀέρος surely renders this indefensible.' As we have seen [1] the editor may be right in his construction, but the reason given for it is entirely wrong; the remark on the interposition of ὑπ' ἀέρος ignores the ordinary feature of hyperbaton. In the 'intermingling of grammatical governments' a member of one construction is intruded among those of another. It is a mistake to suppose that the resulting ambiguity makes the construction 'indefensible.' On the contrary, it is well known that the use of hyperbaton is often harsh, and does cause obscurity, in prose as well as poetry. Cf. Eur. Medea 12, ἀνδάνουσα μὲν φυγῇ πολιτῶν ὧν ἀφίκετο χθόνα. Kühner remarks specially on this fact (one of his instances seems wrong) and refers to Poppo on Thucydides. Again in 68 A Plato gives an awkward position to genitives which might have easily been avoided, τὸ δὲ τούτων αὖ μεταξὺ πυρὸς γένος (not hyperbaton). Compare again Gorg. 469 D, κἄν τινα δόξῃ μοι τῆς κεφαλῆς αὐτῶν κατεαγέναι δεῖν—where αὐτῶν belongs to τινα (Riddell). The editor might have learnt something from the considerable number of undoubted cases of hyperbaton in this very dialogue. To what we have already quoted may be added 17 B, χθές που τῶν ὑπ' ἐμοῦ ῥηθέντων λόγων περὶ πολιτείας ἦν τὸ κεφάλαιον : 50 B, ὁ αὐτὸς δὴ λόγος καὶ περὶ τῆς τὰ πάντα δεχομένης σώματα φύσεως : 53 D, τὰς δ' ἔτι τούτων ἀρχὰς ἄνωθεν θεὸς οἶδε (quoted by Riddell also): 51 A, τῷ τὰ τῶν πάντων ἀεί τε ὄντων κατὰ πᾶν ἑαυτοῦ πολλάκις ἀφομοιώματα καλῶς μέλλοντι δέχεσθαι πάντων ἐκτὸς αὐτῷ προσήκει πεφυκέναι τῶν εἰδῶν :

---

[1] Paragraph 35.

60 A, τέτταρα δέ, ὅσα ἔμπυρα εἴδη, διαφανῆ μάλιστα γενόμενα εἴληφεν ὀνόματα αὐτῶν: 70 A, ὁπότ' ἐκ τῆς ἀκροπόλεως τῷ ἐπιτάγματι καὶ λόγῳ μηδαμῇ πείθεσθαι ἑκὸν ἐθέλοι.

In the present passage the hyperbaton would not be particularly difficult, and the editor contradicts his note by actually rendering in the translation in the manner which the note pronounces indefensible, 'a stroke transmitted through the ears by the air and passed through the brain and the blood to the soul.' In the De Plac. Phil. the words are also thus construed[1]. The grammatical reason which there seems to be in favour of the view in the note has been overlooked by the editor. It would be natural that τε and καί should be correlative (ἐγκεφάλου τε καὶ αἵματος), and then τε would not couple ἐγκεφάλου and ὤτων.

We may give some further specimens of the editor's difficulties with hyperbaton.

35 A, τῆς ἀμερίστου καὶ ἀεὶ κατὰ ταὐτὰ ἐχούσης οὐσίας καὶ τῆς αὖ περὶ τὰ σώματα γιγνομένης μεριστῆς, τρίτον ἐξ ἀμφοῖν, ἐν μέσῳ ξυνεκεράσατο οὐσίας εἶδος, τῆς τε ταὐτοῦ φύσεως καὶ τῆς θατέρου, καὶ κατὰ ταῦτα ξυνέστησεν ἐν μέσῳ τοῦ τε ἀμεροῦς αὐτῶν καὶ τοῦ κατὰ τὰ σώματα μεριστοῦ.

'First,' says the editor, 'a word concerning the Greek. The genitives τῆς ἀμερίστου ... μεριστῆς might well enough be taken with Proklos as dependent on ἐν μέσῳ. I think, however, they are to be considered as in a somewhat loose anticipative apposition to ἐξ ἀμφοῖν, with which words the construction becomes determinate.' Proclus is obviously right, and completely confirmed by the repetition just below of the same thing—ἐν μέσῳ τοῦ τε ἀμεροῦς αὐτῶν καὶ τοῦ κατὰ τὰ σώματα μεριστοῦ. The editor's view is another specimen of a priori scholarship, and is indeed 'somewhat loose.' An 'anticipative' construction should certainly be of the same form as that which it anticipates, and so here the genitive τῆς ἀμερίστου κ.τ.λ. should have the same preposition (ἐκ) as ἀμφοῖν. An exact parallel to what is proposed by the editor would be τοῖς ποτάμοις καὶ τοῖς ὄρεσι τῆς Ἀσίας ἐν ἀμφότεροις εὑρίσκεται χρυσός or τῶν χρησίμων καὶ τῶν καλῶν πλείστη περὶ ἀμφοτέρων ἀμφισβήτησίς ἐστι, where the construction of the genitives would not 'become determinate' till the words περὶ ἀμφοτέρων[2]. This one may venture to think impossible Greek.

[1] See above, par. 35.
[2] The known poetical idiom whereby the second only of two nouns has a preposition which belongs to both does not apply here and is not what the editor means.

The reader will have observed that the editor seldom makes one mistake at a time. In the present passage he makes another, and a conspicuous one. He translates τῆς αὖ περὶ τὰ σώματα γιγνομένης μεριστῆς 'that which *becomes* divided in material bodies.' The phrase just quoted is opposed to τῆς ἀμερίστου καὶ ἀεὶ κατὰ ταὐτὰ ἐχούσης οὐσίας: thus γιγνομένης is opposed to ἀεὶ κατὰ ταὐτὰ ἐχούσης, and as the latter means 'belonging to the world of changeless Being,' so the other means 'belonging to the world of change and Becoming,' exactly as if τῆς αὖ περὶ τὰ σώματα μεριστῆς καὶ γιγνομένης were written.

The editor adds, 'Stallbaum is certainly wrong in connecting them (i. e. the genitives τῆς ἀμερίστου κ.τ.λ.) with εἶδος [1].'

It is not absolutely clear how Stallbaum construes. He joins ξυνεκέρασατο εἶδος τῆς ἀμερίστου κ.τ.λ., and it certainly looks as though the genitive τῆς ἀμερίστου κ.τ.λ. was taken as a kind of genitive of material (especially as he supposes ἐξ ἀμφοῖν per redundantiam quandam interjectum), which is at least Greek.

29 B, τοῦ μὲν οὖν μονίμου καὶ βεβαίου καὶ μετὰ νοῦ καταφανοῦς μονίμους καὶ ἀμεταπτώτους, καθ' ὅσον οἶόν τε ἀνελέγκτοις προσήκει λόγοις εἶναι καὶ ἀκινήτοις, τούτου δεῖ μηδὲν ἐλλείπειν· τοὺς δὲ τοῦ πρὸς μὲν ἐκεῖνο ἀπεικασθέντος, ὄντος δὲ εἰκόνος, εἰκότας ἀνὰ λόγον τε ἐκείνων ὄντας· ὅ τί περ πρὸς γένεσιν οὐσία, τοῦτο πρὸς πίστιν ἀλήθεια.

The note is—
Some corruption has clearly found its way into this sentence. It seems to me that the simplest remedy is to reject οἷον, which I think may have arisen from a duplication of ὅσον. By the omission the sentence becomes perfectly grammatical. Stallbaum, reading καὶ before καθ' ὅσον, alters ἀνελέγκτοις, λόγοις, ἀκινήτοις to the accusative and writes δὲ for δεῖ. This method does indeed produce a sentence that can be construed; but it involves larger alterations of the text, and the position of the word λόγους seems extremely unsatisfactory. I cannot therefore concede his claim to have restored Plato's words. According to my version of the sentence εἶναι must be supplied with μονίμους καὶ ἀμεταπτώτους.

The position of the word λόγους, instead of being extremely unsatisfactory, is greatly in favour of Stallbaum, for it would be an idiomatic and elegant hyperbaton, such as might be found in any Greek writer. The predicates μονίμους, ἀμεταπτώτους are naturally put first so as to be near to μονίμου and βεβαίου, and the sentence with so many acc. masculines is made less heavy by associating

---

[1] This seems an echo of Martin 'M. Stallbaum, par une inversion non moins forcée et non moins utile, prétend faire dépendre ces deux génitifs du substantif εἶδος.'

λόγους, which would be expected in the place proper to the subject, with the other two predicates. The hyperbaton is rather apparent than real, for probably the strict grammatical analysis is that τοὺς λόγους understood from the preceding context is subject, and λόγους ἀνελέγκτους is predicate [1]. This then is another instance of the author's misunderstanding of the order of words. But there are several other matters to note. It is after all an advantage in an emendation that it 'produces a sentence which can be construed;' the editor's may just construe, but that is all. It is as clumsy and obscure as Stallbaum's is elegant and clear. In the editor's version we must supply not merely εἶναι, as he says, but δεῖ λόγους εἶναι, and not only here, but in the next sentence (τοὺς δὲ ... ὄντος). It is doubtful whether Plato could have written a sentence with such harsh construction and harsh rhythm. (The editor commends his view of the interpretation of 41 A fin. on the ground that it suits the 'majestic flow of Plato's rhythm.')

As the editor minimises what has to be supplied to help out his text, so he exaggerates the changes Stallbaum makes. Stallbaum does not insert καί and change δέ to δεῖ merely on his own authority, as the note would certainly make the reader suppose. καί is found in a number of MSS. (13) according to Stallbaum, though not in Paris A; it could easily have been lost before κατά: δέ, as Stallbaum says, is the correction of δεῖ in Paris A itself. The editor's omission of οἷον is not quite original, for Stallbaum says the vulgate before him omitted οἷόν τε.

There is another circumstance in favour of Stallbaum's reading which he himself has not perceived. In τούτου δὲ μηδὲν ἐλλείπειν he takes τούτου as referring to the whole condition μονίμους καὶ ἀμεταπτώτους καὶ ἀνελέγκτους καὶ ἀκινήτους εἶναι. But we get an excellent sense if τούτου refers to τοῦ μονίμου καὶ βεβαίου. 'The arguments which deal with what is lasting and stable, must in no way be inadequate to it (τούτου μηδὲν ἐλλείπειν), but be themselves like it, lasting and stable (μονίμους καὶ βεβαίους).' This sense of τοῦτο is

---

[1] A somewhat similar position of the subject is found in 36 E, καὶ τὸ μὲν δὴ σῶμα ὁρατὸν οὐρανοῦ γέγονεν, αὐτὴ δὲ ἀόρατος μέν, λογισμοῦ δὲ μετέχουσα καὶ ἁρμονίας ψυχή, τῶν νοητῶν ἀεί τε ὄντων ὑπὸ τοῦ ἀρίστου ἀρίστη γενομένη τῶν γεννηθέντων. On which the editor says, 'Notwithstanding Stallbaum's defence of ψυχή, I feel strong misgivings as to its genuineness: its position is strange, and disturbs the connexion.' From the preceding context it follows that αὐτή means ἡ ψυχή, but the word has not been used in the last five lines, being represented by pronouns. Clearness is gained by the insertion of ψυχή in the middle of the somewhat long sentence; point also is gained because σῶμα has intervened. In the present passage (29 B) it follows from the preceding context that τοὺς λόγους is the subject of ἀμεταπτώτους, but this is made clearer by the insertion of λόγους in the middle of the rather long sentence.

rather confirmed by the next following words, τοὺς δὲ τοῦ πρὸς μὲν ἐκεῖνο (i. e. τὸ μόνιμον) ἀπεικασθέντος, ὄντος δὲ εἰκόνος, εἰκότας ἀνὰ λόγον τε ἐκείνων ὄντας.

The editor joins τοῦ μονίμου καὶ βεβαίου λόγους, 'the words of that which is abiding,' but the genitives are governed by ἐξηγητάς, understood from the preceding clause—διοριστέον, ὡς ἄρα τοὺς λόγους, ὧνπέρ εἰσιν ἐξηγηταί, τούτων αὐτῶν καὶ ξυγγενεῖς ὄντας.

Lastly, in the clause quoted a few lines back he renders ἀνὰ λόγον τε ἐκείνων ὄντας, 'and duly corresponding with their subject.' But as ἐκεῖνο means τὸ μόνιμον καὶ βέβαιον, so ἐκείνων probably refers to the corresponding λόγοι, the μόνιμοι καὶ βέβαιοι λόγοι; and this receives strong confirmation from the clause which follows and explains the ἀνὰ λόγον, viz. ὅτί περ πρὸς γένεσιν (i. e. τὸ ἀπεικασθέν) οὐσία (i. e. τὸ μόνιμον) τοῦτο πρὸς πίστιν (i. e. τοὺς εἰκότας λόγους) ἀλήθεια (i. e. οἱ μόνιμοι λόγοι).

20 C, ὥστε καὶ χθὲς εὐθὺς ἐνθένδε ἐπειδὴ παρὰ Κριτίαν πρὸς τὸν ξενῶνα, οὗ καὶ καταλύομεν, ἀφικόμεθα, καὶ ἔτι πρότερον καθ' ὁδὸν αὐτὰ ταῦτ' ἐσκοποῦμεν. The editor, putting a comma after ἐνθένδε, translates, 'In fact yesterday, immediately on leaving this spot, when we reached the guest-chamber at the house of Kritias where we are staying, and even before that on our way thither, we were discussing this very matter.'

The confusion of this is obvious. The distance to the house of Kritias was sufficiently great for a philosophical conversation, and yet 'immediately on leaving this spot' is in the above translation contemporaneous as it were with arrival at Kritias' house. Now Plato might speak in this way treating the action as a whole, but it would be absurd then to add 'even *before this* while we were on the road.' What happened on the road could not well be 'even before' what happened 'immediately on leaving this spot.'

The fact is there is a hyperbaton of ἐνθένδε, which word must be construed as if after ἐπειδή. The obvious meaning is 'as soon as we arrived from here at the house of Critias, and even before we got there,' &c. The hyperbaton is neatly explained by Stallbaum, 'Male vulgo post ἐνθένδε commate distinguunt. Nam εὐθὺς ἐνθένδε cohaeret cum ἐπειδὴ ἀφικόμεθα atque eodem modo dicitur quo alibi junctum cum participio.'

26 B, οὐκ ἂν οἶδ' εἰ δυναίμην. Here the editor recognises the hyperbaton which it would be hard to miss, and comments, 'For the construction and position of ἂν see Euripides' Alcestis 48, Medea 941. I have not noted another instance in Plato.'

It may be confessed that the study of the editor's work would not incline anyone to attach importance to his report of what he has not observed in Plato. If he had read Riddell he would have found this passage treated under hyperbaton of ἄν, and not isolated but put in its logical place as a member of a class well represented in Plato. The general account of this class is, that with verbs of thinking and judging ἄν belonging to an object clause after them is taken out of that clause and associated with the principal verb.

Apart from Plato, the note is another specimen of the crudeness we have before had occasion to remark upon. Instead of an explanation of the principle, and of its idiomatic character where the verb is οἶδα, or (better still) of a reference to some one who treats it adequately, we have merely a reference to two passages given along with this present passage from the Timaeus in Liddell and Scott. These again are from poetry, whereas there is a sufficiency of prose instances, and are thus misleading to the student for whom such a note may be supposed to be written.

Better information, both about the principle and its illustration, may be found in the ordinary helps—Liddell and Scott, or a standard Grammar.

59. Leaving hyperbaton we will give some more instances of lack of knowledge of Riddell's Digest of Platonic idioms.

24 C. The Egyptian priest, speaking of the foundation of Athens by Athene, says, ταύτην οὖν δή τοτε ... τὴν διακόσμησιν ... ἡ θεὸς προτέρους ὑμᾶς διακοσμήσασα κατῴκισεν, ἐκλεξαμένη τὸν τόπον ἐν ᾧ γεγένησθε, τὴν εὐκρασίαν τῶν ὡρῶν ἐν αὐτῷ κατιδοῦσα, ὅτι φρονιμωτάτους ἄνδρας οἴσοι. The translation makes εὐκρασία τῶν ὡρῶν nominative to οἴσοι. The true nominative is τόπος, as Riddell has pointed out in his chapter on 'Binary Structure.' The editor has gone out of his way to make this mistake, for here, as in some of the cases we have mentioned, the very next sentence in the text might have set him right, τὸν προσφερεστάτους αὐτῇ μέλλοντα οἴσειν τόπον ἄνδρας. The translation given of the first part is 'With all this constitution and order the goddess established you when she founded your nation first.' This is misleading, for προτέρους means 'before the founding of our nation.' Cf. 23 D fin.

Again in 40 B there is a remarkable construction, ἐξ ἧς δὴ τῆς αἰτίας γέγονε κ.τ.λ. The editor translates 'from which cause have been created' without any comment whatever, though it is far more worthy of a note than many of the points he has chosen to discuss. It is treated by Riddell under 'Binary Structure.'

Connected with the same chapter of Riddell is the following. In 61 A Plato explains the dissolution of a mass of earth in water by the penetration of the water particles in a certain way between those of the earth. In 61 B he explains similarly the dissolution of a substance combined of earth and water by the action of fire. As in the former case the watery particles penetrated between those of earth, so in this the particles of fire penetrate between the particles of water. The reading of the MSS. in 61 B is τὰ δὲ πυρὸς εἰς τὰ τῶν ὑδάτων διάκενα εἰσιόντα, ὅπερ ὕδωρ γῆν τοῦτο πῦρ ἀέρα ἀπεργαζόμενα κ.τ.λ. This of course gives the wrong sense, but if ὕδωρ is written for ἀέρα, we have exactly what is wanted. The corruption does not seem an improbable one—

ΠΥΡΥΔΩΡΑΠΕΡΓΑΖΟΜΕΝΑ
ΑΕΡΑ

The editor omits πῦρ ἀέρα entirely from his text, and has this note: 'The words πῦρ ἀέρα ... I have rejected for more than one reason: the chief of which is that they are absolute nonsense.... What conceivable sense is there in introducing air? &c.... A minor though still substantial reason for rejecting the words is the grammar. If we retain πῦρ ἀέρα, not only is πῦρ out of all construction, but ἀπεργαζόμενα is left forlorn of any substantive wherewith to agree. On the other hand, the rejection of these two words, which I conceive to have been inserted by a copyist in an over antithetical frame of mind, restores both sense and grammar.'
The remarks on the grammar are not quite sound. It is the grammar which is in favour of the text, and makes the expulsion of the words unsafe. In sense the only word wrong is ἀέρα. The grammatical form is an instance of 'Binary Structure.' In comparison 'there is,' says Riddell, 'a great tendency to the Binary Structure,' and this is virtually a comparison. Riddell does not discuss this precise type of passage. The original or primary construction is τὰ δὲ πυρὸς εἰς τὰ τῶν ὑδάτων διάκενα εἰσιόντα ἀπεργαζόμενα (τὸ ὕδωρ) ὅπερ ὕδωρ γῆν; then the first of the contrasted clauses is repeated in a different form, and in a structure accommodated to the second, and so we get τοῦτο πῦρ ὕδωρ, which is all the easier because τὰ τοῦ πυρός the subject of ἀπεργαζόμενα is = τὸ πῦρ. The position of ἀπεργαζόμενα need cause no difficulty: Riddell gives striking examples of intermixture of

clauses. For the repetition in another form of the first of the two contrasted clauses, compare Rep. 413, καὶ θεατέον (τοὺς νέους), ὥσπερ τοὺς πώλους ἐπὶ τοὺς ψόφους τε καὶ θορύβους ἄγοντες σκοποῦσιν, εἰ φοβεροί, οὕτω νέους ὄντας εἰς δείματα ἄττα κομιστέον ... βασανίζοντας ... εἰ κ.τ.λ.

It is to the last degree unlikely that an interpolating copyist would have produced anything so idiomatic. On the other hand, it is possible that ἀέρα may be a copyist's alteration of ὕδωρ, perhaps mechanical, from a remembrance of the proportion of the four elements in 32 B–C.

If we keep τοῦτο, as the editor does, then since this corresponds to ὅπερ, it is at once felt that something is wanted to balance the rest of the clause introduced by ὅπερ. The editor himself so far feels this that though he prints τοῦτο ἀπεργαζόμενα, he concludes his note thus, 'I suspect, however, that Plato's original words were τοῦθ' ὕδωρ ἀπεργαζόμενα, and that ὕδωρ was expelled by the two intruding elements, πῦρ ἀέρα: its insertion would be a gain to the text.'

The last conjecture as to the alteration of the text is complicated and entirely improbable: if the copyist found ὅπερ ὕδωρ γῆν, τοῦτο ὕδωρ ἀπεργαζόμενα, he would be very unlikely to introduce into the last clause πῦρ ἀέρα.

18 C, τί δὲ δὴ τὸ περὶ τῆς παιδοποιίας; ἢ τοῦτο μὲν διὰ τὴν ἀήθειαν τῶν λεχθέντων εὐμνημόνευτον, ὅτι κοινὰ τὰ τῶν γάμων καὶ τὰ τῶν παίδων πᾶσιν ἁπάντων ἐτίθεμεν, μηχανωμένους, ὅπως μηδείς ποτε τὸ γεγεννημένον αὐτῷ ἰδίᾳ γνώσοιτο, νομιοῦσι δὲ πάντες πάντας αὐτοὺς ὁμογενεῖς κ.τ.λ.

Accepting μηχανώμενοι (Stephanus' conjecture) instead of the MSS. reading μηχανωμένους, with Stallbaum and others, the editor translates, 'This, I think, is easy of recollection because of the novelty of our scheme. We ordained that the rights of marriage and of children should be common to all, to the end that no one should ever know his own offspring, but that each should look upon all as his kindred,' &c.

His note is—'Hermann's defence of μηχανωμένους is vain; nor is Buttmann's μηχανωμένοις very satisfactory. I agree with Stallbaum in receiving the nominative.' The editor then feeling μηχανωμένοις is not 'very satisfactory' seems to consider μηχανωμένους out of the question: and it is therefore very doubtful indeed whether the editor understands the distinguished scholar whose view he so curtly dismisses. Hermann's note in full is as follows, 'idemque (sc. Cod. Par. A) mox cum ceteris fere omnibus μηχανωμένους, cui frustra B[ekker] ex Buttmanni conj. μηχανωμένοις, ST ex Stephani μηχανώμενοι substituerunt; me ut cum Schneidero vulg. retinerem, movit imprimis Legg. VI. 7 [=759 B] τούτων δὴ πάντων τὰ μὲν αἱρετὰ χρή, τὰ δὲ κληρωτὰ γίγνεσθαι, μιγνύντας κ.τ.λ.' The latter clause is more fully μιγνύντας πρὸς φιλίαν ἀλλήλοις δῆμον καὶ μὴ δῆμον ... ὅπως ἂν μάλιστα ὁμονοῶν ᾖ.

μηχανωμένοις of course would have to agree with πᾶσιν: but in Plato it is common after such expressions of necessity or obligation as would naturally be followed by a dative participle, to change from the dative to an accusative, or to use the accusative alone. This is most usual perhaps with verbals in -τέος. The sentence quoted by Hermann is a similar construction with χρή, and it is remarkably parallel to the present passage; for τίθεμεν is a word of ordinance parallel to χρή; and μιγνύντας referring to the persons to whom the ordinance is addressed, and expressing something delegated to them, is parallel to μηχανωμένους, which would have precisely the same function. This view is strongly confirmed by the part of the Republic itself to which the Timaeus here refers (460 C), where μηχανώμενοι is applied to the magistrates who are to carry out this particular, οὐκοῦν καὶ τροφῆς οὗτοι ἐπιμελήσονται ... πᾶσαν μηχανὴν μηχανώμενοι ὅπως μηδεμία (τῶν μητέρων) τὸ αὑτῆς αἰσθήσεται κ.τ.λ., the parallelism of which to the Timaeus passage is obvious.

The editor's notes on the MSS. have their usual value. The only information they impart is that μηχανωμένους is the reading of A, and μηχανώμενοι the correction of Stephanus. Stallbaum tells us that μηχανωμένους is found in far the greater number of MSS., and that the nominative is found in four.

The editor does not even construe rightly the reading which he adopts. μηχανώμενοι ὅπως ... γνώσοιτο, of course does not express the object of the ordinance, but on the contrary one of the means by which it is carried out, and should not therefore be rendered 'to the end that,' &c., but 'contriving some way by which'.

Even if μηχανωμένους were referred to the subject of ἐτίθεμεν, which the parallel passage from the Republic makes improbable, it would have been dangerous to alter the lectio difficillima, against the best MS. authority, considering the Platonic idiom pointed out by Riddell, § 279 d.

60. We will close this list of errors as to Platonic usages with one which relates not so much to grammatical idiom, as to a formula of Plato's philosophical language.

In 52 B–C Plato maintains that a sensible thing being but a semblance (εἰκών) of reality cannot exist independently like the idea, the true reality, but requires a substrate, viz. space, in which to inhere. In 52 C is this difficult passage, ... τἀληθὲς λέγειν, ὡς εἰκόνι μέν, ἐπείπερ οὐδ' αὐτὸ τοῦτο, ἐφ' ᾧ γέγονεν, ἑαυτῆς ἐστίν, ἑτέρου δέ τινος ἀεὶ φέρεται φάντασμα, διὰ ταῦτα ἐν ἑτέρῳ προσήκει τινι γίγνεσθαι κ.τ.λ. The translation has, ' . . . affirm the truth ; namely, that to an image it belongs, seeing that it is not the very model of itself on which it has been created, but is the ever fleeting semblance of another, in another to come into being.' The note is—

> I believe the true construction of these words has escaped all the editors and translators, who are consequently in sore straits what to make of ἑαυτῆς. The construction seems to me a very simple and very Platonic σχῆμα πρὸς τὸ σημαινόμενον. What is meant by αὐτὸ τοῦτο ἐφ' ᾧ γέγονε? of course the παράδειγμα, and the whole phrase governs ἑαυτῆς just as if παράδειγμα had been written: 'since it is not the original upon which it is modelled of itself.'

This is neither the 'true construction,' nor has it 'escaped all the editors and translators.' It is given in Cousin's translation, in his annotated version of Plato's dialogues, a book well known and referred to often enough, for instance, by Martin. Cousin (vol. 12, p. 159) renders—

> Cependant comme toute image n'est pas la même chose que le modèle sur lequel elle est faite, sans relever non plus d'elle-même, mais qu'elle est toujours la représentation d'un être différent d'elle, et que par conséquent elle doit avoir lieu au sein d'un autre être.

But, besides this, the editor's confident solution is quite wrong, and his criticism of others is wrong. It is not accurate to say that the editors are in 'sore straits' what to make of ἑαυτῆς. Stallbaum's view of the passage ('quandoquidem nec ipsum hoc, cujus causâ exstitit, ipsius est') seems wrong, but causes him no difficulty with ἑαυτῆς. Stephanus wished to read αὐτῆς : on which Stallbaum says, 'ne quis in posterum vitiosum et cum Stephano in αὐτῆς mutandum censeat, hunc in modum accipe "sui ipsius est proprium, ad ipsum pertinet."' The difficulty the editor appears to find, is that in Stallbaum's view ἑαυτῆς does not refer to the subject of the clause in which it occurs (αὐτὸ τοῦτο). But a scholar like Stallbaum was of course aware that the reflexive pronoun in a subordinate clause might refer not to the subject of that clause, but to the subject of the principal clause ; and here εἰκόνι, to which ἑαυτῆς is referred, is the logical subject of the principal clause.

The editor's construction is neither 'very simple' nor 'very Platonic.'

The editor really construes ἐφ' ᾧ γέγονε '*in the likeness of which* it was made.' In the first place, neither grammar nor dictionary records such a use of ἐπί. The only thing at all like it is the use with verbs of naming, κεκλῆσθαι ἐπί τινι. And even if this were extended to the sense given by the editor (of which there is no sign), it would have to be followed by a word definitely expressing imitation, and not by so vague a word as γέγονε. Secondly, the editor is himself unconsciously in sore straits with ἑαυτῆς. He says that by αὐτὸ τοῦτο ἐφ' ᾧ γέγονε is meant 'of course the παράδειγμα,' but he really makes it as he construes mean not merely παράδειγμα but 'παράδειγμα ἑαυτῆς,' 'the original of itself,' and thus the addition afterwards of ἑαυτῆς is most awkward, and is ill concealed in the note and translation. In fact it is obvious that the rendering in the former 'since it is not the original-upon-which-it-is-modelled of itself'='since it is not the original of itself, of itself.'

Thirdly, the editor is 'in sore straits' with οὐδέ, and also with the emphatic αὐτό which follows it. It will be observed that in his rendering in the translation he omits οὐδέ altogether, and in the rendering in the note he omits both οὐδέ and αὐτό. It is clear that as the editor joins the words (with εἰκών as subject, ἐστί as copula, and αὐτὸ τοῦτο κ.τ.λ. as predicate) οὐδ' αὐτό ought to introduce something which the εἰκών might at the very least be expected to be: whereas they introduce what an image could not be, viz. its own original. We have indeed the bathos—'an image, seeing that it is not even its own original.'

For the explanation of the passage we must refer to the well-known distinction and definition of relative terms made in the Republic. Plato has this formula for a relative term: it is οἷόν τινος εἶναι τοῦτο ὅπερ ἐστί. 'Its nature is to be what it is (τοῦτο ὅπερ ἐστί) *of* or in relation to something else (τινός, ἄλλου τινός).' For instance, thirst is what it is *of* something else, i. e. thirst is thirst *of* drink.

There is a certain paradox intended in the definition more evident in Greek than in English, from the ambiguity of the genitive case. A thing would be expected to have its own essence, τοῦτο ὅπερ ἐστί, all to itself, not to be *of* another what it is, or, in this phraseology, not εἶναι τοῦτο ὅπερ ἐστί τινος (ἑτέρου), but εἶναι τοῦτο ὅπερ ἐστὶν ἑαυτοῦ (where ἑαυτοῦ is in the same construction as τινός). But, on the contrary, the peculiarity of these terms (relatives) is that they are *not even* their own essence *of* (or in relation to) *themselves*, but *of something else*, i. e. ἔστιν οὐδ' αὐτὸ τοῦτο ὅπερ ἐστὶν ἑαυτῶν. Now an image or semblance (εἰκών) is what it is (i. e. a semblance) of something else, and therefore of it, as of every relative term, it is true that ἔστιν οὐδ' αὐτὸ τοῦτο ὅπερ ἐστὶν ἑαυτῆς. Thus we have the very formula of the text—except that instead of ὅπερ ἐστίν we find ἐφ' ᾧ γέγονε. The difference only seems to be then that instead of saying 'the very thing it is,' Plato says 'the very thing it was meant for.' The rendering given to the whole clause seems exactly what is wanted, and its correctness seems proved by the next clause, ἑτέρου δὲ τινὸς φέρεται φάντασμα; ἑτέρου τίνος corresponding to the τινός of the Republic, and being opposed to ἑαυτῆς.

This interpretation, however, was anticipated long ago in Kühner's Grammar, 'Ein Bild ist nicht einmal das, wozu es hervorgebracht ist, seiner selbst.' See Kühner, § 414, 5, b.

61. The author's emendations will next be considered: some have been incidentally treated already, and some of them as well as of those which follow may deserve the judgment which the editor, after his manner, pronounces on an emendation of Stallbaum's—' Stallbaum not understanding this sentence desires to corrupt it.'

47 C, φωνῆς τε δὴ καὶ ἀκοῆς περὶ πάλιν ὁ αὐτὸς λόγος, ἐπὶ ταὐτὰ τῶν αὐτῶν ἕνεκα παρὰ θεῶν δεδωρῆσθαι (i. e. that we may have knowledge of the rational movements of the heavens, and imitate them in 'the revolutions' of our own thoughts). λόγος τε γὰρ ἐπ' αὐτὰ ταῦτα τέτακται, τὴν μεγίστην ξυμβαλλόμενος εἰς αὐτὰ μοῖραν, ὅσον τ' αὖ μουσικῆς φωνῇ χρήσιμον πρὸς ἀκοήν, ἕνεκα ἁρμονίας ἐστὶ δοθέν. The editor brackets πρὸς ἀκοήν in the text and says, 'The words πρὸς ἀκοήν appear to me superfluous and unmeaning: I conceive them to be a marginal gloss on φωνῇ.'

The text is probably right. Two uses of sound are here distinguished. First, sound as language where its value is not as sound but as symbol of thought, this is referred to in the clause λόγος τε γὰρ κ.τ.λ. The second is a musical sound, where it is the sound as such which is of value. This distinction is brought out clearly in the second clause by the words πρὸς ἀκοήν. The first use is for the understanding, the later for the hearing. Just as we say 'a pleasure of the ear.' (This pleasure of the ear it appears in the sequel is to be however not the true end of music, but a means to effecting 'harmony' in the mind.)

Stallbaum, among his references, mentions a passage in which Plutarch refers to this place.

Plut. De Superst. 167 B, μουσικήν φησιν ὁ Πλάτων ἐμμελείας καὶ εὐρυθμίας δημιουργόν, ἀνθρώπων ὑπὸ θεῶν οὐ τρυφῆς ἕνεκα καὶ κνήσεως ὤτων δοθῆναι ἀλλὰ διὰ τὸ τῶν τῆς ψυχῆς περιόδων καὶ ἁρμονιῶν ταραχῶδες κ.τ.λ., where will be found the phrase κνῆσις ὤτων, which corresponds to the above idea.

Now it must be observed that Plutarch's words οὐ τρυφῆς ἕνεκα καὶ κινήσεως ὤτων δοθῆναι ἀλλὰ κ.τ.λ. correspond to the words of Plato in the continuation of the present passage, 47 D, οὐκ ἐφ' ἡδονὴν ἄλογον, καθάπερ νῦν εἶναι δοκεῖ χρήσιμος, ἀλλ' ἐπὶ τὴν γεγονυῖαν ἐν ἡμῖν ἀνάρμοστον ψυχῆς περίοδον... δέδοται κ.τ.λ. Thus χρήσιμος ἐφ' ἡδονὴν ἄλογον is made equivalent to χρήσιμος πρὸς κνῆσιν ὤτων, which answers to χρήσιμος πρὸς ἀκοήν. Thus the reading is doubly supported, for it will be seen that the sentence quoted from the text itself, 47 D, is in favour of it, even without the Plutarch.

It is a rule that a supposed corruption of a text should not be attributed to a gloss, without considering whether such a gloss was likely to be made. From the editor's point of view, at least, there could be no reason for glossing φωνῇ. We find, as so often, another inaccuracy in the same passage. The editor translates his own text 'But all such music as is *expressed in sound* has been granted for the sake of harmony.' This is an impossible rendering of ὅσον τ' αὖ μουσικῆς φωνῇ χρήσιμον. If the editor omits πρὸς ἀκοήν, he ought to translate 'all that part of music which is useful to us by means of sound': for Plato is speaking of the usefulness to us of sight and sound.

It is clear that the addition of πρὸς ἀκοήν gives clearness, and prevents an ambiguity the passage might else have had: the other part of μουσική is also 'useful to us by means of sound': it is intellectual instruction (cf. Rep. 376 E, μουσικῆς δ' εἰπὼν τίθης λόγους), and thus corresponds to the first use of sound, as speech in service of reason, which is referred to the first clause, λόγος τε γάρ κ.τ.λ. It might be described as ὅσον μουσικῆς φωνῇ χρήσιμον πρὸς λόγον. Chalcidius (see above) omits πρὸς ἀκοήν in translating, but it is easy to see that this might well be due to his not seeing the special meaning of it. C. F. Hermann puts the comma before πρὸς ἀκοήν instead of after it, but this does not seem to yield so good a sense.

The editor represents Stallbaum as reading φωνῆς: but Stallbaum's later edition has φωνῇ.

59 D–E. Here the process of freezing is described. Water, ὑγρὸν ὕδωρ, in the ordinary liquid state is, with Plato, mingled with fire, and is congealed by the separation of the fire from it. τοῦτο ὅταν πυρὸς ἀποχωρισθὲν ἀέρος τε μονωθῇ, γέγονε μὲν ἀμαλώτερον, ξυνέωσται δὲ ὑπὸ τῶν ἐξιόντων εἰς αὐτό, παγέν τε κ.τ.λ. This is, in the first place, translated by an apparent oversight, 'When relinquished by fire and

deserted of air, becomes more uniform, and is compressed by the outgoing elements; thus it is congealed.' This of course would necessitate ἀποχωρισθῇ. The words ἀερός τε are attacked in the note : ε probably not genuine. 'It is in this hard to see what air has to do with matter, no air entered into the composition of the ὑγρὸν ὕδωρ.... May not ἀερός τε be an interpolation from the hand of some copyist who thought it necessary to separate water from both kindred elements? The copyists have an unconquerable desire to drag in all the elements, whether they are wanted or not; see note on 61 B, where there is an indisputable interpolation.'

The editor seems to have forgotten a passage in which he himself has put in the element of air—a note or two back. In 59 D, Plato, speaking of bronze, says it is lighter than gold, τῷ μεγάλα ἐντὸς αὑτοῦ διαλείμματα ἔχειν. 'These,' according to the note, 'would appear to be cavities in the substance of metal *filled with air*.' Plato says nothing whatever about air filling these cavities. But no doubt the editor supposes it must do so because Plato maintains in 58 A seqq. that there is compressing force in nature tending to fill up all empty space by driving the smaller particles into the interstices of the larger—διὸ δὴ πῦρ μὲν εἰς ἅπαντα διελήλυθε μάλιστα, ἀὴρ δὲ δεύτερον, ὡς λεπτότητι δεύτερον ἔφυ. It is not therefore 'so hard to see what air has to do with the matter.' When the 'water mingled with fire' parts with its contained fire, it might happen, on Plato's principle, either that air penetrated into the vacant spaces, or that the watery particles themselves were forced closer together. Plato intends the latter, and thus the suspected words are relevant, for they exclude the former case. It may well be admitted that the words are not necessary, for they are omitted in the similar account of the solidification of molten metal, 59 A. On the one hand, however, the editor could not well argue from the latter place, because he assumes that air does get into the metal (in the case of bronze at least), and on the other hand, it is specially important to mention the expulsion of air in the case of freezing water, because according to 61 A the feeblest congelation of water (τὴν ἀσθενεστέραν ξύνοδον) can be melted by air getting into the interstices (τὰ διάκενα). The words do not look like an interpolation. An interpolator would be more likely to have added them after πυρός. There is a certain elegance in their position, and the rhythm of the sentence is spoiled if they are taken out.

Charges against the defenceless copyist are easily made. What evidence is there of his 'unconquerable desire to drag in all the elements, &c. ?' The editor gives but one single instance, and the 'indisputable interpolation' there is the supposed introduction of the two words πῦρ ἀέρα, in 61 B, where we have seen that it is the editor's grammar which is probably at fault; and that there is hardly reason to suppose more than the change (possibly by corruption) of one of these words (ἀέρα) from ὕδωρ.

In 61 C all the other editors read τὰ παθήματα ὅσα αἰσθητικά, and no variant is given. The editor substitutes αἰσθητά for αἰσθητικά, and prints αἰσθητά alone in his text. To explain this we must give his notes on this passage and one a few lines earlier. 61 C, καὶ τὰ μὲν δὴ σχήμασι κοινωνίαις τε καὶ μεταλλαγαῖς εἰς ἄλληλα πεποικιλμένα εἴδη σχεδὸν ἐπιδέδεικται· τὰ δὲ παθήματα αὐτῶν δι' ἃς αἰτίας γέγονε πειρατέον ἐμφανίζειν.

'The word πάθημα is here used in a rather peculiar manner. Elsewhere it denotes the impression sustained by the percipient subject from the external agent—see 64 B—C. But here πάθημα signifies a quality pertaining to the object which produces the impression on the subject.'

The note on παθήματα αἰσθητικά is—' I have taken upon me to make this correction of the MS. αἰσθητικά, which appears to me unmeaning. The two subjects to be handled are (1) the structure of the flesh, &c., how it is capable of receiving impressions; (2) the properties of objects, how they are capable of producing impressions. But the latter is expressed by αἰσθητά, not αἰσθητικά: how can the objects in the relation be termed sentient? The corruption has arisen, I doubt not, from failure to apprehend the peculiar significance of παθήματα. A similar confusion is found in 58 D, κινητικόν for κινητόν.'

Even if the editor were right as to the 'peculiar' significance of παθήματα, the alteration of the text is not a necessary inference from it, and is another instance of defective logic. In 61 C the words above quoted are followed by πρῶτον μὲν οὖν ὑπάρχειν αἴσθησιν δεῖ τοῖς λεγομένοις ἀεί. Thus the sensible qualities themselves are said to have αἴσθησις belonging to them. The editor, like Martin, calls attention to this, for to the note on the peculiar use of παθήματα he adds, 'We have a similar unusual significance in ὑπάρχειν αἴσθησιν below, where αἴσθησις denotes the property of exciting sensation.' Now if Plato departs so far from usage as to transfer the name of the subjective impression (πάθημα) to the quality in the object which causes it, and to extend what properly designates a state of the subject (αἴσθησιν ἔχειν) to the object which causes the state, it would only be a continuation of this extended usage to call αἰσθητικόν that which he has virtually called αἴσθησιν ἔχον. αἰσθητικόν is indeed nearly equivalent to αἴσθησιν ἔχον, and the one

H

expression might well share the ambiguity of the other. αἴσθησιν ἔχον is implied not only here in ὑπάρχειν αἴσθησιν but also below, 64 A, in κεκτῆσθαι αἴσθησιν—ὅσα διὰ τῶν τοῦ σώματος μορίων αἰσθήσεις κεκτημένα καὶ λύπας ἐν αὑτοῖς ἡδονάς θ' ἅμα ἑπομένας ἔχει.

Again through want of consistency the editor has missed a great opportunity. [1] In 37 B the text has λογιστικόν where νοητόν would have been expected—ὅταν μὲν περὶ τὸ αἰσθητὸν γίγνηται . . . ὅταν δὲ αὖ περὶ τὸ λογιστικὸν ᾖ. Instead of changing λογιστικόν (which is indeed sound) the editor presses the MS. reading into the service of his mistaken views about the existence of (modern) idealism in the Timaeus. He gravely maintains that λογιστικόν is substituted by Plato for νοητόν in order to convey the doctrine that thought is identical with its object. The value of the remark may be considered later; it is enough now to point out that the editor passes over the difficulty that if Plato had substituted λογιστικόν for νοητόν he would of course have put αἰσθητικόν for αἰσθητόν in the corresponding clause. The present passage, 61 C, gives a chance for doing something to help this defect. If the editor had thought of it, he might, from his habit in such subjects, have expounded the deep philosophic significance of the reading he has unluckily rejected as 'unmeaning': and shewn that this intentional substitution of αἰσθητικόν for αἰσθητόν could not have been made 'until he (Plato) had reached a period in his metaphysic where he deliberately affirmed the identity of thought and its object.' But it is pretty clear that if there had been a word λογιστόν used by Plato related to λογιστικόν as αἰσθητόν to αἰσθητικόν, the editor would have altered λογιστικόν there to λογιστόν (just as he alters αἰσθητικά here to αἰσθητά) and never thought of his idealism.

But apart from the fact that the MS. reading αἰσθητικά is not, as the editor supposes, inconsistent with his interpretation of παθήματα, that interpretation is erroneous. Martin has rightly said in his note that τὰ παθήματα αὐτῶν means (not the affections or qualities of bodies

---

[1] As we are upon this passage we may notice that it is not rightly construed by the editor: λόγος δὲ ὁ κατὰ ταὐτὸν ἀληθὴς γιγνόμενος περί τε θάτερον ὂν καὶ περὶ τὸ ταὐτόν, ἐν τῷ κινουμένῳ ὑφ' αὑτοῦ φερόμενος ἄνευ φθόγγου καὶ ἠχῆς, ὅταν μὲν περὶ τὸ αἰσθητὸν γίγνηται καὶ ὁ τοῦ θατέρου κύκλος ὀρθὸς ὢν εἰς πᾶσαν αὐτὰ τὴν ψυχὴν διαγγείλῃ, δόξαι καὶ πίστεις γίγνονται βέβαιοι καὶ ἀληθεῖς· ὅταν δὲ αὖ περὶ τὸ λογιστικὸν ᾖ καὶ ὁ τοῦ ταὐτοῦ κύκλος εὔτροχος ὢν αὐτὰ μηνύσῃ, νοῦς ἐπιστήμη τε ἐξ ἀνάγκης ἀποτελεῖται. The translation has 'This word of hers is true alike whether it deal with Same or with Other . . . and when she is busied with the sensible . . . then are formed true opinions &c., and when she is busied with the rational.' Here ψυχή (understood) is made subject of the clause ὅταν . . . γίγνηται and of the clause ὅταν ᾖ κ.τ.λ., whereas the subject of them both is λόγος. Thus λόγος is left without construction.

but) the affections *which they cause* in the percipient, and translates 'les impressions qu'elles produisent sur nous.' The context shews indeed that πάθημα is used in its ordinary sense: the editor has got into difficulty through the genitive. A few lines below heat is mentioned as one of these παθήματα, and it is said ὅτι μὲν γὰρ ὀξύ τι τὸ πάθος πάντες σχεδὸν αἰσθανόμεθα where the editor himself rightly translates πάθος by 'sensation.' Thus the text has not been corrupted by someone's 'failure to apprehend the peculiar significance of παθήματα.' But even if the editor had taken παθήματα rightly he would have had a difficulty with αἰσθητικά, from the meaning he supposes the word must have—'sentient,' i.e. with faculty of perception ('how can the object ... be sentient?'). The usual meaning is certainly 'sentient,' but αἰσθητικός also means sometimes 'what is connected with αἴσθησις.' For instance, in the Aristotelian expression φαντασία αἰσθητική the adjective has this general meaning. Here παθήματα αἰσθητικά are affections of the perceiving subject which belong to sense-perception: i.e. the sensations through which perception takes place.

Another matter has been pointed out to me which I had overlooked here, in which the editor again measures himself with C. F. Hermann with an unfortunate result. In 70 D Plato assigns to the lungs the function of cooling the heat of the heart. The MSS. reading is— καὶ περὶ τὴν καρδίαν αὐτὸν (sc. τὸν πλεύμονα) περιέστησαν οἷον ἅλμα μαλακόν, ἵν' ὁ θυμὸς ἡνίκα ἐν αὐτῇ ἀκμάζοι, πηδῶσα εἰς ὑπεῖκον καὶ ἀναψυχομένη πονοῦσα ἧττον, μᾶλλον τῷ λόγῳ μετὰ θυμοῦ δύναιτο ὑπηρετεῖν. For ἅλμα μαλακόν Hermann reads in his text μάλαγμα. Of this the editor says 'Hermann's μάλαγμα is as inappropriate as arbitrary. μάλαγμα means a poultice or fomentation; but the function of the lungs is distinctly stated just below, πηδῶσα εἰς ὑπεῖκον.' We have already given instances which shew how little trouble the editor takes to understand the text (Hermann's) on which he bases his own, and his imperfect acquaintance with Hermann's apparatus criticus. But here the editor surpasses himself. If he had read the note on this passage in Hermann's preface he might have discovered that μάλαγμα is entirely 'appropriate' and so far from 'arbitrary' that it has most important external testimony. Hermann in fact informs us that μάλαγμα means not only '*fomentum* apud medicos, sed apud mechanicos quoque velut *culcitas* coriaceas sive pelles alga farctas significat, quibus tormentorum ictus frangerentur.' That is, μάλαγμα means a 'fender' or a 'buffer,' and this is precisely the sense wanted in the passage: as appears even in the editor's translation 'as it were a soft *cushion* to spring upon.' Nor is Hermann's reading a mere conjecture. He got it out of the reproduction of this passage in Longinus de Sublimitate and the Isagoge of Alcinous—'ex Longino de Sublim. xxxii. 5 et Alcinoi Isagoge c. 23 restitui.' If the editor read this sentence, he must have done so without understanding that Hermann was not appealing to a usage of these authors, but to a reproduction by them of this very part of the Timaeus. But the same information might have been got from Liddell and Scott, who not only give the meaning of 'fender or buffer' to μάλαγμα, but actually add 'Longin. 32. 5 *quotes* Plat. (Tim. 70 C), where our MSS. give ἅλμα μαλακόν.' Add to this that Lindau also mentions the reading in Longinus and Alcinous, and, though he does not adopt it, rightly explains its meaning. Hermann explains how easily the corruption could have arisen. μαλακόν may easily have been substituted for the less familiar μάλαγμα, and then the correction αγμα written over the last two syllables of μαλακόν would easily become ἅλμα.

The editor explains the MSS. reading thus, 'There is certainly no reason for altering the text: Plato might very well say "a soft leap" for "a soft place to leap upon."' One cannot think Plato would have said anything of the kind. This is another piece of a priori scholarship—this time however 'a priori to the individual but not a priori to the race,' for it is found in Lindau, whom the editor does not mention. and in Martin who quotes Lindau ('comme un lieu mou pour y bondir') with just disapproval.

39 B, ἵνα δ' εἴη μέτρον ἐναργές τι πρὸς ἄλληλα (i.e. the planets) βραδυτῆτι καὶ τάχει, καὶ τὰ περὶ τὰς ὀκτὼ φορὰς πορεύοιτο, φῶς ὁ θεὸς ἀνῆψεν ἐν τῇ πρὸς γῆν δευτέρᾳ τῶν περιόδων, ὃ δὴ νῦν κεκλήκαμεν ἥλιον, ἵνα ὅτι μάλιστα εἰς ἅπαντα φαίνοι τὸν οὐρανὸν μετάσχοι τε ἀριθμοῦ τὰ ζῷα. This is the MSS. reading, Hermann proposed ὡς τά for καὶ τά. The editor reads καθ' ἅ in his text, with the sole remark 'καθ' ἅ scripsi.' This scarcely differs from the conjecture καθ' ὅ due to Wagner, whose book the editor has quoted in another place. The conjecture is also given as Wagner's in the note to the Engelmann translation which the editor uses so much. The reason the editor gives in his note is characteristic. The poetry and (as we shall see presently) the humour of Plato alike cause him difficulties.

'I have ventured upon this correction of MS. reading καὶ τά, which certainly cannot stand, involving as it does the *absurd hypothesis* that the heavenly bodies could not see their way until their orbits were illumined by the sun.' The reader with the passage quoted before him will not need a comment on this amusing faux pas, especially if he remembers that the planets are ζῷα with Plato. It is a part of the same mistake that the editor wrongly renders 'that there might be some *clear* measure'—it should of course be as in Jowett's translation 'some *visible* (ἐναργές) measure.' One may venture to think that no emendation is needed, and that the text is an easy hendiadys—'that the planets might have some visible measure of relative speed, and proceed on the course of their eight orbits '='that they might have some visible measure for their relative speed in their eight orbits.'

66 E. Speaking of odours Plato says δύ' οὖν ταῦτα ἀνώνυμα τὰ τούτων ποικίλματα γέγονεν, οὐκ ἐκ πολλῶν οὐδ' ἁπλῶν εἰδῶν ὄντα, ἀλλὰ διχῇ τὸ C' ἡδὺ καὶ τὸ λυπηρὸν αὐτόθι μόνω διαφανῆ λέγεσθον.

The editor prints in his text δι' οὖν. 'Although' he says 'all the MSS. agree in giving δύ' οὖν it is impossible to retain it. For the δύο εἴδη could only refer to the two divisions specified below, which are not ἀνώνυμα but ἡδύ and λυπηρόν.' He says nothing of the origin of the emendation, which he probably took from Hermann's text. Hermann's preface gives it as the reading of Stephanus. Stallbaum gives διὰ οὖν as the reading of the old editions. It is doubtful whether 'all the MSS. agree,' for Hermann says 'ex codicibus *fere* omnibus,' and it appears from Bekker that δύ' οὖν is in one of the MSS. a correction only. Whether the emendation is right or not, the editor's reason for it is wrong. The δύο εἴδη, which he rightly says would be referred to in the text, *are* ἀνώνυμα quâ odours; they have not designations which belong to them as such, as, e. g. red and blue to colours, and can only be distinguished by the attributes 'pleasant' and 'painful,' which they share with other sensations different to them in kind. Thus it is so far from being 'impossible' to retain the MSS. reading, that, if there were no other objection beside the editor's, there would be the strongest probability of its soundness. The first clause would state that there are δύο εἴδη and that they are ἀνώνυμα. The following clauses would expand and explain both these statements and are just of the form suited to do so.

38 C, ἐξ οὖν λόγου καὶ διανοίας θεοῦ τοιαύτης πρὸς χρόνου γένεσιν, ἵνα γεννηθῇ χρόνος, ἥλιος καὶ σελήνη καὶ πέντε ἀλλὰ ἄστρα, ἐπίκλην ἔχοντα πλανητά, εἰς διορισμὸν καὶ φυλακὴν ἀριθμῶν χρόνου. The editor brackets ἵνα γεννηθῇ χρόνος, because the words appear to him 'so unmistakably a mere gloss on πρὸς χρόνου γένεσιν.' As he rightly says they are not represented in Cicero's translation. But there is hardly

sufficient difficulty in πρὸς χρόνου γένεσιν to call for such a gloss; and no account is taken of the tendency to repetition, sometimes sententious, in the style of the personated Timaeus. The other editors were probably right in resisting the obvious temptation.

The following are illustrations of the tendency to repetition in the Timaeus.

42 C, μὴ παυόμενός τε ἐν τούτοις ἔτι κακίας, τρόπον ὃν κακύνοιτο, κατὰ τὴν ὁμοιότητα τῆς τοῦ τρόπου γενέσεως εἴς τινα τοιαύτην ἀεὶ μεταβάλοι θηρείον φύσιν. Where κατὰ τὴν ὁμοιότητα τῆς τοῦ τρόπου γενέσεως is a mere repetition in expanded form of τρόπον ὃν κακύνοιτο.

40 B, τὰ δὲ τρεπόμενα καὶ πλάνην τοιαύτην ἴσχοντα, καθάπερ ἐν τοῖς πρόσθεν ἐρρήθη, κατ' ἐκεῖνα γέγονε. Here κατ' ἐκεῖνα is redundant and means the same as καθάπερ ἐν τοῖς πρόσθεν ἐρρήθη.

42 E, ἔμενεν ἐν τῷ ἑαυτοῦ κατὰ τρόπον ἤθει. κατὰ τρόπον is somewhat superfluous.

In the next two passages words are supplied which are usually omitted as needless.

60 D, ᾧ γένει κέραμον ἐπωνομάκαμεν, τοῦτο γέγονεν which the editor himself notices as a 'rather elaborate form of expression,' and compare 40 B.

67 B, ἐν τοῖς ὕστερον λεχθησομένοις ἀνάγκη ῥηθῆναι.

Compare also the following: 35 A, τῆς ἀμερίστου καὶ ἀεὶ κατὰ ταὐτὰ ἐχούσης οὐσίας καὶ τῆς αὖ περὶ τὰ σώματα γιγνομένης μεριστῆς τρίτον ἐξ ἀμφοῖν ἐν μέσῳ ξυνεκεράσατο οὐσίας εἶδος, τῆς τε ταὐτοῦ φύσεως καὶ τῆς θατέρου, καὶ κατὰ ταὐτὰ ξυνέστησεν ἐν μέσῳ τοῦ τε ἀμεροῦς αὐτῶν καὶ τοῦ κατὰ τὰ σώματα μεριστοῦ.

In the very passage we are considering (38 C) διανοίας is added to λόγου. The repetition which occasions the emendation is not so difficult if πρὸς χρόνου γένεσιν is joined closely with what goes before it, and ἵνα γεννηθῇ χρόνος joined closely with what follows—pretty much as is done in the Engelmann translation, 'Zufolge solcher Betrachtung und der Ueberlegung Gottes in Beziehung auf die Entstehung der Zeit sind, damit die Zeit erzeugt würde, Sonne, Mond und die übrigen 5 Sterne ... entstanden.'

It may be noted that at the beginning of this chapter (38 B) the particles δ' οὖν are not rightly rendered—χρόνος δ' οὖν μετ' οὐρανοῦ γέγονεν: 'time *then* has come into being along with the universe.' δ' οὖν here resumes what has been interrupted by a digression, for χρόνος μετ' οὐρανοῦ γέγονεν repeats τότε ἅμα ἐκείνῳ ξυνισταμένῳ τὴν γένεσιν αὐτῶν μηχανᾶται, after which had come some discussion on the proper application of such differences of tense as 'is,' 'was,' 'shall be.' The sense is—'Well then, however that may be, time came into being with the universe.' Stallbaum has a note by which the editor might have profited, 'Ponitur δὲ οὖν quum dubitationi alicui imponitur finis atque dein ad aliud quid transitur.'

Against the failures among these somewhat confident condemnations of the text may be set a suggestion of the editor which seems valuable. In 40 D the vulgate is τὸ λέγειν ἄνευ διόψεως τούτων αὖ τῶν μιμημάτων μάταιος ἂν εἴη πόνος. Proclus quotes this passage and gives in one place ἄνευ τῶν δι' ὄψεως μιμημάτων, and in another αὐτῶν instead of αὖ τῶν. The editor proposes to introduce both these changes into the text. But he says nothing whatever of the fact that both of these variants in Proclus are pointed out by Lindau in his commentary, where special attention is drawn to them though they are not accepted. Again, the editor adds, 'Ficinus seems to have read αὐτῶν to judge from the word "ipsorum" in his rendering,' and this too is given in Lindau's note, 'Ficin. *absque* simulacrorum *ipsorum* inspectione. Junctum igitur is legit αὐτῶν,' &c. The editor does not cite Proclus quite accurately. He gives the reading as αὐτῶν τούτων; it should be τούτων αὐτῶν.

With the exception of some of the emendations, the mistakes we have been discussing are mainly grammatical; we may leave these, not that the list is exhausted, and proceed to consider some other mistakes of translation which for the most part do not depend on grammatical issues.

62. Though the editor supposes himself, as we have seen, to have observed an irony in a certain place which had generally escaped the commentators [1], he is not always successful in seeing the 'points' of a passage. For instance, in describing the human nails, Plato (76 D) says their true use was prospective. Men, the first human beings created, are destined to pass into the form of *women* and of the lower animals (γυναῖκες καὶ τἆλλα θηρία—in accordance with the rule that they who live unworthily are to degenerate), and the creating gods knew that many animals would find much use for their nails, therefore they formed nails in a rudimentary way as a foreshadowing of this future use (ὅθεν ἐν ἀνθρώποις εὐθὺς γιγνομένοις ὑπετυπώσαντο τὴν τῶν ὀνύχων γένεσιν). The sly allusion to the natural weapons of women—the

[1] Par. 18 above.

inferior animals are to find the true use of the nails—is entirely lost on the editor, who can only see ' a curious approximation to Darwinism in his statement.' We may return to the sequel of this amusing note hereafter.

Again, in the account of Atlantis, Plato, to give an idea of the size of the great ocean, makes the Mediterranean but a *harbour* in comparison. 25 A, τάδε μὲν γάρ, ὅσα ἐντὸς τοῦ στόματος οὗ λέγομεν (i. e. the pillars of Hercules), φαίνεται λιμὴν στενόν τινα ἔχων εἴσπλουν. ἐκεῖνο δὲ πέλαγος ὄντως κ.τ.λ.

The rendering given is, ' For those regions that lie within the strait aforesaid seem to be but a *bay* having a narrow entrance.'

In the same context (25 C) the point of a passage is spoilt by the rendering. The Egyptian priest is describing the successful resistance made by Athens to the invasion from Atlantis.

πάντων γὰρ προστᾶσα εὐψυχίᾳ καὶ τέχναις ὅσαι κατὰ πόλεμον, τὰ μὲν τῶν Ἑλλήνων ἡγουμένη, τὰ δ' αὐτὴ μονωθεῖσα ἐξ ἀνάγκης τῶν ἄλλων ἀποστάντων, ἐπὶ τοὺς ἐσχάτους ἀφικομένη κινδύνους, κρατήσασα μὲν τῶν ἐπιόντων τρόπαια ἔστησε.	' For being foremost upon earth in courage and the arts of war, sometimes she was leader of the Hellenes, sometimes she stood alone perforce, when the rest fell away from her; and after being brought into the uttermost perils, she vanquished the invaders and triumphed over them.'

The editor is aware of what others have remarked on—the likeness of the legend to the facts of the Persian invasion. The clause τὰ μὲν τῶν Ἑλλήνων ... ἀποστάντων represents the particular events of the war with Atlantis, whereas the translation coordinates it with πάντων προστᾶσα κ.τ.λ., a general account of the preeminence of Athens, as it would be if it described Athenian history in general. This collocation has also the awkwardness of putting the clause ' sometimes she stood alone ' and ' being foremost upon earth ' in the apparent relation of consequence and reason. The sense is ' For being foremost in courage and warlike arts, she conquered the invader, fighting sometimes at the head of the Greeks, and sometimes single-handed when the rest deserted her.'

In the same context there are some mistakes also of rendering.

25 C, ὑστέρῳ δὲ χρόνῳ σεισμῶν ἐξαισίων καὶ κατακλυσμῶν γενομένων, μιᾶς ἡμέρας καὶ νυκτὸς χαλεπῆς ἐπελθούσης, τό τε παρ' ὑμῖν μάχιμον πᾶν ἀθρόον ἔδυ κατὰ γῆς κ.τ.λ.

This is wrongly rendered, ' But in later time, *after* there had been exceeding great earthquakes and floods, there fell one day and night of destruction.' The clauses σεισμῶν ... γενομένων and μιᾶς ... ἐπελθούσης are put in a wrong relation. The day and night of destruction must have been a time of earthquake and flood, and not have come *after* these. Indeed, it can hardly be doubtful that the clauses are in entire apposition, and that Plato intends to represent the earthquake and flood as the events of one day. The passage thus gains in point.

24 E, τότε γὰρ πορεύσιμον ἦν τὸ ἐκεῖ πέλαγος· νῆσον γὰρ πρὸ τοῦ στόματος εἶχεν κ.τ.λ. The editor translates 'For in those days the sea could be crossed, *since* it had an island before the mouth of the strait, &c.' and explains, 'Plato means that since the Atlantic was thickly studded with large islands, it was possible for mariners to pass from one to another by easy stages until they reached the transatlantic continent.' It is evident from what comes later that this is not the meaning of πορεύσιμον. The editor has mistaken the force of the second γάρ, which introduces the whole account of the island of Atlantis and its disappearance. τότε πορεύσιμον is contrasted with the muddy and (possibly) shoaly state of the water caused by the subsidence of the island. Cf. 25 D, ἥ τε Ἀτλαντὶς νῆσος ὡσαύτως κατὰ τῆς γῆς δῦσα ἠφανίσθη· διὸ καὶ νῦν ἄπορον καὶ ἀδιερεύνητον γέγονε τὸ ἐκεῖ πέλαγος, πηλοῦ κάρτα βραχέος ἐμποδὼν ὄντος, ὃν ἡ νῆσος ἱζομένη παρέσχετο. Cf. also Critias 108 E, which Stallbaum quotes, νῦν δὲ ὑπὸ σεισμῶν δῦσαν ἄπορον πηλὸν τοῖς ἔνθενδε ἐκπλέουσιν ἐπὶ τὸ πᾶν πέλαγος.

In the passage of the Timaeus last quoted (25 D) the editor is not altogether happy. He may be right in following Hermann, who rejects βαθέος (as Stallbaum does), the reading of A for βραχέος. But he observes, 'A gives βαθέος, which is pointless: surely the question that would interest a sailor is how near the mud was to the surface: its depth he would regard with profound indifference.' The editor is obviously no sailor; the amateur of the Broads could have told him better. The note is an amusing instance of the confidence of his deliverances in all departments alike. The translation and continuation of the note shews that he does not see the point of πηλοῦ. 'There is little more to be said for Stallbaum's suggestion τραχέος. Accordingly I retain πηλοῦ κάρτα βραχέος in the sense of very shoaly mud.' The mud does not appear at all in the translation, which is 'being blocked by very shallow shoals.' Stallbaum's emendation is probably wrong, but it proves (see his note) that he saw what the editor has missed, viz. that the navigation was impeded, not only by the shallowness, but by the thick muddy state of the water which made it difficult to get through. Cf. ἄπορος πηλός in the Critias above quoted. It is probably some such tradition as to the state of the water of the Atlantic which is represented in Tacitus' Agricola x. 6 'sed mare *pigrum* et *grave remigantibus*, perhibent, ne ventis quidem perinde attolli,' though Tacitus himself says nothing about muddiness, and conjectures a different reason. This explanation, as well as the reading βαθέος, is confirmed by the translation of Chalcidius—'nisi quod pelagus illud *pigrius* quam caetera, *crasso* dehiscentis [desidentis?] insulae limo, et superne fluctibus concreto, habetur.' The editor's inaccurate account of the MS. reading, &c. has been noticed above.

22 B. Solon, after telling the Egyptians of Phoroneus and of Deucalion and Pyrrha, goes on τοὺς ἐξ αὐτῶν γενεαλογεῖν, καὶ τὰ τῶν ἐτῶν, ὅσα ἦν οἷς ἔλεγε πειρᾶσθαι διαμνημονεύων τοὺς χρόνους ἀριθμεῖν. Thus rendered, 'And he reckoned up their descendants, and tried by *calculating the periods*, to count up the number of years that *passed during* the events he related'—ὅσα ἔτη ἦν οἷς ἔλεγε of course means 'how many years ago were the events he related[1].' Cf. Jowett, 'how many years old were the events of which he was speaking.' The true sense of διαμνημονεύων τοὺς χρόνους is also missed: it means 'recalling the several periods or dates;' i.e. he tried to get back to the time of Deucalion through the periods or epochs corresponding to the stages of the genealogical list.

68 D, τὰ δὲ ἄλλα ἀπὸ τούτων σχεδὸν δῆλα αἷς ἂν ἀφομοιούμενα μίξεσι διασώζει τὸν εἰκότα μῦθον. Here the point of ἀφομοιούμενα and of μῦθον is missed in the translation, 'And for the remaining colours it is pretty clear from the foregoing to what combinations we ought to *assign* them so as to preserve the probability of our *account.*'

Plato uses ἀφομοιούμενα intentionally, and with reference to that tentative character of his physical speculation on which he strongly insists from time to time in the course of the dialogue. He calls them mere εἰκότα; and this sense of ἀφομοιούμενα is made the clearer by the following εἰκότα (μῦθον). It is also made perfectly clear in the next sentence, where he contrasts this mere approximation, which is all that is possible for men, with the divine knowledge. The sense is 'it is clear what combinations they may with probability be likened to.' μῦθον is used with the same association, and should be translated 'story.'

It is very doubtful whether it is right to join ἀπὸ τούτων δῆλον. It is more likely that τὰ δ' ἄλλα ἀπὸ τούτων should be joined, meaning 'the other combinations derived from the foregoing.'

46 A. In explanation of dreams it is said καταλειφθεισῶν δέ τινων κινήσεων μειζόνων, οἷαι καὶ ἐν οἵοις ἂν τόποις λείπωνται τοιαῦτα καὶ

---
[1] Cf. Herod. II. xiii. 2.

τοσαῦτα παρέσχοντο ἀφομοιωθέντα ἐντὸς ἔξω τε ἐγερθεῖσιν ἀπομνημονευόμενα φαντάσματα. This is rendered ' but if some of the stronger motions are left, according to their nature and the places where they remain, they engender visions . . . . which are within us, and when we awake *are remembered as outside us.*' The last words are without sense; perhaps they originate in some misunderstanding of Lindau. Quite a different explanation is given in the note, and no attempt made to relate it to the translation. ' The text may, I think, be explained as it stands : the images are copied within—that is, in the dream-world, and recalled to mind without—that is, when we have emerged from the dream-world.' This explanation seems not improbable, but it is not new. It is in Jowett—'which are remembered by us when we are awake and in the external world.' The editor mentions Martin's translation, with which he disagrees, but says nothing of Jowett's.

In 44 C is another instance of a priori scholarship—' τοῦ βίου διαπορευθεὶς ζωήν] " βίου ζωὴ = the conscious existence of his lifetime," ζωὴ being a more subjective term than βίος. Compare on the other hand Eurip. Herc. Fur. 664, ζωᾶς βιοτάν.' ζωὴ βίου is here simply the substantive corresponding to the verbal phrase ζῆν βίον, in which the two words differ no more than their equivalents do in the corresponding English phrase ' to live one's life.'

When ζῆν and βίος are distinguished, there is no mystery of ' subjectivity' or consciousness in the matter, for ζῆν is ascribed to plants. The distinction is well understood, and is e. g. fairly represented in Liddell and Scott (who, by the way, give the passage from Eurip. Herc. Fur. along with the passage of the Timaeus, under ζωή). See especially under βίος, βιόω, and ζάω. βίος refers to life as a state or a whole period ; ζῆν refers to life as an activity at any moment.

63. The discussion of this subject may be concluded by an examination of the editor's treatment of a passage upon vision (45 B).

The Greek must be given at some length. τοῦ πυρὸς ὅσον τὸ μὲν καίειν οὐκ ἔσχε, τὸ δὲ παρέχειν φῶς ἥμερον, οἰκεῖον ἑκάστης ἡμέρας, σῶμα ἐμηχανήσαντο γίγνεσθαι. τὸ γὰρ ἐντὸς ἡμῶν ἀδελφὸν ὂν τούτου πῦρ εἰλικρινὲς ἐποίησαν διὰ τῶν ὀμμάτων ῥεῖν λεῖον καὶ πυκνὸν ὅλον μέν, μάλιστα δὲ τὸ μέσον ξυμπιλήσαντες τῶν ὀμμάτων, ὥστε τὸ μὲν ἄλλο ὅσον παχύτερον στέγειν πᾶν, τὸ τοιοῦτον δὲ μόνον αὐτὸ καθαρὸν διηθεῖν. ὅταν οὖν μεθημερινὸν ᾖ φῶς περὶ τὸ τῆς ὄψεως ῥεῦμα, τότ' ἐκπῖπτον ὅμοιον πρὸς ὅμοιον, ξυμπαγὲς γενόμενον, ἓν σῶμα οἰκειωθὲν συνέστη κατὰ τὴν τῶν ὀμμάτων εὐθυωρίαν, ὅπηπερ ἂν ἀντερείδῃ τὸ προσπῖπτον ἔνδοθεν πρὸς ὃ τῶν ἔξω συνέπεσεν.

At the beginning of the passage the editor departs from Hermann's punctuation, omitting the comma after ἑκάστης ἡμέρας, and inserting one after πυκνόν. He translates the first part thus:—'Such sort of fire as had the property of yielding a gentle light but not of burning, they contrived to form into a substance akin to the light of every day. The fire within us, which is akin to the daylight, they made to flow pure smooth and dense through the eyes, having made close the whole fabric of the eyes and especially the pupils, so that they kept back all that was coarser and suffered only this to filter through unmixed and pure. Whenever then there is daylight surrounding the current of vision, then this issues forth as like into like, and coalescing with the light is formed into one uniform substance in the direct line of vision, wherever the stream issuing from within strikes upon some external object that falls in its way.'

The note is—

This punctuation is due to Madvig, who by merely expunging a comma has restored sense to the passage. Ordinarily a comma is placed after ἡμέρας, leaving us to face the inconvenient problem, how could the gods make into body that which was body already? For Martin's attempt to specialise the use of σῶμα in the sense of 'definitely formed matter' is hopeless. Eschewing the comma however, we get quite the right sense—they made it into a substance similar to the daylight, which is a subtle fire pervading the atmosphere. Thus too the γὰρ immediately following, to which Stallbaum takes exception, is justified; it introduces the explanation how the gods made the fire within us similar to the fire without.

The editor's explanation quite deserves the epithet he has applied to Martin. He himself is wrong in all the points which he so confidently maintains. The remark about the inconvenient problem as to how that could be made into a body which was a body already shews an entire misunderstanding of the drift of the passage. Plato obviously means that the gods took light (or 'the fire which does not burn') as a material, and out of it constructed a particular organ of sense—the ὄψεως ῥεῦμα in fact, for which reference may be made to what has been said above in par. 37, p. 64: just as out of flesh, &c. in general is made a particular organ, the hand, e. g. which is a σῶμα. The ὄψεως ῥεῦμα is as much a σῶμα as the hand, and like it adheres to our body. Compare the author's own note, 'The ὄψεως ῥεῦμα is just as much a part of ourselves as the brain or hand: this is clear from 64 D.' Looking at the Greek, it will be seen that the words τὸ γὰρ ἐντὸς κ.τ.λ. do not introduce an account of how the fire in our eyes is made like the light of day—they are assumed to be already alike in the word ἀδελφόν—but how a σῶμα is made out of this light and what σῶμα it is. The process described is not represented as terminating in any assimilation, but as having the formation of a σῶμα (ἓν σῶμα συνέστη) for its result by the union of the inner and outer light.

The imaginary difficulty about σῶμα in the first sentence being removed, it is clear that οἰκεῖον ἑκάστης ἡμέρας is coordinate with the preceding (ὅσον ἔσχε) τὸ παρέχειν φῶς ἥμερον, and like it belongs to the description of τοῦ πυρὸς ὅσον τὸ καίειν οὐκ ἔσχε. Indeed, apart from the proof which the passage as a whole gives, the first two sentences contain evidence enough of the untenableness of the editor's view. The 'fire' in the first sentence could not, according to that view, be the same in kind as the light of day, or there would be no reason for the contrivance to make the one like the other. Yet it is defined by general expressions which naturally describe the light of day, and not something to be distinguished from it—τὸ καίειν οὐκ ἔσχε, τὸ δὲ παρέχειν φῶς ἥμερον. Again Stallbaum says that there is here a play on the words ἡμέρα and ἥμερος, and refers to the etymology in the Cratylus. The editor repeats this (without acknowledgment), and with his usual logic does not perceive how strongly this confirms the construction which he rejects. If there is a play on the words it is hardly conceivable that οἰκεῖον ἑκάστης ἡμέρας could be anything but in apposition to παρέχον φῶς ἥμερον, or rather ὅσον ἔσχε τὸ παρέχειν φῶς ἥμερον. The rendering of the first sentence is too harsh to be probable. It is difficult to believe, also, that Plato can have intended οἰκεῖον ἑκάστης ἡμέρας (which naturally means 'light proper to day') to mean 'akin to the light of day' ('a substance akin to the light of every day'). It is the harsher, because in the next sentence τούτου (τὸ ἐντὸς ἡμῶν ἀδελφὸν ὂν τούτου) naturally refers back to τοῦ πυρὸς ὅσον κ.τ.λ., whereas the editor really refers it to τὸ ἑκάστης ἡμέρας πῦρ, which he has to get out of ἑκάστης ἡμέρας.

'Eschewing the comma' was a misfortune: the insertion of a comma after πυκνόν is another, and a serious one. The editor has misunderstood the construction. He makes λεῖον καὶ πυκνόν predicate of τὸ ἐντὸς ἡμῶν πῦρ: see the above quoted translation. But πυκνόν ('dense' as the editor rightly translates) is the exact opposite of what this 'fire' is to be, as is most evident from what follows: it is to be strained through the close structure (ξυμπιλ.) of the eye and refined,—ὥστε τὸ μὲν ἄλλο ὅσον παχύτερον στέγειν, τὸ τοιοῦτον δὲ μόνον αὐτὸ καθαρὸν διηθεῖν. The editor's confusion is shewn by the note (p. 153) which gives the argument of this context. While the translation has 'they made to flow smooth, pure and *dense* through the eyes,' the note has 'from the eyes issues forth a stream of clear and *subtle* fire.' It ought to be 'subtle'; but that cannot be πυκνόν, the meaning of which is illustrated below, 75 A, πυκνὸν ὀστοῦν, 'bone of dense structure.' πυκνόν should of course be joined with ξυμπιλήσαντες, and refers to the eyes; the same is true of λεῖον, and the construction is 'having compressed the whole texture of the eyes, and especially the middle part of it, so as to be smooth and dense.' The combination πυκνὸν καὶ λεῖον is also used in the Republic to describe a substance with smooth reflecting surface, 510 E, ὅσα πυκνά τε καὶ λεῖα καὶ φανά. Cf. also here 46 A, (κάτοπτρα) καὶ πάντα ὅσα ἐμφανῆ καὶ λεῖα.

The editor gets wrong also in the remainder of the passage. He renders ὅπηπερ ἂν ἀντερείδῃ κ.τ.λ., 'wherever the stream issuing from within strikes upon some external object that falls in its way.' It should be, 'When it thrusts directly against the light from the external object which meets it.' The editor seems to think that the passage ὅταν οὖν μεθημερινόν κ.τ.λ. only treats of the coalescence between the light from the eyes and the daylight in general which surrounds us, but obviously the latter clause of it, at least, treats of the coalescence between the light from the eyes and the rays of light which emanate from the object. This is what Theophrastus understood Plato to mean, and it becomes still clearer in the following passage on mirrors. The editor himself is there (46 A) obliged to assume two coalescences, one of the light from the eyes with daylight in general, and a second between this combination and the rays from the object: and yet according to his rendering Plato would have said nothing of the latter in his general account of vision. His rendering also makes no sense: for if the coalescence were only between the light from the eyes and the daylight in general, it would also happen when the 'stream issuing from within' did *not* strike on an external object, and thus the condition ὅπηπερ ἂν κ.τ.λ., as interpreted by the editor, would be meaningless [1].

At the end of the discussion of reflection which follows the passage we have quoted, the editor's rendering seems very improbable. Speaking of the reversed position of the image in concave mirrors (cylindrical not spherical) Plato says (46 C), τοῦτο δέ, ὅταν ἡ τῶν κατόπτρων λειότης, ἔνθεν καὶ ἔνθεν ὕψη λαβοῦσα, τὸ δεξιὸν εἰς τὸ ἀριστερὸν μέρος ἀπώσῃ τῆς ὄψεως καὶ θάτερον ἐπὶ θάτερον. κατὰ δὲ τὸ μῆκος

---

[1] It has been assumed in the above criticism that Plato may have intended two coalescences. And that some understood him so would be gathered from 'Plutarch' de Plac. Phil. IV. xiii. But the natural interpretation of ὅταν οὖν μεθημερινόν κ.τ.λ. is that the only daylight with which the 'stream of vision' coalesces is that which comes from the object seen. It seems likely therefore that the theory of the two coalescences is a mistake. It does not seem to be found in Aristotle or Theophrastus.

στραφὲν τοῦ προσώπου ταὐτὸν τοῦτο ὕπτιον ἐποίησε πᾶν φαίνεσθαι, τὸ κάτω πρὸς τὸ ἄνω τῆς αὐγῆς τό τ' ἄνω πρὸς τὸ κάτω πάλιν ἀπῶσαν.

The second sentence is rendered 'but if it is turned lengthwise to the face, it makes *the same reflection appear* completely upside down.' ταὐτὸν τοῦτο, however, is the configuration of the mirror described above (ἡ τῶν κατόπτρων λειότης ἔνθεν κ.τ.λ.) and στραφέν agrees with it. In the editor's translation the latter has nothing to agree with either before or after, and he has to get κάτοπτρον for it out of κατόπτρων. 'Lengthwise to the face' is also incorrect.

The sense appears to be 'but if turned *in the direction of the length of* the face this *same configuration of the mirror* makes everything appear upside down.'

A little above in the same passage (46 A fin.) occur the words πολλαχῇ μεταρρυθμισθέντος, referring to the reflected light (or 'fire' as Plato calls it). This is translated 'in manifold ways deflected' with the note 'πολλ. μετ. refers, I conceive, to the various angles at which the rays are reflected, corresponding to the different angles of incidence.' Perhaps this is an unguarded inference from 'variam intelligit lucis reflexionem vel refractionem' &c. in Stallbaum from whom he appears to have derived the preceding part of his note with reference to Seneca (see above, par. 3).

μεταρρυθμισθέντος simply means 'having had its form changed.' The word is used thus in Aristotle (cit. Bonitz, Liddell and Scott), and in Herodotus (cit. Liddell and Scott). It is used in a similar sense in this very dialogue, 91 D.

Lastly, there is in these notes a severe and contemptuous criticism of Aristotle's objection to Plato's theory of vision. The editor entirely mistakes the point, and his failure is exemplary. It may be discussed later.

64. In closing the unfavourable review of the editor's scholarship, it is but fair to record the few instances which have been observed, where he seems really to have improved on a commonly accepted translation or reading. We have seen that his claims in this respect are sometimes very ill founded.

[1] 50 A, θερμὸν ἢ λευκὸν ἢ καὶ ὁτιοῦν τῶν ἐναντίων. Here some of the

---

[1] A little above 49 E the text has φεύγει γὰρ οὐκ ὑπομένον τὴν τοῦ τόδε καὶ τοῦτο καὶ τὴν τῷδε καὶ πᾶσαν ὅση μόνιμα ὡς ὄντα αὐτὰ ἐνδείκνυται φάσις. The article (τοῦ) would be expected before τῷδε: and the latter word itself may be suspected. It may be doubted whether it occurs in this kind of formula in Plato, or whether it could be trans-

other translators (perhaps including Lindau whose rendering is not clear) take ἐναντία as opposites of 'hot' and 'white,' but the editor rightly notes 'Not the opposites to hot and white, but any of the ἐναντιότητες which are the attributes predicable of matter.'

Chalcidius took the same view. (See above par. 50.) It is however not new among modern interpreters. Cousin understands ἐναντία in the same way.

61 C, καὶ τὰ μὲν δὴ σχήμασι κοινωνίαις τε. Here the editor makes a much needed correction.

<small>For σχήμασι the editors from Stallbaum onwards, with the exception of Martin, read σχήματα *sub silentio.* This reading is not mentioned by Bekker, and no ms. testimony is by any one cited for it. It is by no means an improvement; and since I can find neither its origin nor its authority I have suffered it ἐρήμην ὀφλεῖν and reverted to the old reading. Ficinus translates 'eas species, quae figuris commutationibusque invicem variantur.'</small>

This is, however, not quite complete. Stallbaum, it is true, reads σχήματα in the text, and in the heading of his note. But the editor should have mentioned that Stallbaum in his app. crit. quotes the text rightly—καὶ τὰ μὲν δὴ σχήμασι, so that perhaps the change in his text is some accident.

In 60 B, a valuable correction is made. The editor translates ὅσον δὲ διαχυτικὸν μέχρι φύσεως τῶν περὶ τὸ στόμα ξυνόδων by 'that which expands the contracted pores of the mouth to their natural condition,' and seems only right in saying 'the construction and meaning of these words seem to have escaped all the editors.'

The others have been misled by comparing what is said of salt, a little below, 60 D—τὸ δ' εὐάρμοστον ἐν ταῖς κοινωνίαις ταῖς περὶ τὴν τοῦ στόματος αἴσθησιν, for they suppose that the ξύνοδοι περὶ τὸ στόμα are the same probably as κοινωνίαι περὶ τὴν τοῦ στόματος αἴσθησιν. The editor, on the other hand, has rightly seen that the true comparison is with 66 C, τὰ δὲ παρὰ φύσιν ξυνεστῶτα κ.τ.λ. He is perhaps, however, hardly first in the field. The key to the passage lies in ξύνοδοι, the true meaning of this is found by comparing a group of passages in this dialogue where it means 'junction' or 'contraction.' The editor quotes some of these. But the association of this passage with the group had already been made by Liddell and Scott.

<small>lated 'relative to this,' as in the editor's rendering. One may venture to suggest τοῦ ὧδε in place of τῷδε. Compare the parallel passages Theaetet. 157 B, 183 A (quoted by the editor), in the latter of which is found δεῖ δὲ οὐδὲ τοῦτο τὸ οὕτω λέγειν· οὐδὲ γὰρ ἂν ἔτι κινοῖτο τὸ οὕτω κ.τ.λ.</small>

PART IV.

THE EDITOR'S NOTE ON THE MOTION OF THE PLANETS VENUS AND MARS, AND SOME POINTS IN HIS REPLY.

65. The matter of this Part would properly be reserved for the discussion of the editor's note on the scientific subjects, but it is added here in order to complete the answer to the editor's reply.

In the 'Classical Review' the editor's note on the motions of Venus and Mercury was cited as a case where he puts forward a theory, which from his manner would be thought new, though it is far from being so. This is one of the criticisms to which he has replied.

The passage is in 38 D, ἑωσφόρον δὲ καὶ τὸν ἱερὸν Ἑρμοῦ λεγόμενον εἰς τοὺς τάχει μὲν ἰσόδρομον ἡλίῳ κύκλον ἰόντας, τὴν δ' ἐναντίαν εἰληχότας αὐτῷ δύναμιν· ὅθεν καταλαμβάνουσί τε καὶ καταλαμβάνονται κατὰ ταὐτὰ ὑπ' ἀλλήλων ἥλιός τε καὶ ὁ τοῦ Ἑρμοῦ καὶ ἑωσφόρος.

There are two main explanations of the words ἐναντίαν εἰληχότας αὐτῷ δύναμιν. The first is, that Plato supposes the planets Mercury and Venus to revolve in a direction opposite to that of the sun, and explains in this way the fact that these planets are sometimes in advance of the sun (in the direction of the apparent rotation of the heavens) and sometimes behind it.

According to the second theory the ἐναντία δύναμις does not refer to a difference in direction of revolution. The difference supposed to be meant is, that the two planets shew a variation in their orbits, due to what is called retrogradation, to which the sun is not liable. As is well known, a planet, in its apparent path in the heavens, sometimes seems to stop, and then to go backwards, relative to the general direction of its motion; it stops again, and then resumes what is called its 'direct motion.' The Greeks were aware of this, and after Plato's time came to invent the theory of epicycles to account for it.

The editor speaks of the first theory, which he rejects, as if it were the usual one—'These words are usually understood to mean that Venus and Mercury revolve in a direction contrary to that of the sun.' He introduces the second, with which he agrees, in a way which might make the reader suppose it was its first appearance in literature.

This is rather an inversion of the relation between the theories. As to the first—it does not seem to have been held by the ancient commentators. Chalcidius, of whose views Martin speaks, did not hold it, nor did Proclus, nor the commentators mentioned by Proclus— Theodorus, Porphyry, Iamblichus, and certain 'mathematicians.' Cicero's translation does not shew how he took the passage, Martin even thinks it may indicate an opinion like that of Proclus. Alcinous (quoted by Martin) alters the Greek. The theory of contrary revolution does not even seem to be mentioned by the ancient commentators above named. One of the opinions quoted by Chalcidius (cviii.) is a little like it, but is not the same, for it depends on epicycles : and it would make no difference, because the editor seems unacquainted with Chalcidius. Of the modern editors Lindau and Stallbaum neither hold it nor notice it. Martin, who is probably right, maintains it at some length, and is perhaps the first editor who did so, though the passage is translated in this sense (apparently) in Cousin's translation, which appeared two years before Martin's edition.

Information about the second theory, shewing that it was held in ancient times, is given in Martin's note on this passage. He says (vol. ii. p. 72) 'Proclus nous apprend que quelques astronomes prétendaient trouver dans le *Timée* la théorie des excentriques et des épicycles appliquée à l'explication des mouvements de Vénus et de Mercure.'

Now as the epicycles were invented to account for the retrogradations (according to Martin, with special reference to those of Mercury and Venus), it follows that these astronomers (or mathematicians, as Proclus calls them) thought that Plato, in the passage before us, was referring to those peculiarities in the form of the planet's apparent orbit caused by retrogradation.

Among other places, Proclus refers to these mathematicians in 259 A (one of Martin's references)—ἐναντιοῦνται δὲ (sc. Ἀφροδίτη καὶ Ἑρμῆς) πρὸς αὐτὸν (sc. ἥλιον) οὐ κατὰ τὴν ἐν τοῖς ἐπικύκλοις μόνον φοράν, ὡς εἴπομεν πρότερον καὶ οἱ μαθηματικοί φασιν.

ἐναντιοῦνται πρὸς αὐτόν of course corresponds to Plato's ἐναντίαν εἰληχότας αὐτῷ δύναμιν. These 'mathematicians' then thought that the characteristic in which the two planets according to Plato are 'opposed' to the sun lay in the kind of motion which they accounted for by epicycles. Whether they supposed really that Plato himself explained this motion by epicycles may well be doubted, for though Iamblichus (Procl. 258 E) and Proclus apparently thought they did, there may easily have been some misunderstanding: this, however, does not concern the present argument.

But whatever uncertainty there may be about this or any other point in the interpretation of these mathematicians, the view that Plato is speaking of the phenomena of alternate 'retrograde' and 'direct' motion, without any reference to epicycles, is also represented in Proclus.

Martin says that Proclus rejected the idea that the theory of epicycles was referred to in the Timaeus. In fact Proclus (258 E) quotes Iamblichus with seeming approval thus—ὁ δέ γε θεῖος Ἰάμβλιχος οὔτε τὰς τῶν ἐπικύκλων παρεισκυκλήσεις ἀποδέχεται ὡς μεμηχανημένας καὶ ἀλλοτρίως τοῦ Πλάτωνος εἰσαγομένας, οὔτε κ.τ.λ. And he says on his own account (221 F—one of Martin's references) ἀλλ' οὐδὲ Πλάτων ἢ ἐν τούτοις ἢ ἐν ἄλλοις ἐπικύκλων ἢ ἐκκέντρων ποιεῖται μνείαν.

On the other hand he gives as one of the ways in which the δύναμις of the two planets may be called ἐναντία to that of the sun, the following (259 B)—εἴποις δ' ἂν καὶ διότι ὁ μὲν ἥλιος οὔτε ἀφαιρέσεσιν οὔτε προσθέσεσι χρῆται τῶν κινήσεων οὔτε στηριγμοῖς, Ἑρμῆς δὲ καὶ Ἀφροδίτη προποδισμοῖς χρῶνται καὶ στηριγμοῖς καὶ ὑποποδισμοῖς, ἐναντίας αὐτοὺς εἰληχέναι πρὸς τὸν ἥλιον κατὰ τὸ φαινόμενον δυνάμεις. This of course means that the two planets have an alternation of 'retrograde' and 'direct' motion which the sun has not. Cf. also 221 E.

This ancient explanation is the same as that given by the editor. 'What I believe,' he says, 'it [i.e. the ἐναντία δύναμις] to be may be understood from the accompanying figure,' &c. Then after describing retrogradation by the figure, he continues, 'Now this is just what I believe is the ἐναντία δύναμις, this tendency on the part of Venus, as viewed from the earth, periodically to retrace her steps.' This 'retracing of her steps' is exactly ὑποποδισμός.

Now though the editor calls the view which hardly seems to have been maintained before Martin the usual one, he says nothing of the antiquity of the one which he adopts: and it was pointed out in the Classical Review that he gave it even with an appearance of originality. Also, that though he might not have read it in Proclus, attention was called to it in Martin's note which he had before him, and which he had made use of.

In reply the editor says '*this view* [i. e. that which he adopts] *is to be found neither in Martin's note nor in that of Proclus.*' [!]

66. There is another point which may be conveniently treated here, because it arises on this passage (38 D) and is one of the subjects of that part of the editor's reply with which the preceding paragraph is concerned.

The criticism in the Classical Review contained the following remark on the note about retrogradation.

<small>The bit of modern astronomy (illustrated by a woodcut) which the editor quite needlessly adds, illustrates once more the dangers of unfamiliar ground. So also do the notes he adventures, in 31, on the mathematical sense of δύναμις and Greek treatment of number.</small>

The editor in reply quotes this, omitting the last sentence, and says—

<small>Hereupon it is only to be remarked, first that it is this *quite needless* ' bit of modern astronomy' which alone contains my view of the passage; secondly that this view is to be found neither in Martin's note nor in that of Proclus.</small>

With this is associated the following personality in a note—

<small>Woodcuts, by the way, seem to have an alarming effect upon Mr. Wilson: he always charges, head down and eyes shut, whenever he meets one.</small>

There are two points in my criticism: the first is the needlessness of the modern astronomy inserted in the note, and the second is the danger of it to the editor. His answer here on the first point is merely verbal ('alone contains my view'): he must know the meaning and justice of the criticism.

The part of his note which was referred to is this:

<small>What I believe it (i. e. the ἐναντία δύναμις) to be may be understood from the accompanying figure, which is copied from part of a diagram in Arago's *Popular Astronomy*. This represents the motion of Venus relative to the earth during one year, as observed in 1713. It will be seen that the planet pursues her path among the stars pretty steadily from January to May; after that she wavers, begins a retrograde movement, and then once more resumes her old course, thus forming a loop, which is traversed from May to August. After that she proceeds unfaltering on her way for the rest of the year. This process is repeated so that five such loops are formed in eight years. Mercury behaves in precisely the same way, except that his curve is very much more complex and the loops occur at far shorter intervals. Now this is just what I believe is the ἐναντία δύναμις, this tendency on the part of Venus, as viewed from the earth, periodically to retrace her steps.</small>

It will be evident from the last paragraph (65) that the editor could have stated his views quite simply and generally, and was under no obligation whatever to put in this detailed account with a figure shewing the positions held by the planet Venus in the year 1713, in every month from January to December. Even if such a note were right, it would be particularly out of place in this edition, for, as we have said, the editor in his Preface excuses the omission of far more important matters on the ground that 'the commentary would have been swelled to an unwieldy bulk.' The editor might have referred to some manual, if he wished anything further; but such additions are as tempting to some writers as they are unsafe for them. The editor includes in his quotation, without comment, the second part of the criticisms 'the dangers of unfamiliar ground,' and is as unconscious of its possible meaning as he is of the remark on his mistake about the De Ossium Natura. The note in fact has a characteristic which has been already observed: it gives information useless to those acquainted with the subject, and misleading to those who are not.

In the first place the lay reader would carry away the impression which the editor clearly has himself, that the effect of retrogradation is always to loop the planet's apparent path; but this is not so. The effect is sometimes, as in the case of this very planet (Venus), to produce not loops, but a sort of zigzag, or a sinuation in shape like the letter S. See, for instance, Lockyer's Elementary Lessons in Astronomy, fig. 34, 'Path of Venus among the constellations.'

But there is a more serious mistake. The editor appears to have confused two very different diagrams.

The proper figure to illustrate Plato's text would be a representation of the apparent path which a planet 'as viewed from the earth,' describes 'among the stars,' which is a mere matter of observation, and might be made with more or less accuracy by a Greek of Plato's time. This is also such a figure as the reader would expect, and it is evidently such as the editor thinks he is giving from the way in which he speaks of it.

But unfortunately he has taken from Arago a diagram representing a different matter, through a confusion not unnatural to one unaccustomed to the subject. It is not the apparent path of the planet in the heavens, but a plan of what may be called the real motion of the planet relative to the earth [1]. It is not such a figure as Plato could

---

[1] Approximately it may be described as the path traced by the foot of an ordinate from the planet upon the plane of the ecliptic considered as fixed relative to the earth's centre and axis.

have had before him, but a result of the discoveries of modern astronomy on the heliocentric system, and is derived by calculation from a knowledge of the true elliptic paths described by the earth and Venus round the sun.

It is a plan not of the path of a planet as it would look to a spectator on the earth, but a calculation of the path as it would look to a spectator considerably above the earth on a line through its centre perpendicular to the ecliptic. What would appear to such a spectator as a loop, would sometimes appear to a spectator on the earth sometimes as an open sinuation, sometimes as a very flat loop, because the eye of the spectator on the earth being so near the plane of the planet's orbit, the loop is seen nearly edgeways,—so flat that it might escape the early observers, and probably did so: e.g. there is no proof whatever that Plato knew of these apparent loops at all.

The figure given by the editor might have been used by a writer acquainted with the subject to shew the *real* relative motion, and to explain from it the appearances which Plato or the astronomers of his time might have observed; though it would not have been much to the purpose for the interpretation of the text, as not only is there no evidence that Plato knew even roughly that the motion of the planet relative to the earth is of this kind, but all his explicit statements in the Timaeus about planetary motion are incompatible with it. Such a writer however using the figure in such a way would of course have distinguished it from the *apparent* path. The absence of this necessary distinction and explanation is due to the confusion which the editor has made.

His mistake appears in another expression. He says the figure 'represents the motion of Venus relative to the earth during one year, as *observed* in 1713.' So far from representing anything 'observed' in 1713, it represents no observation at all, but the result of a calculation, and it was published in 1709, four years before the time when the editor supposes the observation to have been made. The dates, at least, he might have learned from the book whence he took the diagram. Cassini (who made the calculation) died in 1712, that is a year before the time when, according to the editor, he made the observation. The kind of diagram which the editor really wanted, he would have found in the Plates added at the end of vol. i. of Arago, Nos. xiii. and xiv.

The editor will at length understand the nature of the 'alarming effect' produced by his woodcuts.

67. In the note on 22 D there are some peculiarities which, when the nature of some of the inaccuracies already observed is considered, suggest there has been some slip about the meaning of ῥυόμενος.

In the text the priest explaining how Egypt is saved at periods when the rest of the earth is devastated by fire, is made to say ἡμῖν δὲ ὁ Νεῖλος εἴς τε τἆλλα σωτὴρ καὶ τότε ἐκ ταύτης τῆς ἀπορίας σῴζει λυόμενος (v. l. ῥυόμενος).

The note is as follows:—

λυόμενος] The explanation given of this word by Proklos is utterly worthless: λύεται γὰρ Ἀττικῶς ὅτι λύει τῆς ἀπορίας ἡμᾶς ὁ Νεῖλος. Even conceding the more than doubtful Atticism of λυόμενος = λύων (the only authority Stallbaum can quote is a very uncertain instance in Xenophon *de venatu* I 17), the clumsy tautology of the participle, thus understood, is glaring. It appears to me that the right interpretation has been suggested by Porphyrios, whom Proklos quotes with disapprobation [1]. Πορφύριος μὲν δή φησιν, ὅτι δόξα ἦν παλαιὰ Αἰγυπτίων τὸ ὕδωρ κάτωθεν ἀναβλυστάνειν τῇ ἀναβάσει τοῦ Νείλου, διὸ καὶ ἱδρῶτα γῆς ἐκάλουν τὸν Νεῖλον, καὶ τὸ ἐπανιέναι κάτωθεν ταὐτὸ τῷ Αἰγυπτίῳ δηλοῦν καὶ τὸ σῴζειν λυόμενον, οὐχ ὅτι ἡ χιὼν λυομένη τὸ πλῆθος τῶν ὑδάτων ποιεῖ, ἀλλ' ὅτι λύεται ἀπὸ τῶν ἑαυτοῦ πηγῶν καὶ πρόεισιν εἰς τὸ ἐμφανὲς ἐπεχόμενος πρότερον. Nothing can be more natural than that the Egyptians should have believed that the 'earth is full of secret springs,' which by their breaking forth gave rise to the inundation. It is true that there is still need of an explanation why the springs burst forth at a certain season: but the ancient Egyptians do not stand alone in supposing that they solve a difficulty by removing it a stage further back. λυόμενος will therefore mean 'being released' by the unsealing of its subterranean founts. This explanation also gives a good and natural sense to κάτωθεν ἐπανιέναι below. I hold it then undesirable to admit ῥυόμενος, which is the reading of some inferior MSS.

It will be observed that in the first part of this note λυόμενος in the sense of 'delivering' is rejected with emphasis. [2] The chief reason is that 'the clumsy tautology of the participle ... is glaring' when joined to a verb σῴζει of kindred meaning. It might be expected that here the reading ῥυόμενος would be dismissed for the same reason and with the same emphasis: for obviously being equivalent to the rejected sense of λυόμενος it would produce the same tautology[3]. But in this part of the note nothing is said of ῥυόμενος.

In the second part of the note a scarcely possible interpretation, of the kind not unusual with a scholiast, is adopted (λυόμενος = 'being released from its subterranean founts') and what is said of ῥυόμενος appears closely connected with this. At the end of the argument in favour of keeping λυόμενος in this sense, is im-

---

[1] This interpretation (Porphyry quoted by Proclus) is quoted in Lindau's note here.
[2] The soundness of this reason will be discussed hereafter.
[3] Thus e. g. Stallbaum after defending the meaning of λυόμενος = delivering, immediately adds the rejection of the equivalent ῥυόμενος 'Itaque nihili est quod alii habent ῥυόμενος.'

mediately added as if part of the subject, 'I hold it then undesirable to admit ῥυόμενος,' &c. This is just the place and the manner in which a reading would be rejected which would give the same general sense to the passage as λυόμενος with the meaning proposed. After saying that such a meaning would suit the context, it would be natural to add in such words as the editor uses, the rejection of a reading nearly equivalent but with less MSS. authority as 'undesirable.'

It is true that though the first part of the note would be a natural place for rejecting ῥυόμενος rightly understood, yet the editor might very well reserve what he had to say of it till he had done with λυόμενος. Then, however, it is difficult to think (1) that he would not give as a strong reason against it the fact that it would be a tautology, and (2) that he would not use some stronger expression than 'undesirable.' The emphatic condemnation 'the clumsy tautology of the participle is glaring' would, as already said, apply to it as much as to the first discussed meaning of λύομενος. Nor is it the editor's manner to speak so leniently of what he has (as he thinks) such reason to condemn. Cf. his expression in this same note 'The explanation given of the word by Proclus is utterly worthless.'

Thus it remains that ῥυόμενος is rejected in the connection and in the manner appropriate to a word supposed equivalent to λυόμενος = released from its founts.

It becomes then worth while to look at the authorities used by the editor, because peculiarities in his notes seem often thus accounted for.

In one of these, the Engelmann translation, is found a note which looks like a confirmation, and seems also to explain the nature of the supposed slip.

The translation follows the reading ῥυόμενος and refers it to the flooding of the Nile 'indem er austritt.' To this is appended a note which will be given with the editor's beside it—omitting non-essentials, such as the remark on the wisdom of the Egyptians.

> Wir haben zwar die von den meisten und besten Handschriften gebotene Lesart λυόμενος beibehalten, können aber nicht umhin, einzugestehen, dass uns die in einigen Codd. erhaltene Lesart ῥυόμενος den Vorzug zu verdienen scheine. Denn λυόμενος ist nicht nur aus anderen Gründen anstössig, sondern gewährt auch keinen passenden Sinn.

Even conceding the more than doubtful Atticism of λυόμενος = λύων (the only authority Stallbaum can quote is a very uncertain instance in Xenophon *de venatu* I 17), *the clumsy tautology of the participle thus understood is glaring.*

It appears to me that the right interpretation has been suggested by Porphyrios, whom Proklos quotes &c., &c. . . . λυόμενος will therefore mean 'being released' by the unsealing of its subterranean founts. This explanation also gives a good and natural sense to κάτωθεν ἐπανιέναι below. I hold it then undesirable to admit ῥυόμενος, which is the reading of some inferior MSS.

Zwar sagen der Scholiast und Suidas: λυόμενος Ἀττικῶς ἀντὶ τοῦ λύων τῆς ἀπορίας ὁ Νεῖλος ἡμᾶς [quoted by Stallbaum along with de Venatu], doch ist diese Bemerkung wohl erst zu Gunsten dieser Stelle erdacht. *Indess sollte dies auch nicht der Fall sein*, so enthält doch λυόμενος einen höchst unnützigen und schleppenden Zusatz zu den Worten ἐκ ταύτης τῆς ἀπορίας σώζει.

Man erwartet vielmehr die Art und Weise bezeichnet, durch welche gerade der Nil, und nicht auch andere Flüsse, ein Retter gegen jene Feuersgefahr wird, und dies geschieht ja eben durch den zu gewissen Zeiten regelmässig wiederkehrenden Austritt desselben. Wir sind daher in unserer Uebersetzung der Lesart ῥυόμενος gefolgt.

The correspondence of the argument in the first part of the English note with the German is obvious, and the similarity of expression in the emphatic passage is striking.

The second part of the English note gets out of the reading λυόμενος the same meaning in effect as in the corresponding part of the German note is got out of ῥυόμενος, and the form of this part of the English note is what would be natural if intended really to answer such an argument in favour of ῥυόμενος as is expressed in the German note—an answer tacitly admitting that the interpretation of ῥυόμενος was right in the German, but shewing it 'undesirable' to admit the inferior reading (cf. beginning of German note) because the better reading gave the required sense.

If this were so, it would quite clear up all the peculiarities first remarked in the English note.

There is a further corroborative circumstance. The correspondence in one part pointed out makes it likely that the editor had read the German note: and it is likely also because, as he expressly says, the book containing it is one which he has used, and he would naturally look at it in such difficult places as the present, if he looked at it at all. But if so, and if he saw ῥυόμενος was wrongly taken, it is more than likely that he would have pointed out the mistake. There is a tendency in his edition to go out of the way to point out mistakes or supposed mistakes in other books.

To this may be added that the error would be a slip far more venial than some others made in the edition.

[138]

There are some other matters of interest here. The sentence 'The explanation [of λυόμενος] gives a good and natural sense to κάτωθεν ἐπανιέναι below' illustrates the frequently defective logic of the editor. He is trying to make out in favour of his view of λυόμενος that it explains κάτωθεν ἐπανιέναι. But the latter phrase is clear enough in its context, and it is really on the very probable interpretation of it that the very doubtful interpretation given to λυόμενος has to depend, as is clear from the commentary quoted by the editor, καὶ τὸ ἐπανιέναι κάτωθεν ταὐτὸ τῷ Αἰγυπτίῳ δηλοῦν καὶ τὸ σῴζειν λυόμενον ... ὅτι λύεται ἀπὸ τῶν ἑαυτοῦ πηγῶν. As to the objection to Stallbaum's view, the reading is not really uncertain in the De Venatu. The variants rather confirm the text. Modern editors indeed pronounce the preface to the De Venatu spurious, although one may suspect this was unknown to the editor, for else he would hardly have missed the opportunity of sneering at Stallbaum, and according to his practice elsewhere he would probably have written Pseudo-Xenophon. But if this sense of the middle voice of λύω is doubtful, the sense of 'ransoming' seems near enough. And Suidas, quoted by Stallbaum, actually has λυόμενος, ἀντὶ τοῦ λυτρούμενος καὶ ἀπολύων, οὕτω Πλάτων. Too much should not be made of the tautology, for as we have seen (page 118), the style of the Timaeus inclines to a certain sententious repetition. The view Stallbaum follows, condemned as 'utterly worthless' by the editor, is at least better than what he himself adopts. It is scarcely probable that λυόμενος standing alone and without anything before to lead up to it could have the interpretation maintained by Porphyrius, which is artificial, though not surprising in a Greek commentator.

Is it possible that the text is unsound? ΛΥΟΜΕΝΟϹ could be easily corrupted from ΑΥΞΟΜΕΝΟϹ, a word used of the Nile in a scholium (cit. Stallb.) on this context.

Yet perhaps the text is sufficiently defended, as above indicated, by that very peculiarity of repetition which, looked on only as 'clumsy tautology,' leads the editor and others to reject it.

68. The evidence that the English note was written under some misconception about the meaning of ῥυόμενος is circumstantial; but the chain seems so complete that, though I did not expect the reader merely with the edition before him would see at once the ground for my remark in the Classical Review [1], I thought the editor would be the

[1] See next note.

last person to dispute it, and I confess that I was at first surprised at his reply[1].

Under ordinary circumstances I should have felt the reply must be accepted as a denial, and that it shewed this to be a case where strong circumstantial evidence had failed, and the coincidences remarked to be only curious accidents. I should therefore have thought it proper to withdraw the criticism expressly, not merely to drop it in silence: though I should have pointed out that I had so far done no injustice, seeing that the evidence was strong and the argument of a kind to which the editor's work is fairly liable from what is proved of it.

But the circumstances are not ordinary. In the first place, the most charitable explanation of much which the editor says is defect of memory and confusion of mind. In the second place, the editor has point blank denied statements in my review about the commentary of Proclus and the notes of Martin, where the evidence is not circumstantial, but an ocular demonstration can easily be given, and has been given[2]. On what verbal ambiguity he can be relying in order to vindicate in any shape his denial of those statements I do not know. There is room therefore for a similar doubt about what may be behind his reply here also.

It should be observed further that there is not really here a point blank denial. The editor seems only to appeal to the absence in his note of any direct statement of the meaning of $ῥυόμενος$ (cf. 'there is not a word more'), but he does not deny that he made some slip or other about its meaning. Ordinarily one would say it was a mere quibble to distinguish such an answer as the editor makes from a complete denial. This, however, cannot be securely maintained after what has just been referred to. And besides, an instance can be given where also there is not an actual categorical denial, and where also from the editor's tone the reader would certainly suppose a complete denial conveyed, where nevertheless it can be shewn that the categorical denial which was not given could not be given.

---

[1] The editor refers to the criticism as an 'extraordinary mare's nest' and continues:—In 22 D I retain in my text the vulgate $λυόμενος$, which in the note (following a suggestion of Porphyry's quoted by Proclus) I support, contending that although it cannot bear the sense of 'delivering,' which is given to it by some, it is admissible and appropriate in the sense of 'being released.' And having thus, in my judgment, sufficiently defended the reading, I end with these words: 'I hold it then undesirable to admit $ῥυόμενος$, which is the reading of some inferior MSS.' There is not a word more. Hereupon Mr. Wilson is inspired with the following happy thought: 'In 22 D the note shews that $ῥυόμενος$ "delivering" is taken for something like "flowing" or "overflowing," a mistake evidently from the German translation used by the editor!'

[2] Par. 65.

69. The case is as follows. In the Classical Review among other remarks of mine on the editor's note to 38 D occurs this—

> The editor's attack here on Martin is an instance of the method which vitiates his interpretation everywhere. He assumes Plato couldn't mean anything which would get him into a certain kind of difficulty, and makes rash generalisations about his infallibility in this respect which the *Timaeus* itself confutes.

In his reply the editor says—

> Furthermore it might be interesting to learn wherein consists an 'attack upon Martin,' which our critic attributes to me. I refer to Martin three times in this connexion, and each time with approval.

Here there is no actual denial that Martin was attacked, but the impression which the reply is certain to convey to the reader is (1) that the editor was blamed for attacking Martin, and (2) that he was so far from attacking Martin's view that he only spoke of it with approval, and that therefore he had been the victim of a deliberate misrepresentation.

Now (1) from what is above quoted of the criticism passed on the editor, it will be at once evident that the point of it was not that he attacked Martin, but that the attack was unsuccessful. And (2) as for what the reply would convey of the editor's attitude, the truth is that he did not 'approve' at all of Martin's view as to the motion ascribed by Plato to Mercury and Venus (the point in question), a view which he had before him in a note which he uses and quotes from.

Martin held that in 38 D the words τὴν ἐναντίαν εἰληχότας αὐτῷ δύναμιν mean that the two planets revolve in a direction contrary to that of the sun: the editor, as already seen, disagrees entirely with this. Not only so, but he attacks Martin's view, and attacks it in rather strong terms. His words (in which 'the contrary motion' is the kind Martin means) are as follows—

> If the contrary motion of the two planets is insisted on, the result follows that we have here the one theory in the whole dialogue which is *manifestly*[1] *and flagrantly inadequate*. Plato's physical theories, however far they may differ from the conclusions of modern science, usually offer a fair and reasonable explanation of such facts as were known to him: they are sometimes singularly felicitous, and never *absurd*. *I cannot then believe that he has here presented us with a hypothesis so obviously futile.*

Thus the editor has done the very thing which his reply would be supposed emphatically to deny. What can be the meaning of this? A conjecture may be offered.

---

[1] The italics are not in the original.

The editor in the place where he attacks the view in question does not mention Martin's name. Perhaps, then, he means he has not attacked Martin, but would admit he attacked Martin's view. Or perhaps he would say it is not Martin's view because others beside Martin have held it. (For instance, the first sentence of his note is 'These words are *usually* understood to mean that Venus and Mercury revolve in a direction contrary to that of the sun. This view I believe to be untenable.') This would not only be an evasion, but an unfortunate one. For, as said above, Martin is the principal, if not quite the first, representative of this theory, which is not in the chief ancient commentators, and which appears in modern editions for the first time in Martin, though Cousin had translated in this sense two years before Martin's edition. Besides a comparison of the editor's note with that of Martin which he had before him, and otherwise quotes, shews that it was Martin whom he had in mind in the attack quoted [1].

But what can the 'approval' mean? for after what has been quoted from the editor's own note, it may be wondered how such an expression can be explained. The answer this time is simple. The approval which the reader would suppose, if it were at all relevant to the editor's defence, to be approval of the view which he was said to have attacked, is not approval of that view at all, but of something else.

Apparently the editor gets *three* instances of approval ('I refer to Martin three times in this connection, and each time with approval'), by taking in the preceding note where he had quoted as probably true a remark of Martin's which has nothing at all to do with the question of the 'contrary motion.' It refers to something in the same passage, and thus the editor gets it in under the general expression 'in this connection.'

The second reference to Martin is a quotation of 'his statement of the facts which it is supposed the contrary motion is intended to explain.' Here there is no expression of approval. Indeed, while the facts as facts are subject neither to disapproval or approval, the editor would on his theory apparently disapprove of Martin's view that they are the facts Plato wishes to explain.

The third reference to Martin is an approval not of Martin's view, but of what the editor considers a serious objection to it, stated by Martin himself:—'Now, as Martin observes, the theory of contrary

---

[1] It is in fact so natural to speak as I did that it never even occurred to me that I had used a phrase the editor would object to.

motion' [Plato's theory according to Martin's view] 'is flagrantly inadequate to account for these facts.'

These seem to be the only three places to be found in which Martin's name is mentioned 'in this connexion;' and it turns out that the only instance of approval relevant to the matter before us, is one where the editor does not approve of Martin's view. ('*I cannot then believe that he has here presented us with a hypothesis so obviously futile.*' For the whole passage, see above, page 140.)

Here, then, is a clearly proved case of apparent denial, seeming even to amount to the opposite of the statement which is traversed ('approval,' in fact, instead of 'attack'), so that the fact that there happens to be no categorical denial would never be noticed: where nevertheless, as has been shewn, a real denial could not be made, and reliance appears to have been put on some mere verbal distinction.

70. The argument in the preceding paragraph, against the editor's first reply, has been purposely retained, though since it was written he has given a second reply in the Classical Review. (See Class. Rev., May, 1889.)

In my first short answer I gave as a test of the value of the editor's statements the part of his reply criticised in the foregoing paragraph.

The editor accepted this test. In the more than confident tone of his reply and in the personalities which accompany it the editor has again run a great risk, for failure would mean disaster. His words are as follows—

I have but a few words to add in reference to Mr. Wilson's attempt at replying to my criticisms. I am in no wise concerned, as I have already said, with his opinion of my scholarship and philosophy, but only with his imputations of *mala fides*. I therefore refrain from all comment on his remarks, except as regards the point which he puts forward as a test question between himself and me and which beyond doubt answers that purpose admirably.

In attempting to justify his assertion that I attack Martin in a certain passage, he quotes part of my animadversions upon the contrary motion which, as is commonly thought, Plato assigns to Venus and Mercury. This is no theory of Martin's, but a popular and obvious interpretation of Plato's words, which Martin repeats, presumably because he saw nothing better for it, but to which he urges the gravest objection. The passage cited from my note strongly emphasises the objection which Martin felt, and which any one must feel, to this astronomical hypothesis, and simply amplifies a sentence in the very same note, which is this: 'Now, *as Martin observes*, the theory of contrary motion is flagrantly inadequate to account for those facts.' The 'attack upon Martin' is actually and expressly an argument on Martin's side.

Now Mr. Wilson either saw this or he did not: the inference in either case need not be precisely specified. He may then write a pamphlet, or (as perhaps his style would lead us to expect) a stout quarto, without being troubled by any more observations on my part. Far be it from me to interfere with this austere moralist in the execution of what he 'conceives a public duty.'

Here the editor takes the line which had been in anticipation described in the foregoing paragraph as 'an unfortunate evasion.' He says the theory is not Martin's because Martin 'repeats' it from others. He even gives the reader the impression that Martin merely repeated it as the best he knew of, that he was dissatisfied with it, and urged a strong objection to it, and that (so far) he is himself 'actually and expressly on Martin's side.' All this constitutes an incredible perversion of the facts: facts which are most obvious to anyone with Martin before him.

(1) Martin 'repeats' this theory from no one. As already said, he is the principal exponent of it. Without citing anyone else's authority he puts it forward on his own account, and bases it on the natural sense of the words and on the evidence of another passage, 36 D. He just notes the fact that Cousin agreed with him quite at the end of his note and incident to a criticism of Cousin [1].

(2) The theory is Martin's in the fullest sense. He adopts it entirely and unreservedly, he decides for it in the most positive and unmistakable language. In the very remarks to which the editor replies, I quoted the following sentence from Martin which is by itself decisive, 'Platon a voulu dire *bien positivement* que ces deux planètes suivent *une direction opposée à celle du soleil.*'

'Now' (to speak in the editor's language) 'either he saw this sentence in the Classical Review or he did not: the inference in either case need not be precisely specified.' To prevent even the possibility of doubt on the issue it is only necessary to quote some of the context from which the above sentence is taken.

'La phrase de Platon signifie donc *évidemment*, que Mercure et Vénus vont *dans le sens contraire à celui où va le soleil*. En effet, plus haut [2], après avoir dit que le cercle de la nature de l'autre et le cercle de la nature du même vont en deux sens contraires, Platon a ajouté que les sept cercles dont se compose le cercle de la nature de l'autre, c'est-à-dire les sept cercles des planètes vont en des sens contraires les uns aux autres, ἀλλήλοις. Quels sont donc ceux qui ne *vont pas dans le même sens* que la majorité? Platon nous l'apprend ici: ce sont ceux de Mercure

---

[1] Martin merely says of Cousin's interpretation of another clause in the passage 'le sens que M. Cousin a adopté, serait parfaitement conforme à l'hypothèse de Proclus, mais est inconciliable avec celle que M. Cousin a reconnu comme moi dans le *Timée.*'

[2] The passage referred to is 36 D.

et de Vénus. Dans ce même passage, Platon nous avait dit que quatre de ces cercles font leurs révolutions avec des promptitudes diverses, trois avec des promptitudes égales. Nous voyons maintenant que ces trois derniers sont ceux du soleil, de Mercure et de Vénus. Ces deux passages, ainsi rapprochés, s'expliquent l'un par l'autre, et *établissent d'une manière incontestable* le sens de la théorie des mouvements de Vénus et de Mercure d'après le Timée. *Platon a voulu dire bien positivement que ces deux planètes suivent une direction opposée à celle du soleil*; d'ailleurs la suite de la phrase *le prouve*, " C'est pour cela, ajoute Platon, que ces trois planètes s'atteignent et sont atteintes semblablement, κατὰ ταὐτά, les unes par les autres." En effet, quand deux corps *vont à la rencontre* l'un de l'autre, ils s'atteignent mutuellement; or, d'après la phrase de Platon, *c'est ce qui a lieu pour le soleil d'une part, et de l'autre pour Mercure et Vénus.*'

(3) The difficulty of which Martin speaks, and of which the editor makes so much capital, has been entirely misrepresented by him.

It is simply untrue that Martin 'urges' the difficulty 'as the gravest objection' to the view that Plato means Mercury and Venus to move in a direction opposite to that of the sun. On the contrary, as we have seen, he holds the view 'incontestable:' instead of supposing it wrong, he holds that Plato himself made a mistake, and gave a theory in disagreement with some obvious phenomena. So far from the editor being 'on Martin's side,' Martin actually condemns those commentators who, like the editor, have allowed this disagreement with facts to prevent them from giving the words what is, according to Martin, their natural and necessary meaning.

To make quite clear the extent of the editor's misrepresentation, we must again quote a passage from Martin.

' Platon au sujet des mouvements de Mercure et de Vénus, paraît s'être arrêté surtout à cette observation, qu'au bout de la révolution annuelle du soleil, elles se trouvent toujours à une assez faible distance de cet astre, et en avoir conclu que leurs révolutions, quelles qu'en puissent être les irrégularités, s'effectuent toujours à peu près dans un an. S'il en était resté là, son opinion eût été du moins à peu près d'accord avec les premières apparences; mais *il ajoute que leur mouvement est dans le sens contraire à celui du mouvement annuel du soleil.* Il avait sans doute remarqué que ces deux planètes avancent souvent sur cet astre; mais, si ce qu'il dit était vrai, elles devraient prendre toujours de plus en plus de l'avance sur lui, puisque leur mouvement planétaire serait dans le sens du mouvement diurne; et après s'être écartées de lui suivant tous les angles possibles, et avoir gagné sur lui un jour, elles devraient paraître en même temps que lui sur l'horizon, puis le devancer encore. Or, au contraire, elles ne s'écartent de lui qu'à une faible distance. Cette hypothèse, *énoncée si brièvement par Platon en deux endroits du Timée,* est donc en contradiction évidente avec les faits les plus faciles à observer.

On conçoit que les commentateurs aient fait difficulté de voir dans ce dialogue une opinion si denuée de vraisemblance,' &c.

In what follows Martin gives the various interpretations to which commentators have been reduced in order to make Plato's words agree with facts, and calls them forcées and fausses.

At the end of his long note he points out further that Cicero's translation of 36 D (contrariis inter se motibus) gives a new verification of the interpretation of the passage which he has maintained. 'Sans rentrer dans la discussion d'une question déjà résolue plus haut, je me contente de faire remarquer cette autorité nouvelle et peu suspecte, en faveur de l'interprétation que j'ai donnée.'

In an important essay published years after his Commentary on the Timaeus—an essay which, it may be remarked, the editor never seems even to have heard of—Martin emphatically reaffirms the same interpretation, calling it 'le seul sens possible des mots.'

K

Oxford
HORACE HART, PRINTER TO THE UNIVERSITY

THE

CLASSICAL

REVIEW.

VOLUME XVIII

London:
DAVID NUTT, 57-59 LONG ACRE.
1904.

RICHARD CLAY AND SONS, LIMITED,
BREAD STREET HILL, E.C., AND
BUNGAY, SUFFOLK.

ON THE PLATONIST DOCTRINE OF THE ἀσύμβλητοι ἀριθμοί.

§ 1. ARISTOTLE *Nic. Eth.* I. vi. and *Metaph.* M. vi.

AN interesting article in the February number of the *Classical Review* discusses what is said to be 'a well-known difficulty,' amounting to 'seeming contradiction'[1] between the following passages :—*Nic. Eth.* I. vi. 1096^a 17 οἱ δὴ κομίσαντες τὴν δόξαν ταύτην οὐκ ἐποίουν ἰδέας ἐν οἷς τὸ πρότερον καὶ ὕστερον ἔλεγον, διόπερ οὐδὲ τῶν ἀριθμῶν ἰδέαν κατεσκεύαζον : *Metaph.* M. vi. 1080^b 11 οἱ μὲν οὖν ἀμφοτέρους φασὶν εἶναι τοὺς ἀριθμούς, τὸν μὲν ἔχοντα τὸ πρότερον καὶ ὕστερον τὰς ἰδέας, τὸν δὲ μαθηματικὸν παρὰ τὰς ἰδέας καὶ τὰ αἰσθητά, καὶ χωριστοὺς ἀμφοτέρους τῶν αἰσθητῶν. The difficulty, surely, is imaginary, and only due to one of those slips of interpretation sometimes made by distinguished critics in very plain matters. The writer of the article must pardon a fellow-student for thinking that in it the true nature of the mistake has not been made clear, and that—perhaps in consequence—the simplicity of the issue and of its solution have not been realised : further that the interpretation given of the passage from the *Ethics* is not correct, owing to a misunderstanding of the drift of a passage referred to from *Metaph.* B. iv.

The seeming contradiction arose simply from a misinterpretation of the first clause in the passage from the *Ethics*. According to the *Metaphysics*, the Ideal numbers stand in the relation of πρότερον καὶ ὕστερον. The words in the *Ethics*, on the other hand, οὐκ ἐποίουν ἰδέας ἐν οἷς τὸ πρότερον καὶ ὕστερον ἔλεγον were taken to mean that there were no 'Ideas' at all[2] in the case of things related as πρότερον and ὕστερον. This would necessitate that the numbers referred to in the *Metaphysics* as having in them the πρότερον καὶ ὕστερον could not be Ideas, and so would contradict the statement in the *Metaphysics* that they were.

But the first clause of the *Ethics* passage means, not that the Platonists allowed no Ideas at all in the sphere of the πρότερον καὶ ὕστερον, but that in the case of a group whose members were in this relation, there was no one single Idea to correspond to the group as such. Aristotle uses the plural ἰδέας and not the singular ἰδέαν, because he is thinking of such groups in general. There is no implication that the members of a group of the kind could not be themselves Ideas. And with this the whole difficulty disappears.

The second clause means that the Platonists in consequence of the doctrine ascribed to them in the first clause did not recognise one Idea of the Numbers, as they held the Numbers stood in the relation of πρότερον καὶ ὕστερον.

Thus if we had no other passage from the *Metaphysics* except that which was supposed to contradict the *Ethics*, we should by combining the two places arrive at this perfectly coherent result :—The later Platonists held that the Ideal numbers were in the relation of πρότερον καὶ ὕστερον to one another (*Met.*). They also held that when the members of a group stood in that relation there was no one Idea corresponding to the group (*Eth.*). Consequently they held that the Ideal numbers had no one Idea of number corresponding to them as a group ; *i.e.* there was

---

[1] Cp. Trendelenburg, *Platonis de ideis et numeris doctrina ex Aristotele illustrata*, p. 80 : 'locos duos inter se, ut videtur, repugnantes.' Zeller, *Plat. Stud.* p. 243 : 'mit welcher Stelle, die ihr widersprechende,' etc.

[2] Cp. Trend. *l.c.*: 'his inter se collatis, alterum, ideas eum definiri numerum, qui habeat prius et posterius, altero, non ideas factas eorum in quibus sit prius et posterius, prorsus repugnat.' Brandis, *Rhein. Mus.* 2 (1828), p. 563. Zeller, *Phil. d. Gr.*, 3rd ed., II. i. p. 571 : 'Wie lässt sich nun aber mit dieser Auffassung...die Angabe vereinigen dass Plato und seine Schule von demjenigen in dem Vor und Nach stattfindet, *keine* Ideen angenommen haben?' Zeller himself, who at first followed Trendelenburg, but eventually realised the essentials of the interpretation of the *Ethics* passage, does not happen to say that the difficulty was merely due to this mistranslation, his attention being taken up with the questions about the meaning of τὸ πρότερον καὶ ὕστερον raised by those who misunderstood the *Ethics* text.

no 'Idea' corresponding to ἀριθμός in general (*Eth.*). There would then be no disagreement, and we need nothing further for the reconciliation of the two passages taken alone.

But there is another passage in the *Metaphysics* itself (999ᵃ 6) which when combined with the above passage from the same treatise gives exactly the same result as the combination of that passage with the *Ethics*.

Met. B iii. 999ᵃ 6 ἔτι ἐν οἷς τὸ πρότερον καὶ ὕστερόν ἐστιν, οὐχ οἷόν τε τὸ ἐπὶ τούτων εἶναί τι παρὰ ταῦτα. οἷον εἰ πρώτη τῶν ἀριθμῶν ἡ δυάς, οὐκ ἔσται τις ἀριθμὸς παρὰ τὰ εἴδη τῶν ἀριθμῶν.' According to this if a group of things stand in the relation of πρότερον καὶ ὕστερον, their common predicate (τὸ ἐπὶ τούτων) cannot be some common element distinguishable (παρά) from them. What this more exactly means will be considered later, for the moment we are only concerned with the application made of it in the context, which is that since the εἴδη τῶν ἀριθμῶν stand in the relation of 'prior and posterior,' there is no ἀριθμός distinguishable from these εἴδη. If the Platonists accepted this sort of reasoning—and we learn from the *Ethics* that they did, then since they held the Ideal numbers stood in such relation, they would necessarily hold that there was no one Idea corresponding to this group as such, *i.e.* that there was no Idea of ἀριθμός. Thus the result of the two passages from the *Metaphysics* agrees entirely with the passage from the *Ethics*, and there is not the smallest discrepancy between the two treatises.

The foregoing is all that is relevant to shew the unreality of the supposed difficulty. Nothing turns upon what the exact meaning of τὸ πρότερον καὶ ὕστερον may be, and it is not necessary to enquire, for instance, if it refers to some process of γέννησις, or even to discuss it at all for the real issue between the passages, however otherwise interesting. Nor is it right to suppose the meaning of the *Ethics* to be that 'the Idealists did not view the higher (logically soluble) *genera* as Ideas.' 'Logically soluble' appears to stand for 'capable of differentiation into species,' so that the meaning would be 'the Idealists allow no Idea except for *infimae species.*' This doctrine is not really contained in the passages before us. All that is ascribed to the Idealists is the doctrine that when species are related to one another as 'prior and posterior' there could be for them no one Idea. Thus for instance, it is not a true inference from *Metaph.* 999ᵃ 6, above quoted, that ''Ἀριθμός does not constitute in itself an ἰδέα because it is divisible into a variety of εἴδη.' The principle stated in this passage is not applied to the Platonic Ideas at all; and if it were, the result would be that there was no ἰδέα of ἀριθμός, not because ἀριθμός was divisible into εἴδη, but because its εἴδη stand to one another in the relation of πρότερον καὶ ὕστερον. The εἴδη meant are the δυάς, τριάς, τετράς, etc., etc., of which the δυάς is prior to the τριάς and all the rest, the τριάς, to the τετράς and all the rest, and so on. The bearing of the whole passage of which 999ᵃ 6–9, is a part will be considered later.[1]

§ 2.—*Current views on the ἀσύμβλητοι ἀριθμοί and the doctrine of τὰ μεταξύ.*

We may turn to some questions of somewhat greater difficulty.

What is the true meaning, and what is the origin of the doctrine that the Ideal numbers were ἀσύμβλητοι, and of the doctrine associated with it that the objects of mathematics, τὰ μαθηματικά are μεταξύ—between the Ideas and the world of sense?

According to the theory of Ideas represented by Plato's writings, there were of course Ideas of number. In a later development of Platonism, of which we hear through Aristotle, all 'Ideas' were somehow identified with Numbers. The Ideas of numbers, ἰδέαι τῶν ἀριθμῶν, of the earlier theory, and the Idea-numbers of the later may both be called 'Ideal numbers,' and this general expression has been used in the foregoing for a reason which will appear hereafter.

It is perhaps the generally accepted view that ἀσύμβλητοι ἀριθμοί was a designation only applied to the Idea-numbers of the later theory and suited to them alone. It might seem that 'Ideas' would only be called numbers in some metaphorical way, and that the name ἀριθμοὶ ἀσύμβλητοι indicated the Idea-numbers had not the properties of true number; for to say they could not be added would be to say that no arithmetical relation was possible between them. Bonitz expressly remarks (Comm. on *Metaph.* p. 540) that the name ἀσύμβλητοι shews nothing numerical was really intended :—hos numeros, qui idearum exprimerent naturam a mathematicis ea distinxit ratione, quae revera ipsam numerorum naturam penitus tolleret. Cp. p. 541 Nimirum quum numeris abstractis illud, ut sint συμβλητοί, inde accidat, quod nullum in iis est qualitatis discrimen sed unice quanti-

[1] § 7.

tas diversa, ad idem prorsus redit utrum numeros dixeris ἀσυμβλήτους esse an qualitate inter se differre. He thinks the numbers were mere symbols of notions : cp. p. 543 Etenim Plato quod ἀσυμβλήτους dixit numeros suos ideales, qualitatis diversitatem, quae in iis cerneretur, significavit et ipsam quantitativam numeri naturam ita sustulit, ut eorum vis non amplius penderet unitatum a multitudine ... sed numeri modo signa quaedam et quasi symbola fiant notionum. Thus it would be assumed without question that the Ideal numbers of the earlier theory being Ideas of number in the literal sense were not the ἀριθμοὶ ἀσύμβλητοι, that these latter belonged to the later theory, and were, of course, but a paradox of Platonism without any value for thought in general.

It must be contended that these views are erroneous. The theory of the ἀσύμβλητοι ἀριθμοί contained an important truth, though it was not appreciated by Aristotle : and it is a theory which, in the nature of the case, belonged essentially to the earlier Platonism, arose out of that and not out of anything peculiar to the later theory.

It seems also to be supposed that the doctrine of the μαθηματικὸς ἀριθμός, as something μεταξύ τοῦ εἰδητικοῦ καὶ τοῦ αἰσθητοῦ (1090^b 35) was a peculiar adjunct of the later Idea-number theory ; probably because it is thought that as the Idea-numbers did not relate to true numbers at all some place had to be found for true, or mathematical number, and for this *Metaph.* 991^b 26 [1] might be appealed to. But the origin of this doctrine again, which cannot be dissociated from the view that geometrical figures were also μεταξύ, lies in conditions which belong not to the later theory but to the earlier, and has nothing whatever to do with the Idea-numbers as such.

§ 3.—*Meaning and origin of the conception of ἀσύμβλητοι ἀριθμοί.*

We may consider first the ἀσύμβλητοι ἀριθμοί.

Plato's ἰδέα is of course the Universal. We are not concerned here with what is peculiar to his view of its nature, but with a part of it, which all must accept, and upon which Plato laid great stress : namely, the assertion that the Universal is one—a unity, that is, in contrast with the manifold to which it corresponds. This means that whereas there are many circles, for instance, Circularity, the Universal, is one—there is only one Circularity. It is not necessary to repeat here the familiar *reductio ad absurdum* of the hypothesis that there could be more than one. ' *The* circle,' with the definite article, is an equivalent expression for circularity, and even if we give several definitions of 'the Circle' we suppose them all definitions of one and the same thing. ' *The* number Two,' as we call it, is a Universal: it is 'twoness' in general, and there is only one 'twoness.' It is because there is only one that we use the definite article in the expression '*the* number Two.' Now 'the number Two' thus accurately understood cannot enter into a process of summation like a particular two. 'Two and two make four' means two things (= a particular two) added to two other things of the same kind amount to four things. The proposition is a universal one because it stands for 'any two things added to any other two things, etc., etc.,' but not because it means an addition of Universals. It does not mean, that is, that twoness added to twoness is fourness. There is only one 'twoness' and thus the expression 'twoness added to twoness' has no sense. This is the same as saying that 'two and two make four' does not mean that 'the number Two' added to 'the number Two' is 'the number Four.' Nor does anyone ever express the proposition in this way. As before, we must say there is only one 'number Two,' and that 'the number Two added to the number Two' is an unmeaning expression. Similarly ' two and three are five' means 'any particular two (*i.e.* any two things) added to any other particular three, etc.' and does not mean twoness added to threeness is fiveness. The latter is an absurd expression, for, as is easily seen, it would involve more than one twoness, and more than one threeness. Or it may be put thus :—if twoness (= the number Two) could be added to threeness (= the number Three) so as to produce fiveness (= the number Five) twoness must be conceived as having two units added to three units contained in threeness. But such units cannot be particulars as twoness is universal: they must be Universals, and the Universal of units is oneness. Thus twoness would have to consist of oneness added to another oneness which is absurd as there is only one 'oneness.' Thus 'the number Two,' 'the number Three,' etc., that is the universal twoness, the universal threeness, etc., or, in popular language, the abstractions of twoness and threeness, etc. do not consist of units, and are not capable of numerical addition in the same sense as *a* two and *a*

[1] This passage is considered below, § 4, paragraph 8.

three, by the combination of units. And thus if we call them Numbers (we call them '*the* Numbers') they are certainly numbers which are not addible.[1] This is exactly the Platonic doctrine; for if the ἰδέαι or Universals of number are called ἀριθμοί they must be ἀριθμοὶ ἀσύμβλητοι.

Geometry of course affords an exact parallel. Just as the Universals represented by *the* Numbers cannot enter into arithmetical operation, in the sense explained, so also the Universals represented by *the* figures cannot have geometrical constructions performed upon them, or be elements in such constructions. 'The Circle' as we have said is a Universal, and *e.g.* just as 'the number Two' cannot be added to 'the number Two,' *the* Circle cannot intersect *the* Circle. That is circularity cannot intersect circularity, for there is only one circularity. Accordingly no mathematician would ever think of expressing the proposition 'a circle can intersect another circle in not more than two (real) points' in the form 'the circle can intersect the circle etc.' the absurdity of which would be felt at once. The construction of Eucl. I. 1 is general, and universal in the proper sense, but it is not the construction of the Universal, 'equilateral triangularity,' upon the Universal, 'rectilinearity,' nor the construction of *the* equilateral triangle upon the straight line or upon 'the given straight line.'

The doctrine then of the ἀσύμβλητοι ἀριθμοί, instead of being a mere fantastic product of later Platonism, embodies a truth which depends on nothing peculiar to Platonism. In that philosophy it arises naturally out of the principles involved in that theory of Ideas which is represented in Plato's writings and not out of anything peculiar to the later Idea-number theory.[2]

When in this latter all Ideas were identified with Ideas of number, as Ideas of numbers they would be still ἀσύμβλητοι, and it is exactly on their numerical side and not as mere Ideas that the epithet belongs to them and is relevant. Accordingly when Aristotle attacks the Idea-numbers, he speaks of them as ἀσύμβλητοι ἀριθμοί, and while he of course points out the absurdity of identifying with Ideas of number Ideas of things which cannot be mere number, such as Man and Animal, most of his criticisms have nothing to do with this aspect of the Idea-numbers, but relate to their numerical aspect as Ideas of numbers solely, and the other aspect might be altogether non-existent as far as these criticisms are concerned.

From his treatment of the conception of ἀσύμβλητοι ἀριθμοί it must be gathered that Aristotle did not appreciate the truth conveyed in it. Possibly the form in which he presents it is a perversion current in the Academy, but if he had recognised the valuable side of it, we should expect him to say so.

His attack turns mainly on the assumption that while the units in one Ideal number could not be added to those of another, this constituting them ἀσύμβλητοι, each of them consisted of units which were added together within the number itself. He gives this as if it were but a statement of the Platonists' own view. In his division of possible opinions he gives first the one that the μονάδες were all ἀσύμβλητοι, but

---

[1] About this principle there is no confusion within mathematics proper: indeed no occasion for it arises there. But it is otherwise with what may be called 'reflective mathematics' or 'quasi-philosophic mathematics.' For the attempt to find continuity within number itself (cf. Dedekind) is a mistake which comes from looking on *the* Numbers as magnitudes, and not realising the truth attained so long ago in Greek philosophy that they are Universals. A parallel mistake would be to treat 'triangularity,' 'squareness,' etc., etc., as figures, misled by the linguistic equivalence to them of '*the* Triangle,' '*the* Square,' etc.

[2] As is well known, there are two criticisms in the *Metaphysics* of the Platonic theory of Ideas, one in bk. A, and another in bk. M. The second is a kind of revised and expanded version of the first: in some places it is a mere duplicate, lengthy passages being repeated word for word. It is noteworthy that whereas the version in bk. M has an introduction

which may well imply the writer held it not strictly accurate to speak of the Idea-number theory as if due to Plato himself, as was done in the first version—περὶ δὲ τῶν ἰδεῶν πρῶτον αὐτὴν τὴν κατὰ τὴν ἰδέαν δόξαν ἐπισκεπτέον, μηδὲν συνάπτοντας πρὸς τὴν τῶν ἀριθμῶν φύσιν, ἀλλ' ὡς ὑπέλαβον ἐξ ἀρχῆς οἱ πρῶτοι τὰς ἰδέας φήσαντες εἶναι (1078ᵃ 9), later on in the same book the conception of ἀσύμβλητοι ἀριθμοί is attributed to Plato. Cf. 1083ᵇ 33, εἰ δ' ἐστὶ τὸ ἓν ἀρχή, ἀνάγκη μᾶλλον ὥσπερ Πλάτων ἔλεγεν ἔχειν τὰ περὶ τοὺς ἀριθμούς, καὶ εἶναί τινα δυάδα πρώτην καὶ τριάδα καὶ οὐ συμβλητοὺς εἶναι τοὺς ἀριθμοὺς πρὸς ἀλλήλους. This so far confirms the view which is now put forward. But the important point is the contention that the conception of the ἀσύμβλητοι ἀριθμοί even if formulated by those who originated the Idea-number theory depends on the principles of the earlier theory alone.

The impression that the writer of the second version wishes to dissociate the name of Plato from the Idea-number theory, is confirmed by another interesting circumstance. The second version while repeating the greater part of a long passage at the beginning of the first version nearly word for word, omits a little way down in the context that passage in the earlier version which involves the identification of Plato's Idea theory with the Idea-number theory and substitutes for it some different matter.

says expressly that it was an opinion which no one had held.

Now, as has been shewn above, the considerations which make it impossible that a Universal of number, such as 'fourness,' or 'the number Four,' should consist of Universals of number added together—'twoness to twoness' or 'the number Two' to 'the number Two,' make it impossible that any Universal of number, *i.e.* any one of *the* Numbers, should consist of units added together, for that would involve that there should be more than one universal 'oneness.'

The two thoughts are inseparable; and it is hardly conceivable that the philosopher whose penetration enabled him to appreciate one side of the truth should have failed to see the other. But it is very credible that a conception, so remote from ordinary habits of mind, should be imperfectly understood by disciples.

The alternative, πάσας τὰς μονάδας εἶναι ἀσυμβλήτους, which Aristotle says no one maintained, would not in any case represent the true theory: for of course, as we have seen, that no more admits of a plurality of 'oneness' than of 'twoness': that is, just as there is *the* δυάς but not δυάδες in the plural, so there would be *the* μονάς but not μονάδες.

Bonitz in a footnote (p. 555) to his commentary on *Met.* M. viii. has remarked that Aristotle's criticisms are not well directed because those who held the theory of ἀσύμβλητοι ἀριθμοί would not consider them as each composed of added units. But the objection as Bonitz puts it is mistaken, for it is based upon his view that the ἀσύμβλητοι ἀριθμοί were in no sense numbers and had nothing really numerical about them. Thus he supposes that the Platonists could not represent them as composed of units because they did not mean them to be ideas of real number at all. 'Etenim is qui eos numeros, quos pro principiis ponat, ἀσυμβλήτους esse dicit, ipsam numerorum naturam manifesto tollit.' Owing to the same mistake he supposes Aristotle's proper course would have been to shew that the conception of ἀριθμὸς ἀσύμβλητος was self-contradictory.

§ 4.—*Meaning and origin of the doctrine of τὰ μεταξύ.*

Before discussing the meaning of the πρότερον καὶ ὕστερον and certain other subjects connected with the Ideal numbers, it will be best for the confirmation of the view put forward about the ἀσύμβλητοι ἀριθμοί to pass to another doctrine of later Platonism, that of τὰ μεταξύ; or the doctrine that the objects of mathematical science were neither Ideas nor particulars of sense, but something between the two; for this may be shewn to be the outcome, though a mistaken one, of the same kind of thinking as that which produced the ἀσύμβλητοι ἀριθμοί combined with Plato's theory of the object of scientific knowledge.

The passage of Aristotle which helps most towards ascertaining the real meaning and origin of the conception of τὰ μεταξύ is the following from *Metaph.* A. vi. 987[b] 14:—ἔτι δὲ παρὰ τὰ αἰσθητὰ καὶ τὰ εἴδη τὰ μαθηματικὰ τῶν πραγμάτων εἶναί φησι μεταξύ, διαφέροντα τῶν μὲν αἰσθητῶν τῷ ἀίδια καὶ ἀκίνητα εἶναι, τῶν δὲ εἰδῶν τῷ τὰ μὲν πόλλ' ἄττα ὅμοια εἶναι, τὸ δὲ εἶδος αὐτὸ ἓν ἕκαστον μόνον. cp. 1002[b] 15 τὰ μὲν μαθηματικὰ τῶν δεῦρο ἄλλῳ μέν τινι διαφέρει, τῷ δὲ πόλλ' ἄττα ὁμοειδῆ εἶναι οὐδὲν διαφέρει.

Plato's view as it appears in his writings is that the sciences in the strict sense dealt with Universals only, or, in his language, with 'Ideas' only; with the Idea, *e.g.* of the Circle and not with particular circles. But there is only one 'Idea' of the circle, and so if geometry were of that alone there would be no possibility of a proposition about two or more circles. Similarly in arithmetic, if the only Two to be had was the Idea, there is only one such, and yet in some sense arithmetic requires a plurality of twos. This difficulty is not realised, much less provided for, in the writings of Plato:[1] but it seems to explain both the meaning and the origin of the conception of τὰ μεταξύ. For this can be understood if we suppose it contrived, whether by Plato or a disciple, to meet the difficulty above stated.[2]

It was probably held that geometry could not really be of the Idea of the Circle which was only one, and must be of some plurality of circles. But the Platonic doctrine was retained that the objects of science were eternal, unchangeable (and perfect), and not the fleeting (and imperfect) particulars of sense: so these manifold circles were considered as eternal (and perfect). In this they were like the Idea of the circle, τῷ

[1] See below, § 8, on διάνοια and μαθηματική in the *Republic.*
[2] The writer finds that his friend Mr. J. A. Smith, of Balliol College, has independently arrived at much the same result; and also shares the opinion that the conception of ἀσύμβλητοι ἀριθμοί was connected with Platonism in general, and not specially with the Idea-number theory.

ἀίδια καὶ ἀκίνητα εἶναι, while as a plurality they were so far like the circles of perception, τῷ πόλλ' ἄττα ὅμοια εἶναι. And so for all the objects of mathematics in general whether numbers or figures.[1]

Thus the number with which Mathematics deal was called μαθηματικὸς ἀριθμός in distinction from the ἀριθμοὶ ἀσύμβλητοι and said to be μεταξύ, or between ideal numbers and concrete numbers.

The doctrine may possibly have been developed by the later Platonists who originated the Idea-number theory, but in itself it is the natural product of the line of thought which produced the conception of the ἀσύμβλητοι ἀριθμοί, and has nothing to do with the reduction of all Ideas to Ideas of number.

There were different forms of the Idea-number theory, and of the first form it is said in *Metaph.* M. 1086ᵃ 10, ὁ δὲ πρῶτος θέμενος τὰ εἴδη εἶναι καὶ ἀριθμοὺς τὰ εἴδη καὶ τὰ μαθηματικὰ[2] εὐλόγως ἐχώρισεν. This means as the context shews that whereas a later

[1] τὰ μεταξύ undoubtedly included geometrical figures as well as number. Cp. *Met.* B. ii. 997ᵇ 2 τὰ μεταξύ, περὶ ἃ τὰς μαθηματικὰς εἶναί φασιν ἐπιστήμας, where μαθηματικὰς ἐπιστήμας must include geometry. This seems also the clear implication of what is said of geometry in 997ᵇ 26 *sqq*. Compare also *Metaph.* A. ix. 991ᵇ 27, quoted below,—περὶ δ ἡ ἀριθμητική, καὶ πάντα τὰ μεταξὺ λεγόμενα ὑπό τινων, which shews that τὰ μεταξύ comprises more than ἀριθμητική.

It would not be necessary to mention this were it not that *Met.* B. ii. 992ᵇ 13 *sqq*. might cause a difficulty: οὐδένα δ'ἔχει λόγον οὐδὲ τὰ μετὰ τοὺς ἀριθμούς, μήκη καὶ ἐπίπεδα καὶ στερεά, οὔτε ὅπως ἔστιν ἢ ἔσται οὔτε τίνα ἔχει δύναμιν· ταῦτα γὰρ οὔτε εἴδη οἷόν τε εἶναι, οὐ γάρ εἰσιν ἀριθμοί, οὔτε τὰ μεταξύ, μαθηματικὰ γὰρ ἐκεῖνα, οὔτε τὰ φθαρτά, ἀλλὰ πάλιν τέταρτον ἄλλο φαίνεται τοῦτό τι γένος. Here it is implied that geometrical objects, in some sense, are not included in τὰ μαθηματικά, and so are not among τὰ μεταξύ. But Aristotle is not referring to the ordinary form of the doctrine of τὰ μεταξύ. He is attacking certain Platonists who, while identifying all Ideas with numbers, and retaining the view of the intermediacy of the objects of mathematical science, put, it may be supposed, the Universals of geometrical figures not among the Ideas (which were numbers), but a degree below them (μετά), thus introducing a fourth kind of object between the Ideas and τὰ μαθηματικά. The geometrical figures which were objects of geometry would still be found in the μαθηματικά. For these Platonists see 1080ᵇ 23, where Aristotle, after noticing certain differences among the Platonists about Ideal and Mathematical Number, says there were differences also about geometrical objects: ὁμοίως δὲ καὶ περὶ τὰ μήκη καὶ περὶ τὰ ἐπίπεδα καὶ περὶ τὰ στερεά. οἱ μὲν γὰρ ἕτερα τὰ μαθηματικὰ καὶ τὰ μετὰ τὰς ἰδέας, οἱ δ' ἰδέας, οἱ δ' ἃ shews that they had two kinds of geometrical objects, one the mathematical and the other μετὰ τὰς ἰδέας. Cp. also 1028ᵇ 25, where these philosophers are distinguished from Plato and Speusippus:—ἔνιοι δὲ τὰ μὲν εἴδη καὶ τοὺς ἀριθμοὺς τὴν αὐτὴν ἔχειν φασὶ φύσιν, τὰ δ' ἄλλα ἐχόμενα, γραμμὰς καὶ ἐπίπεδα κ.τ.λ.

[2] Omitting with Christ the εἶναι after μαθηματικά.

form of the Idea-number theory abandoned the distinction between Ideal number and mathematical number (1086ᵃ 6, *sqq*.), the earliest form (cf. ὁ πρῶτος) maintained it. This does not necessarily imply that the distinction itself originated with the Platonists in question.

In *Metaph.* A. ix. 991ᵇ 27, Aristotle criticising the Idea-number theory objects to it that it would necessitate the invention of another kind of number for the purpose of ἀριθμητική, and indeed the whole sphere of τὰ μεταξύ, a conception which he holds fraught with difficulty :—ἔτι δ' ἀναγκαῖον ἕτερόν τι γένος ἀριθμοῦ κατασκευάζειν, περὶ ὃ ἡ ἀριθμητική, καὶ πάντα τὰ μεταξὺ λεγόμενα ὑπό τινων.[3]

This objection does not the least necessitate that the μεταξύ theory should have been a special consequence of the Idea-number theory as such. Aristotle is attacking the latter generally,—finding all the objections he can to it, and this objection would be relevant because the Idea-numbers in this later theory were of course ἀσύμβλητοι ἀριθμοί[4] and as such seemed to provide no object (as has already been explained) for mathematical operations. Any wrong inference from this passage is corrected by Aristotle's own statements, above quoted from *Metaph.* 987ᵇ 14 and 1002ᵇ 15 which simply indicate that the μεταξύ theory simply originated in the necessity of finding a plurality for mathematics as against the absolute unity of the mere Idea of a figure or a number. It is perhaps significant (though no great stress need be laid on it) that in all the passages where τὰ μεταξύ in general, and not merely μαθηματικὸς ἀριθμός, are opposed to the Ideal world, the latter is designated by εἴδη or ἰδέαι not ἀριθμοί (except in one which in a way combines both), and there are a considerable number of them—987ᵇ 14, 995ᵇ 16, 997ᵇ 2, 998ᵃ 7, 1002ᵇ 12, 1028ᵇ 20, 1059ᵇ 6, 1069ᵃ 35. Even in the exceptional passage, 992ᵇ 16, the division is still into εἴδη, τὰ μεταξύ, and τὰ φθαρτά, the text implying in this case that the εἴδη are ἀριθμοί. So that it seems as if in any case the usual formula for the division had εἴδη, not ἀριθμοί. See the discussion below of the phrase εἰδητικὸς ἀριθμός.

In *Metaph.* N. iii. 1090ᵇ 32, ὁ μαθηματικὸς ἀριθμός, which is one part of τὰ μεταξύ, is said to be μεταξὺ τοῦ εἰδητικοῦ (sc. ἀριθμοῦ) καὶ

[3] The editors have a comma after κατασκευάζειν and none after ἀριθμητική which gives what seems a wrong sense.

[4] See above, § 3, paragraph 3.

τοῦ αἰσθητοῦ. The contrast here not being with mathematical Ideas in general but only with Ideal number, the substitution for εἰδῶν of an expression such as εἰδητικὸς ἀριθμός would be natural, even if Aristotle had not, as he may have in this place, the Idea-number theory before him. The expression in itself need not mean anything more than Ideal Number, as will be seen later on.[1] It may indeed refer to the Idea-numbers, but there is nothing in this passage any more than in the one above discussed, *Metaph.* 991ᵇ 27, to prove that the conception of τὰ μεταξύ is only a consequence of the Idea-number theory.

§ 5.—*On* τὸ πρότερον καὶ ὕστερον *in the* ἀσύμβλητοι ἀριθμοί.

We may next consider the meaning of the πρότερον καὶ ὕστερον assigned to Ideal Number. It has been said that the text of *Metaph.* M. vi. 1080ᵇ 11 *sqq.* (quoted above, § 1, init.) is vindicated against Trendenlenburg's insertion of μή before ἔχοντα τὸ πρότερον καὶ ὕστερον [due to his mistake about the interpretation of *N. Eth.* I. vi] and that the statement in it that Ideal Number contains 'the Before and After' is explicable, because 'Bonitz and others have clearly proved that τὸ πρότερον καὶ ὕστερον was a technical term in the ideal arithmetic for the relation of the factor (τὸ γεννῶν) to the product (τὸ γεννώμενον).' It is difficult to understand how this opinion in this precise form could be attributed to Bonitz. Bonitz in consequence of his mistaken notion that there was nothing really numerical about the Idea-Numbers thought their order must be one of quality (de ordine quodam qualitatis agi) and not a numerical one at all. This seems inconsistent with supposing that order to be one of factor and product, nor does there seem to be evidence of such a view in Bonitz' commentary. Zeller, it is true, makes the relation of πρότερον καὶ ὕστερον that of factor and product in some sense; and this passes with him in a confused way into a purely qualitative distinction,[2] with which latter Bonitz would agree. But Zeller's defence of the text turns solely on the circumstance that there is abundant evidence in the *Metaphysics* that some kind of πρότερον καὶ ὕστερον was attributed to the Ideal Numbers and not at all upon his theory of what kind it was.

However there is in any case a misunderstanding. A simple and sufficient explanation of the πρότερον καὶ ὕστερον is indicated by the Aristotelian text itself (in which it may be remarked the technical distinction of γεννῶν and γεννώμενον as factor and product does not even occur) : whereas the one proposed is entirely inapplicable to the ἀσύμβλητοι ἀριθμοί rightly understood, is not really applicable even to the later Idea-number theory, as will be seen, and at any rate is not necessary for either. The Ideas of numbers, as being the Universals of number and therefore ἀσύμβλητοι, are as ἀσύμβλητοι entirely outside one another, in the sense that none is a part of another. Thus they form a series of different terms, which have a definite order (ἔχουσι τὸ πρότερον καὶ ὕστερον). They are nothing but what mathematicians call '*the* series of natural Numbers,' where the definite article is right, because there is only one such series, consisting as it does of Universals each of which is unique. The order of this series is obviously enough to explain the passages in the *Metaphysics*, and enough for the requirements of the argument attributed to the Platonists in the *Ethics*.

This view is fully confirmed by *Metaph.* M. vi, where the order of the Idea-numbers, which, as has been said, are treated on their numerical side as Ideas of number, is closely associated with the fact that they are ἀσύμβλητοι, and not with any sort of γένεσις of them. Thus according to 1080ᵃ 17, if there is a kind of number such that τὸ μὲν πρῶτόν τι αὐτοῦ τὸ δ' ἐχόμενον, the numerical elements in such order must be ἀσύμβλητοι. Two cases are possible. Either the elements are μονάδες, and then, if these have an order of πρότερον καὶ ἐχόμενον, they must be all ἀσύμβλητοι. Or the elements are the Numbers ; and here the Numbers as forming a series with πρῶτον and ἐχόμενον must be ἀσύμβλητοι with one another, that is, the units in any Number must not be συμβληταί with those of another, though its own units are συμβληταί within itself. In this case we have μετὰ τὸ ἓν πρώτη[3] ἡ δυάς, ἔπειτα ἡ τριάς, καὶ οὕτω δὴ ὁ ἄλλος ἀριθμός—*i.e.* 'the series of natural Numbers.' The mutual exclusiveness, caused by their being ἀσύμβλητοι, which enables them to form a series is expressly put

---

[1] See § 8,—On the expression εἰδητικὸς ἀριθμός.
[2] So also Schwegler, note on *Metaph.* B iii. 16. See below note to paragraph 5.
[3] Christ would emend either to ἡ πρώτη δυάς or ἡ δυὰς ἡ πρώτη. But the text is doubtless sound, for πρώτη corresponds to ἔπειτα. That πρώτη should be assigned to δυάς in another sense in the same context ought to cause no difficulty. Such carelessness is common in Aristotle, and there are far harsher instances to be found than this.

thus :—οὗτος δὲ (sc. ὁ ἀριθμός) μετὰ τὸ ἓν δύο ἕτερα ἄνευ τοῦ ἑνὸς τοῦ πρώτου, καὶ ἡ τριὰς ἄνευ τῆς δυάδος, ὁμοίως δὲ καὶ ὁ ἄλλος ἀριθμός. Thus if there is a serial order of the Numbers they must be ἀσύμβλητοι. And the converse of this is put. In contrast to the number which exhibits an order, the number which does not exhibit an order is such that all units in it are συμβληταί (1080ᵃ 20), and this is the μαθηματικὸς ἀριθμός (ᵃ 21 cp. 1081ᵃ 5). The inclusiveness of one number in another in the μαθηματικὸς ἀριθμός, which prevents it from having the πρότερον καὶ ὕστερον,[1] is put thus (1080ᵃ 30) διὸ καὶ ὁ μαθηματικὸς ἀριθμὸς ἀριθμεῖται μετὰ τὸ ἓν δύο, πρὸς τῷ ἔμπροσθεν ἑνὶ ἄλλο ἕν, καὶ τὰ τρία πρὸς τοῖς ·δυσὶ τούτοις ἄλλο ἕν, καὶ ὁ λοιπὸς δὲ ὡσαύτως. Thus clearly the property of being ἀσύμβλητος is sufficient and necessary to constitute a kind of ἀριθμός a series with πρότερον καὶ ὕστερον. A little below in the same context the production of numbers out of certain elements, according to some philosophers is alluded to :—οἱ λέγοντες τὸ ἓν ἀρχὴν εἶναι καὶ οὐσίαν καὶ στοιχεῖα πάντων, καὶ ἐκ τούτου καὶ ἄλλου τινὸς εἶναι τὸν ἀριθμόν : but no attempt is made to connect the πρότερον καὶ ὕστερον with this.

We may now consider what is found on the γένεσις of number in other places, so far as it concerns the question of the priority of factor to product. The derivation of numbers from τὸ ἕν and ἡ ἀόριστος δυάς as elements, whether original or adapted from some Pythagorean source, may perhaps belong to the fantastic Platonism which identified all Ideas with Numbers, and these elements may be accordingly regarded as a sort of arithmetical translation of πέρας and ἄπειρον, owing to the Pythagorean association of the former with τὸ ἕν and the latter with the dyad. The description however of the process did not remain a mere metaphor, but got a kind of arithmetical expression though but a vague one. The ἀόριστος δυάς appears as an operating factor, the effect of which is to double what it operates upon, and so it is δυοποιός (1082ᵃ 10). Thus in distinction from the ὡρισμένη δυάς, which is the number Two and the abstraction of 'Twoness,' it really comes to be the abstraction of 'Twiceness.' Accordingly by combination of τὸ ἕν with the ἀόριστος δυάς is produced the number Two, the δυάς, and by the operation of the ἀόριστος δυάς on this

again, the number Four. By successive operations of this kind on successive results there arises the series of even numbers which are powers of Two. This would not yield the odd numbers, or the even ones which have an odd factor. Aristotle expressly notes this as a difficulty in *Metaph.* M. iii. 1091ᵃ 10 (cf. ᵃ22), and we may infer that the theory was originally vague enough to be open to his objection.

Another passage seems to indicate that an attempt to remedy the defect had been made by adding other principles. In *Metaph.* M. viii. 1084ᵃ 3 Aristotle says, in an objection, ἡ δὲ γένεσις τῶν ἀριθμῶν ἢ περιττοῦ ἀριθμοῦ ἢ ἀρτίου αἰεί ἐστιν, ὡδὶ μὲν τοῦ ἑνὸς εἰς τὸν ἄρτιον πίπτοντος περιττός, ὡδὶ δὲ τῆς μὲν δυάδος (sc. τῆς ἀορίστου) ἐμπιπτούσης ὁ ἀφ' ἑνὸς διπλασιαζόμενος, ὡδὶ δὲ τῶν περιττῶν ὁ ἄλλος ἄρτιος. The odd numbers are produced by the operation of τὸ ἕν on an even number, in the way of addition : the other even numbers (ὁ ἄλλος ἄρτιος) which do not arise from the operation of the ἀόριστος δυάς, above explained, have their γένεσις described in ὡδὶ δὲ τῶν περιττῶν κ.τ.λ. This we might expect to be the operation of the ἀόριστος δυάς on odd numbers, and so Bonitz understands it : but the Greek is not suited to this, and rather suggests τῶν περιττῶν ἐμπιπτόντων εἰς τὸν ἄρτιον, which, understood of multiplication, would give the desired result. However the text is elliptical, for after ἐμπιπτούσης is to be understood εἰς τὸ ἕν as well as εἰς τὸν ἄρτιον. This account involves addition as well as multiplication, and if therefore the πρότερον καὶ ὕστερον had to be explained by it, that formula could not be confined to the relation between 'factor (γεννῶν) and product (γεννώμενον).' Thus the proposed explanation of τὸ πρότερον καὶ ὕστερον, the one which seems to be a part[2] of Zeller's, fails even in the case most favourable to it.

In the case of what may be supposed to be the original meaning of the ἀσύμβλητοι ἀριθμοί such a genesis whether by multiplication or addition is not to be thought of. It may be argued, as before, that the philosopher who grasped the truth expressed in the phrase ἀσύμβλητοι ἀριθμοί, could not have regarded them as generated by multiplication or addition : that would be too crude a misunderstanding of the principle to which his own insight had led him.

---

[1] Hence if *Metaph.* 999ᵃ 6 referred to the Platonist theory, the ἀριθμός there spoken of could only be μαθηματικὸς ἀριθμός. But there is really no reference to Platonism in the passage : see below, § 7.

[2] Zeller's utterances however (*Phil. d. Gr.* 3rd Edn. ii. 1. p. 570) are very confused. It is not necessary to discuss the nature of the confusion, as he has misunderstood the meaning of the ἀσύμβλητοι ἀριθμοί and of the πρότερον καὶ ὕστερον.

It is true that the γένεσις theory of some other Platonists involves a πρότερον καὶ ὕστερον of factor and product and a πρότερον καὶ ὕστερον of part and whole in the way of addition, and Aristotle makes use of the former kind in criticisms, as in 1082ᵃ 26, and elsewhere. But though he often refers to the γένεσις from τὸ ἕν and ἡ ἀόριστος δυάς he never says that the πρότερον καὶ ὕστερον characteristic of the ἀσύμβλητοι ἀριθμοί in the Platonist theory was either relative to multiplication or relative to addition, or relative to any sort of γένεσις; but, as we have seen he connects the order of these numbers solely with the fact that they are ἀσύμβλητοι. To the passages already quoted for this, another *Met.* M. vii. 1081ᵃ 17 *sqq.* may be added, partly misunderstood both by ancient and modern commentators,[1] the key to which is that if *all* μονάδες are ἀσύμβλητοι they necessarily form a series in which one is before another in order, according to the principle already enunciated, as we have seen, in *Met.* M. vi. 1080ᵃ 18. Here of course there could be no question of the production of μονάδες by multiplication.

The Idea-numbers then, as Ideas of number are ἀσύμβλητοι, and as Ideas of number have the πρότερον and ὕστερον of the serial order of 'the natural Numbers.'

§ 6.—*On the meaning of ἀριθμῶν in Nic. Eth.* I. vi.

The question now naturally presents itself, Are the ἀριθμοί in *Nic. Eth.* I. vi the Ideas of number as in the Ideal theory represented by Plato's writings, or are they the Idea-numbers of later Platonism? It is evident that what is said in this chapter of the *Ethics* is true of both stages of the theory, and it is hardly possible to decide which stage Aristotle had in mind. There is no trace either here or anywhere else in the *Ethics* of the Idea-number theory. In the corresponding chapter of the *Eudemian Ethics*, there is a reference to it, but not in the part which corresponds to the passage in the *Nicomachean Ethics* on the πρότερον καὶ ὕστερον in the ἀριθμοί. It is in an argument added by the author of the *Eudemian Ethics* on his own account, and stands in contrast to the *Nicomachean Ethics* because it bases a criticism of the Idea theory upon its later number form, a thing never done in the *Nicomachean Ethics*. But even if the reference had been in a passage which had a counterpart in the *Nicomachean Ethics*, it would not in the least settle the bearing of the Aristotelian text, such additions being quite in the Eudemian manner. But the really important matter is that even if Aristotle had the Idea-numbers in mind, what he says of them, as is evident from the foregoing investigation, applies to their numerical aspect as Ideas of numbers, and not at all to them as Idea-numbers. Besides if he were regarding them as Ideas without any reference to a numerical character and as standing in an order of πρότερον καὶ ὕστερον according to some principle not numerical [2] he would surely have written ἰδεῶν and not ἀριθμῶν, the latter word being in such a context merely irrelevant and confusing.

§ 7.—*On the Interpretation of Metaph.* B iii. 999ᵃ 6.

Some have held that τὰ εἴδη τῶν ἀριθμῶν here refers to the μαθηματικὸς ἀριθμός, others that it refers to the εἰδητικὸς ἀριθμός. If the choice were really between these alternatives, it is obvious that the only possible one would be that εἰδητικὸς ἀριθμός was intended, since, as has been seen (§ 5), μαθηματικὸς ἀριθμός does not admit of the πρότερον καὶ ὕστερον. But the truth is both of these contentions are irrelevant, for in this place Aristotle has not even got the Platonist distinction of μαθηματικὸς ἀριθμός from the ἀσύμβλητος ἀριθμός before him: he is not criticising anything specially Platonic, and he is speaking in the language of his own philosophy.

The passage before us belongs to a series of questions about ἀρχαί raised at the beginning of bk. B of the Metaphysics. In the preceding chapter (ch. 2) Aristotle has considered the Platonic theory. In the present chapter (ch. 3) he passes from that to a general question περὶ τῶν ἀρχῶν which has no special reference to Platonism as such—

---

[1] ἅμα γὰρ αἱ ἐν τῇ δυάδι τῇ πρώτῃ μονάδες γεννῶνται. The meaning of an objection brought in these words is that in the process of γένεσις referred to the μονάδες would have to be coordinate, whereas (ex hyp.) as ἀσύμβλητοι one must be necessarily prior to the other. Christ notices that Alexander thinks ἢ γὰρ ἅμα preferable, and himself conjectures ἅμα γὰρ αἱ ἐν τῇ δυάδι πρώτῃ καὶ αἱ ἐν τῇ τριάδι μονάδες, which can hardly be due to anything else than a misunderstanding. Bonitz appears to have taken the place rightly, but perhaps has not brought the point out clearly enough to prevent Christ's misconception.

[2] The current expression 'logical order,' which we often use for some order not a time order, is vague. It seems properly to mean an order determined by some principle or conception, and thus should include every kind of numerical order, to which nevertheless it is sometimes opposed.

πότερον δεῖ τὰ γένη στοιχεῖα καὶ ἀρχὰς ὑπολαμβάνειν ἢ μᾶλλον ἐξ ὧν ἐνυπαρχόντων ἐστὶν ἕκαστον πρῶτον. After an aporematic discussion of this (998ᵃ20—ᵇ13) he proposes in the present context (998ᵇ 14 *sqq.*) the question whether, supposing the γένη really were ἀρχαί these would be the highest γένη or the 'infimae species,'—πρὸς δὲ τούτοις εἰ καὶ μάλιστα ἀρχαὶ τὰ γένη εἰσί, πότερον δεῖ νομίζειν τὰ πρῶτα τῶν γενῶν ἀρχὰς ἢ τὰ ἔσχατα κατηγορούμενα ἐπὶ τῶν ἀτόμων; On this again there is a set of aporematic arguments, the first part of them being directed against the claims of the highest γένη. To this part belongs the passage on the πρότερον καὶ ὕστερον: and it is immediately preceded by an argument the analysis of which will shew how remote is the consideration of anything Platonic. τὸ ὄν and τὸ ἕν having been given as examples of γένη which might seem suited beyond all others to be ἀρχαί, a subtle attempt is made to reduce the view that τὸ ἕν could be an ἀρχή to a contradiction (999ᵃ 1—6). If, it is said, τὸ ἀδιαίρετον is ἕν, then the infima species as being ἀδιαίρετον (*sc.* κατ᾽ εἶδος) has a better title to be considered a ἕν (and so an ἀρχή) than τὸ ἕν itself, because this latter as a γένος is διαιρετὸν εἰς εἴδη. Then follows the passage in question :—ἔτι ἐν οἷς τὸ πρότερον καὶ ὕστερόν ἐστιν, οὐχ οἷόν τε τὸ ἐπὶ τούτων εἶναί τι παρὰ ταῦτα, οἷον εἰ πρώτη τῶν ἀριθμῶν ἡ δυάς, οὐκ ἔσται τις ἀριθμὸς παρὰ τὰ εἴδη τῶν ἀριθμῶν· ὁμοίως δὲ οὐδὲ σχῆμα παρὰ τὰ εἴδη τῶν σχημάτων. Here τὸ ἐπὶ τούτων means the common predicate of certain species. εἴδη does not mean 'Ideas' but simply species as contrasted with the γένος. Aristotle is maintaining that the common predicate of εἴδη which stand in the relation of πρότερον καὶ ὕστερον cannot be something separable (παρά) from each species and abstractable from it, in the sense that each of them contains not only what this predicate means, but also something more. Thus figure, σχῆμα, is predicated of the various species of figure, τὰ εἴδη τῶν σχημάτων, the triangle, the quadrilateral, etc., but 'triangle' is not figure together with something else other than figure. 'Triangle' contains nothing but what is comprised in 'figure,' so that if we abstract 'figure' from 'triangle,' no differentia of it is left. Or, if we leave any such, what is left is a determination of 'figure,' and so 'figure' is left and has not been abstracted. Similarly for the εἴδη τῶν ἀριθμῶν, the various species of number, that is the Numbers Two, Three, Four, etc, the common predicate number is not τι παρὰ ταῦτα; if we abstract 'number' or numericalness from Two, no differentia of it is left.

This has no connexion whatever with the Platonist distinction of ἀσύμβλητος ἀριθμός and μαθηματικὶς ἀριθμός, nor is there any reference to Platonism as such.

Though the principle ἔτι ἐν οἷς τὸ πρότερον καὶ ὕστερον κ.τ.λ. was, as we learn from the *Ethics*, one recognised by the Platonists, it was also recognised by Aristotle and is here put as his own view. In a familiar passage also from the *Politics* (1275ᵃ 34 *sqq.*) quoted by Zeller, Aristotle puts the view as his own and argues from it. Similarly εἰ πρώτη τῶν ἀριθμῶν ἡ δυάς has nothing to do with Platonism, but simply means that the number Two comes first in the series of Numbers. Nor has the passage anything to do with the notion of a γένεσις not completed till an ἄτομον εἶδος is reached.

The inseparableness of the generic predicate from species which stand in a certain relative order is an example of a more general principle. If a generic notion is such as to include within itself the differentiae of certain given species, then none of the species contain anything outside (παρά) and distinguishable from what is contained in the given notion : so that to abstract the determination represented by that notion from the species is to take the differentiae as well. The species, it is true, may be said to agree with one another in the genus, but what they differ in is not something outside the genus but it also belongs to the genus. What red and blue agree in is colour, but what they differ in is also colour. The general principle is appreciated by Aristotle and is the basis of the argument—perhaps not always understood—which he urges at the end of *Nic. Ethics* I. vi. 1096ᵇ23. The goods agree in goodness, but they do not therefore differ in something which is not goodness but just in goodness. Hence the definition of the goodness of one good is different from the definition of the goodness of another : which of course prevents there being one single criterion of all good.

The case of the πρότερον καὶ ὕστερον falls under this general principle, because the differentiae in respect of order are comprised in the generic notion itself as is obviously the case with the generic notion of number.[1]

---

[1] Eudemus' attempt to explain this case in *Eud. Eth.* I. viii., where he reproduces *Nic. Eth.* I. vi. 1096ᵃ 17 *sqq.*, is an entire misunderstanding.

§ 8.—*On the expression* εἰδητικὸς ἀριθμός.

It seems always assumed, perhaps without a sufficient examination of the evidence, that εἰδητικὸς ἀριθμός was the special designation of the Idea-numbers as such. It may have been so, but it is not clear that this was the original meaning of the phrase or even that Aristotle uses it in this special reference.

The conception of 'mathematical number,' as distinguished from 'Ideal number,' arises, as we have seen, out of the earlier Platonic theory of Ideas and not out of the later Idea-number theory. That number from which 'mathematical number' was distinguished was then simply the 'Ideas,' ἰδέαι or εἴδη, of number, in true reference to number. If a collective expression for the εἴδη τῶν ἀριθμῶν, parallel to the collective μαθηματικὸς ἀριθμός was wanted, εἰδητικὸς ἀριθμός might very naturally suggest itself. It would be neater and more convenient than οἱ ἐν τοῖς εἴδεσι ἀριθμοί which occurs in *Metaph.* N. vi. 1093ᵇ 21, and that such a terminology should spring up in this way is no more than might be expected. If this were so, when later the Ideas of number became the Idea-numbers, they would in opposition to μαθηματικὸς ἀριθμός still be called εἰδητικὸς ἀριθμός in the same sense as before.

The three Aristotelian passages in which εἰδητικὸς ἀριθμός is named, *Metaph.* M. ix. 1086ᵃ 2 *sqq.* and N. iii. 1090ᵇ 32 *sqq.*, are compatible with this view: they favour it but hardly prove it.

In 1086ᵃ 2 there comes first a statement about certain Platonists who acknowledged only one kind of number, the μαθηματικὸς ἀριθμός:—οἱ μὲν γὰρ τὰ μαθηματικὰ μόνον ποιοῦντες παρὰ τὰ αἰσθητά, ὁρῶντες τὴν περὶ τὰ εἴδη δυσχέρειαν καὶ πλάσιν, ἀπέστησαν ἀπὸ τοῦ εἰδητικοῦ ἀριθμοῦ καὶ τὸν μαθηματικὸν ἐποίησαν. The difficulty referred to is not one which arose out of the identification of all Ideas with the Ideas of numbers, but solely out of the distinction of an Ideal number from a mathematical, and there is no reason whatever why εἰδητικὸς ἀριθμός should mean anything but Ideal number, in the sense of Ideas of number proper. εἰδητικός just corresponds to τὰ εἴδη in the preceding clause. Next we are told that certain Platonists who identified all the Ideas with Ideas of numbers acknowledged only the εἰδητικὸς ἀριθμός and rejected the μαθηματικός:—οἱ δὲ τὰ εἴδη βουλόμενοι ἅμα καὶ ἀριθμοὺς ποιεῖν, οὐχ ὁρῶντες δὲ εἰ τὰς ἀρχάς τις ταύτας[1] θήσεται, πῶς ἔσται ὁ μαθηματικὸς παρὰ τὸν εἰδητικόν, τὸν αὐτὸν εἰδητικὸν καὶ μαθηματικὸν ἐποίησαν ἀριθμὸν τῷ λόγῳ, ἐπεὶ ἔργῳ γ' ἀνῄρηται ὁ μαθηματικός. Here again εἰδητικός is defined by its opposition to μαθηματικός. With these Platonists, of course, εἰδητικὸς ἀριθμός, even if properly meaning Ideal number, would include all Ideas because they reduced all Ideas to Ideal numbers; yet it was not from this point of view that they rejected μαθηματικὸς ἀριθμός, but from considerations of number as number: and so in this passage too there is no reason why Aristotle should be using εἰδητικὸς ἀριθμός in any other sense than that of Ideal number.

A second passage, 1090ᵇ 32, is as follows:—οἱ δὲ πρῶτοι δύο τοὺς ἀριθμοὺς ποιήσαντες, τόν τε τῶν εἰδῶν καὶ τὸν μαθηματικόν, ἄλλον, οὐδαμῶς οὔτ' εἰρήκασιν οὔτ' ἔχοιεν ἂν εἰπεῖν πῶς καὶ ἐκ τίνος ἔσται ὁ μαθηματικός. ποιοῦσι γὰρ αὐτὸν μεταξὺ τοῦ εἰδητικοῦ καὶ τοῦ αἰσθητοῦ. εἰ μὲν γὰρ ἐκ τοῦ μεγάλου καὶ μικροῦ, ὁ αὐτὸς ἐκείνῳ ἔσται τῷ τῶν ἰδεῶν κ.τ.λ. Here εἰδητικὸς ἀριθμός is the equivalent of τὸν τῶν εἰδῶν in the previous sentence, and of τῷ τῶν ἰδεῶν in the following one, and corresponds to τὰ εἴδη in the parallel place 987ᵇ 15 (where, as we have seen, the origin of the conception of μεταξύ is not put in connexion with anything which concerns the Idea-number theory, but with a difficulty arising from the ideas of number as such), and the meaning 'Ideal number' is the only one required in the passage and the most suitable.

The remaining passage is 1088ᵇ 29:—ἐάν τε τὸν εἰδητικὸν ἀριθμὸν ἐξ αὐτῶν (*sc.* τοῦ ἑνὸς καὶ τῆς ἀορίστου δυάδος) ποιῶσιν, ἐάν τε τὸν μαθηματικόν. Here also the only meaning of εἰδητικὸς ἀριθμός which is relevant is that of Ideas of number and not that of Idea-numbers.

In this matter the usage of the Greek Commentators does not carry us farther than the Aristotelian text. εἰδητικοὶ ἀριθμοί would be a convenient formula for Idea-numbers as opposed to numbers in the ordinary sense, and may therefore have come to be the equivalent of Idea-numbers with them, and it should be noticed that the plural εἰδητικοὶ ἀριθμοί which they use never seems to occur in Aristotle but only the singular collective εἰδητικὸς ἀριθμός.

§ 9.—*Is the doctrine of* τὰ μεταξύ *to be found in Plato's 'Republic'?*

In the familiar passage at the end of the Sixth Book of Plato's *Republic*, διάνοια which is concerned with the objects of mathematics

---

[1] There is a curious slip here in the Teubner edition:—'ταύτας codd. edd., ταύτας emendavi.'

(though as will be seen not with these alone) is said to be between νοῦς and δόξα, the latter being concerned with the αἰσθητά; and the objects of διάνοια are somehow between the νοητά and αἰσθητά. The field of διάνοια is treated by Ueberweg as if it corresponded to the τὰ μεταξύ of the *Metaphysics*, and accordingly he puts in it τὰ μαθηματικά which are not ἰδέαι, the ἰδέαι being confined to the upper division of νοητά corresponding to νοῦς. If this were right it would be extraordinary that Aristotle should in the *Metaphysics* make no kind of reference to the *Republic* or to its terminology. But there is really no such doctrine in the *Republic*. The objects of διάνοια are ἰδέαι, and διάνοια itself is a faculty of apprehending universals in clear distinction from any perception of particulars. Moreover— though this is of less importance—τὰ μαθηματικά do not constitute the whole of the objects of διάνοια. A careful examination of the text of the *Republic* can hardly leave any doubt on these points. Perhaps some misunderstanding might arise from the fact that one of the distinctions Plato makes between the objects of διάνοια and νοῦς is in the manner in which they are studied and not in the objects themselves. The objects of διάνοια are studied with the help of sensible objects, *i.e.* figures, etc. perceived by the senses. But the text clearly distinguishes between the object really studied and those sensible objects which are but aids to the study. The geometrical object studied is the original of which the sensible figure is but the copy, and this language in Plato shews that the geometrical object is the ἰδέα:—τοῖς ὁρωμένοις εἴδεσι προσχρῶνται ...οὐ περὶ τούτων διανοούμενοι, ἀλλ' ἐκείνων περὶ οἷς ταῦτα ἔοικε, and similar expressions. This is made unmistakeable by the examples given—τετράγωνος αὐτός, διάμετρος αὐτή, which can only be the ἰδέαι of the τετράγωνος and of the διάμετρος respectively. By his reiteration Plato shews his concern lest we should be misled by the use made of the sensible figures into confounding them with the true objects of mathematics, which are these Universals and these alone—ἀλλ' οὐ ταύτης ⟨τῆς διαμέτρου⟩ ἣν γράφουσι. And it is to these objects and just in this sharp distinction from the objects of sense, *i.e.* from the particular figures which are drawn to illustrate them, that διάνοια is assigned, as a faculty which is not of the sensible objects: ο ὐ π ε ρ ὶ τ ο ύ τ ω ν δ ι α ν ο ο ύ μ ε ν ο ι ἀλλ' ἐκείνων περὶ οἷς ταῦτ' ἔοικε, τοῦ τετραγώνου αὐτοῦ, etc. So again ζητοῦντές τε αὐτὰ ἐκεῖνα ἰδεῖν ἃ οὐκ ἂν ἄλλως ἴδοι ἢ τῇ δ ι α ν ο ί ᾳ, where αὐτὰ ἐκεῖνα refers to the ἰδέαι of the τετράγωνος of the διάμετρος and such like. Cp. 529 E ἃ δὴ λ ό γ ῳ μὲν καὶ δ ι α ν ο ί ᾳ ληπτά, ὄψει δ' οὔ; 526 A, ὧν διανοηθῆναι μόνον ἐγχωρεῖ: 511 C, καὶ διανοίᾳ μὲν ἀναγκάζονται ἀλλὰ μ ὴ α ἰ σ θ ή σ ε σ ι ν αὐτὰ θεᾶσθαι οἱ θεώμενοι.

Notwithstanding these express statements confusion may have been caused perhaps by the reflection that on the one hand Plato makes a use of perceived particulars characteristic of the mathematical procedure, and on the other hand seems to assign διάνοια as the special faculty of the mathematician: whence it might seem διάνοια must include the reference to particulars.

But there ought to be no difficulty. The faculty of mathematical study, as a process of investigation, is not διάνοια: if any name is to be given to it μαθηματική would be the most appropriate. This, as the mathematician's procedure, involves αἴσθησις so far as it employs the sensible figure and διάνοια so far as the Universal is apprehended. διαλεκτική as a process stands in a very similar relation to the two 'faculties' of διάνοια and νοῦς: it is neither, but involves both, as will be seen presently.

If Plato had intended that there should be anything of the nature of sensuous intuition in διάνοια, such, for instance, as some plurality distinguishing its object from the unity of the Universal, he could not have failed to say so, and, in such a context, say it with great clearness: certainly he would never have employed expressions the only natural interpretation of which is the very opposite.

If then the objects of διάνοια are ἰδέαι, how does it differ from νοῦς, and how do its objects differ from νοητά, in the narrower sense of that term? To these questions Plato himself, at the end of *Rep.* vi., supplies a clear answer, and one which once more shews that the objects of διάνοια are ἰδέαι.

He holds that all the Ideas are connected with one another in a system which depends on one Idea, the Idea of the Good. This is the absolute and self-sufficient principle or ἀρχή on which they all depend. The knowledge of this system in its completeness, the ideal at which διαλεκτική aims and which a completed διαλεκτική would realise, is called νοῦς; and thus an ἰδέα is not a νοητόν, in the higher sense as object of νοῦς, unless it is known as a member of this system and therefore in connexion with the ἀρχή. If not seen in this connexion (μετ' ἀρχῆς) its full nature is not apprehended, and, its validity is not really known, because it is this connexion which alone guarantees validity.

Now in mathematics the Ideas concerned are not entirely without connexion: for by processes of consistent reasoning groups of Ideas are shewn to depend on a limited number of Ideas. But these latter are not connected with one another and the ultimate ἀρχή, the Idea of the Good. Thus though treated as absolute starting-points (ἀρχαί) in mathematics they are not self-sufficient, therefore not absolute but only ὑποθέσεις, and their validity can only be assured when derived from the Idea of the Good. The connexions then between the Ideas in mathematics are not complete, and thus an Idea in it, though seen in some of its connexions with others, is not seen in the completeness of such connexions in the system which depends on the ultimate ἀρχή, and therefore not in the completeness of its own nature.

On this account obviously an Idea as seen in mathematics is not νοητόν; it is not object of νοῦς: and the faculty which apprehends them in this incomplete way though a faculty of Universals, a faculty of thought, not of sense (διανοίᾳ καὶ μὴ αἰσθήσεσιν), and as thought falling with νοῦς under the general designation νόησις, is inferior to νοῦς. This is the distinction Plato makes between the two faculties when he sums up his result at the end of the sixth book of the *Republic*; and it is the only distinction.

It follows of course that an object of διάνοια when its full nature is apprehended, when, that is, its connexion with the true ἀρχή is seen, is νοητόν in the higher sense, *i.e.* object of νοῦς; and this is exactly what Plato says:—καίτοι νοητῶν ὄντων μετ' ἀρχῆς. This is a confirmation of the view that the objects of διάνοια are ἰδέαι, for nothing but an ἰδέα can be object of νοῦς.

There are certain characteristics of Plato's terminology which also confirm this result. The sphere of διάνοια is a part of the whole sphere of νοητόν, in opposition to the ὁρατόν (= αἰσθητόν), and διάνοια itself is a species of νόησις in opposition to αἴσθησις. Now such a passage as that in 507, where it is said τὰς ἰδέας νοεῖσθαι ὁρᾶσθαι δ' οὔ, taken in connexion with this indicates that the objects of νόησις as such are ἰδέαι. Again in the seventh book of the *Republic* the objects of perception which stimulate the mind to the exercise of thought and the discovery of the Universal are called variously παρακλητικὰ διανοίας and ἐγερτικὰ νοήσεως (p. 524).

διαλεκτική must not be confused with νοῦς. It is a process which begins with Ideas incompletely connected as seen in διάνοια. It therefore involves the use of this faculty. Its work is to effect more and more connexions between the Ideas and finally effect their full connexion with the ἰδέα τοῦ ἀγαθοῦ. Only when this result had been consummated and only when διαλεκτική had finished this work would νοῦς appear. διαλεκτική therefore begins from διάνοια, and its ideal ending is in νοῦς. As already indicated, it is important for the proper interpretation of διάνοια to recognise that διαλεκτική and μαθηματική are processes of investigation to be distinguished from the fourfold division of 'faculties of objects'—as they may be called for want of a better term—νοῦς, διάνοια, πίστις, εἰκασία.

From the general description Plato gives of διαλεκτική taken with the allegory of the Cave it would seem that διαλεκτική in its upward progress brings to light ἰδέαι not found in the field of the sciences. These too, properly speaking, would not be νοητά till the process of διαλεκτική was complete, but Plato has not considered this point. There is another point also omitted in the sixth book, but implied in the allegory of the Cave. From the distinction he makes between διάνοια and νοῦς, it should follow that any ἰδέα whether mathematical or not, before its connexion with the ἰδέα τοῦ ἀγαθοῦ was understood would be object of διάνοια. An important class of these would be the ethical Ideas. Important as these are to him Plato, carried away by his interest in defining the position of the sciences, seems at the end of the sixth book of the *Republic* to have forgotten all about them—great thinkers sometimes do these things. But there is a passage in the Allegory of the Cave which shews that ethical notions are conceived of us having the same kind of gradations in respect of reality and truth as scientific notions:—517 E, περὶ τῶν τοῦ δικαίου σκιῶν ἢ ἀγαλμάτων ὧν αἱ σκιαί, opposed to αὐτὴ δικαιοσύνη.

It may be permissible to add that in a paper read before the Oxford Philological Society in 1892 the writer maintained that the plural γεωμετρίαι in these passages in the *Republic* did not mean Plane and Solid Geometry, but acts or operations of Geometry, and related to γεωμετρεῖν just as θεωρίαι to θεωρεῖν: γεωμετρία by itself, and without qualification indicated by context, standing normally for plane geometry. The plural γεωμετρίαι is thus exactly parallel to λογισμοί with which it is in these passages associated. The same result, if not quite in the same way, has been independently given lately by Dr. Adam in his edition of the *Republic*.

J. Cook Wilson.

ANCIENT PHILOSOPHY

1. Otto Apelt. *Platonis Sophista. Recensuit, Prolegomenis et Commentariis Instruxit*
2. Grace Hadley Billings. *The Art of Transition in Plato*
3. Thomas H. Billings. *The Platonism of Philo Judaeus*
4. Ingram Bywater. *Aristotle on the Art of Poetry. A Revised Text with Critical Introduction and Commentary.*
5. Lewis Campbell. *The Theaetetus of Plato. A Revised Text and English Notes. Second Edition*
6. Henri Carteron. *La notion de force dans le système d'Aristote*
7. Harold Cherniss. *The Riddle of the Early Academy*
8. Ingemar Düring. *Aristotle's De Partibus Animalium. Critical and Literary Commentaries*
9. Ingemar Düring. *Aristotle's Chemical Treatise. Meterologica, Book IV. With an introduction and commentary*
10. Ingemar Düring. *Die Harmonienlehre des Klaudios Ptolemaios* bound with Ingemar Düring. *Porphyrios Kommentar zur Harmonienlehre des Ptolemaios*
11. Ingemar Düring. *Ptolemaios und Porphyrios über die Musik*
12. Wilmer Cave France. *The Emperor Julian's Relation to the New Sophistic and Neo-Platonism: with a study of his style*
13. John Gibb and William Montgomery. *The Confessions of Augustine. Second Edition*

14. Carlo Giussani. *T. Lucreti Cari De Rerum Natura Libri Sex. Revisione del testo, commento e studi introduttivi*
15. Sir Thomas Heath. *Mathematics in Aristotle*
16. William A. Heidel. *Selected Papers.* Edited with an introduction by Leonardo Tarán
17. Roger Miller Jones. *The Platonism of Plutarch and Selected Papers.* Edited with an introduction by Leonardo Tarán
18. Hal Koch. *Pronoia und Paideusis. Studien über Origenes und sein Verhältnis zum Platonismus*
19. Clara Elizabeth Millerd. *On the Interpretation of Empedocles*
20. Constantin Ritter. *Bibliographies on Plato* ("Berichte . . . über Platon erschienenen Arbeiten")
21. Léon Robin. *Pyrrhon et le scepticisme grec*
22. Richard Robinson. *Plato's Earlier Dialectic.* Second Edition
23. W.D. Ross. *Aristotle's Prior and Posterior Analytics. A Revised Text with Introduction and Commentary*
24. Paul Shorey. *Selected Papers.* Edited with an introduction by Leonardo Tarán
25. Paul Shorey. *The Unity of Plato's Thought*
26. G. Stallbaum. *Platonis Opera Omnia.* (This set is published here in fourteen volumes and includes Stallbaum's commentary on Plato's *Parmenides*.)
27. E. Seymer Thompson. *The Meno of Plato, edited with Introduction, Notes, and Excursuses*
28. Eliza Gregory Wilkins. *"Know Thyself" in Greek and Latin Literature*
29. John Cook Wilson. *On the Interpretation of Plato's Timaeus. Critical studies with reference to a recent edition*
    bound with
    John Cook Wilson. "*On the Platonist Doctrine of the ἀσύμβλητοι ἀριθμοί*"
30. Martinus Wohlrab. *Platonis Theaetetus. Recensuit, Prolegomenis et Commentariis Instruxit. Editio Altera et Emendatior*